understanding Sexuality
THE MYSTERY OF OUR LOST IDENTITIES

by Roy Masters

Edited by Dorothy Baker

UNDERSTANDING SEXUALITY:
The Mystery of Our Lost Identities

Previously published under
the title of SEX, SIN & SALVATION
and SEX, SIN & SOLUTION.
Copyright © 1977, 1970 by Roy Masters
Revised Edition Copyright © 1988
All rights reserved, including the right to reproduce
this book or portions thereof in any form.

Published by The Foundation of Human Understanding
Printed in the United States of America

For information, please direct your inquiry to:
The Foundation of Human Understanding
P.O. Box 34036, 8780 Venice Boulevard
Los Angeles, California 90034

or

P.O. Box 811, 111 N.E. Evelyn Street
Grants Pass, Oregon 97526

Cover design: Yuri Teshler
Typographers: Stephanie Lawson and Jeannette Papp

Library of Congress Catalog Card Number 87-83552
ISBN 0-933900-13-9

CONTENTS

Editor's Preface...v

Foreword...ix

1. The Root of the Problem...............................1

2. Bewitched, Blinded, and Bewildered...........13

3. The Fall..31

4. Hypnosis and Animal Magnetism...............43

5. The Tyranny of Sex.....................................57

6. The Many Faces of Love.............................75

7. The Mystery of Our Lost Identity...............93

8. Our Hypnotic Relationships......................113

9. The Marriage Gamble...............................133

10. Who Pulls the Strings?..............................175

11. Mutual Corruption—or Correction...........207

12. Struggling with the Ties that Bind............237

13. Sexual Problems and Aberrations.............267

14. The Tangled Web.......................................309

15. Back to Reality...335

Editor's Preface

This book was first published in 1970, under the title "Sex, Sin & Solution," and it was actually written a year or two before that. When it was republished in 1977, Mr. Masters added the material now contained in the last two chapters and changed the title to "Sex, Sin & Salvation," which was actually the title he preferred in the first place, but elected not to use lest the word "Salvation" discourage people from buying the book on the basis of its "religiosity."

When I heard that The Foundation of Human Understanding was getting ready to republish the book, I asked Roy Masters if I might reedit it and help in the selection of a new title. Although I was the book's original editor, insofar as its main content is concerned, I had offered no suggestions for chapter titles or subtitles, and I was somewhat disappointed in those that appeared in the first editions. While I could see how they got there, I felt that they really detracted from the seriousness of Roy Masters' message.

Nevertheless, I'm sure that no real seeker of

Truth was put off by the editorial word play in the previous editions. We lovers of Truth are drawn to Roy Masters and The Foundation of Human Understanding from all walks of life and all parts of the country, and we all have our own ideas on how best to help Roy with the task of "selling" the message. We keep trying, in our various ways, to lure the uncommitted, the "fringe folk" over to our side, but deep down in our hearts, we know that those who love the Truth will get the message, and those who don't, won't, no matter what we do.

Except for the new title, new chapter headings, and the deletion of subtitles, this is essentially the same book you might already have read under one of the former titles. But whether you are a new reader or a re-reader, you will no doubt get the impression, as I did this time, that Roy Masters was addressing a world that no longer exists today. No doubt some of the worldly ones were planting the seeds that have come to full flower in AIDS and every conceivable kind of addiction, and thinking the thoughts that have led to unisex, the breakup of the home, and the bashing of moral values that we once held dear. But at that time it would have been unthinkable to hear certain practices referred to openly as "sexual preferences," as we do now on almost every news program. How could we have fallen so far so fast?

Under the circumstances, we made no attempt to bring the book up to date. To do so would have necessitated a completely new approach, a rewriting rather than a reediting. In any event, Roy Masters is addressing today's audience and today's problems every single day, both in his writings and in his daily radio and television call-in programs.

"The Moving Finger writes; and, having writ,
Moves on: nor all your Piety nor Wit
Shall lure it back to cancel half a Line,
Nor all your Tears Wash out a Word of it."*

Truth is Truth, in whatever context we find it, and those who love it will surely find a way to it. I don't think I found Roy Masters by accident, and I don't think you have this book in your hands by accident, either. Do read on, and rejoice.

D. B.

*The Rubaiyat of Omar Khayyam. Stanza 71.

Foreword

I can't remember who it was who, when asked what his feelings were concerning sex, answered: "The position is ridiculous, the pleasure only temporary, and the consequence often disastrous."

Whoever he was, I'm certain Roy Masters heartily agrees with his observation. It's not so much that Mr. Masters is against sex, *per se*, it's that he is *for* a proper relationship between man and woman. Who can deny that when sex is used, as it so often is, as a powerful manipulative device, a questionable energy source or as a distraction from one's own wrongness, no meaningful marital relationship can exist.

Shortly before his death in 1939, Sigmund Freud, the founder of psychoanalysis, confessed, "Up to the present I have not yet found the courage to make any broad statements on the essence of love and I think that our knowledge is not sufficient to do so . . . we really know very little about love."

Roy Masters, on the other hand, believes that he knows the true nature of love. More important, he knows what love is *not*. He makes the potent point that too many of us mistake *need* for love.

In this powerful volume, Masters' message is loud and clear; man is pathetically subject to external pressures, a whimpering slave to outer direction, a pig sloshing his life away in a dung heap of emotionalism. All the while arrogantly proclaiming his mastery over body and mind, strutting pridefully in the parade to Hell.

If we are ever to arrive at the final solution to our most pressing problem, the author of *Understanding Sexuality: The Mystery of Our Lost Identities* tells us that we must awaken from a lifelong stupor. He wants us to open our eyes and to see that there's an evil *something* that has an overwhelming appeal to our ego, a certain ghastly something that makes us feel helpless in the face of temptation; something that makes us think it is we who choose to commit adultery or become an alcoholic or a drug addict.

Make no mistake, the price of awareness is not inexpensive. It can only be paid in a currency the Soul understands: *right intent*. That is, a sincere longing to do the right thing in every situation, no matter how costly or ego-deflating, just because it is the right thing to do and not because it's going to make us look or feel good.

This brings us, once again, to that little old three-letter word that has fascinated, frightened and ruled mankind with a cast-iron grip ever since Adam left the Garden. Of course, we're referring to *sex*. Surely, nothing can make a weak and thoroughly wrong male feel more powerful and securely right in his wrongness than a heated sexual encounter with an accommodating partner.

How we have applauded this self-deception. Cleverly we camouflaged our weakness with yet another word that enabled us to justify our actions. *Love* . . . it's what makes the world go round, we loudly boast. And round and round we went, trapped in a vicious circle and unable to break free because up till now, nobody had the courage or clarity to "blow the whistle" on this deadly farce. Make no mistake, the cat has been let out of the bag and you can blame Mr. Masters! From now on we haven't an excuse left. He has opened the lid and the secret is out! Pity the egocentric!

And just what are Roy Masters' credentials for such an epic undertaking? To best answer that often-asked question, I like to recall what the University of Michigan's very famous philosopher, Abraham Kaplan, once said, "The word philosophy means *love of wisdom*. I suppose it's like any other sort of love—the professionals are the ones who know the least about it."

The author of *Understanding Sexuality: The Mystery of Our Lost Identities* has no college degrees to adorn his walls. He has not spent long years in school classrooms listening to the contradictory theories of the so-called experts. In short, Roy Masters is not a professional problem-solver; his insights and understanding, he says, are intuitive and come to him through the Grace of God.

When I started writing my last book, *Healers, Gurus & Spiritual Guides*, I had planned on devoting just one chapter to Roy Masters. But once I began researching my subject in depth, what started out as a single chapter grew and grew. As it turned out, almost half that particular book is devoted either directly or indirectly to him. His influence is considerable.

Roy is a complicated individual of great simplicity and humility. He's an energetic mystic of uncommon sensibility and common sense. Color him prophet, philosopher, metaphysical revolutionary, or voice in the wilderness; he's all that and more. Above all, he's a man hard to ignore.

To the untrained eye and ear, to the uninitiated, this bushy-haired transplanted Englishman, who has an uncanny facial resemblance to the hip-swinging singing star Tom Jones, is just another cultist with a Messiah-complex. Not so to the hundreds of thousands who read his books, listen to him on radio and TV, or flock to his lectures. They appreciate him for being a channel through which the wisdom of the ages is once again being made available. To many, he's the one man willing and able to *tell it like it really is!* And that's what this book is really all about.

—*William Wolff*

1

The Root
of the Problem

The "great white father" of psychiatry, Sigmund Freud, came very close to basic truth, but before he had quite reached it, he veered off into the outer reaches of scientific confusion. If only he had been able to view the facts that his searching mind uncovered by the light of spiritual discernment, he might have discovered the truth about man's nature.

He might have discovered, for instance, that the sex drive in man is somehow linked with and blossoms from a traumatic experience with a parent—long forgotten, of course, but nevertheless there at the core of his being, surrounded and hidden by the concentric growth rings of subsequent traumatic experiences that have blinded him to the original violation of his human identity. The first trauma sets the pattern, and becomes the nucleus for the problems that follow concentrically, one upon the other, until the original experience, the nucleus itself, is lost from the observation of the conscious mind. Notice I have said "observation," not "memory." The "memory" is "synonymous" with the experience itself.

Each emotional reaction is actually a traumatic experience for a human being—essential for animal growth, but not for human development. In fact, "animal" growth is inimical to human development, blunting our human perceptions at the point of unfoldment and supplementing them with the brutish reasoning of an "evolving body."

In the beginning, then, the individual encounters an original traumatic experience that sets the wheel of his development in motion around an axis of emotional "turn-on" experiences. But this growth pattern carries him further from his true identity, or from the possibility of discovering that identity. The real identity of each of us exists as a potential not yet realized, buried somewhere within us, but prevented from expressing itself and unfolding in harmonious obedience to higher law, by the blocking power of *emotion*. Each emotional shock is another traumatic experience, another step away from the calm center of the true Self.

Now, it is an established biological fact that when living protoplasm (flesh) is exposed to stress, the reaction to that stress causes the body to absorb some of the nature (identity) of that stress (presence) permanently. The permanent impression left on an organism as a result of stress is called an "engram." In other words, some of the outside environment gets inside the organism that reacts to it, makes a mark on it, and gives additional development to that life form. Evolutionists would term this process adaptation and evolution. The creature is subject to the impress of its environment, and it takes shape and adjusts according to the severity and type of pressure that is brought to bear on it.

Now, in what position does that place our "free moral agent" called "man"? Certainly, he is not very "free," and stripped of control over the process, he cannot be very "moral." Yet we know that man's consciousness is subject to two distinct "tugs," the tug of nature, and the counter tug of conscience. This tug-of-war for the carcass of man is the basis of his soul's unrest. As the pressures of environment envelop him, he becomes increasingly obliged to obey that environment and dramatize its secret messages, codes, and implications.

We are surrounded by an environment composed not only of nature itself, but of other people with precisely the same problems as our own, subject to the environment that preceded them and fouled up by their forebears even as we have been by our own. All of us dramatize in the flesh the forces that have overshadowed us, and thus our behavior becomes an "environment" with a "message" to others.

Freud recognized that all our problems begin in childhood, and that parents are the primary problem producers. If we are victims of our environment, it is because our parents are wrong, and we shall surely inherit some of that wrong. We are somehow scarred at birth by what I would like to call an inherent error that lurks in the parent undetected. Then the child becomes the parent, and the process continues. Surely this is the meaning of "being born in sin."

There is not one single person who does not have

a crippling problem. The entire human race is made up of emotional cripples who are confused, irrational, or downright cruel. Rich or poor, and of whatever ethnic background, each child comes into the world preceded by tyrants. Let's call them "victim-sinners," as the word "sin" denotes a deviation, while "victim" denotes helplessness. The fleshly presence of this deviation in the form of a parent is the "ministering angel" that shocks the infant to change the course of its development. In time, the child also grows up to be a parent, complete with inherited defects and the authority to relay the error to the next generation.

Perhaps there is some truth to the biblical statement that man is born in sin; that is, we are born subject to powers that are able to corrupt our nature and enslave our minds to serve them in a meaningless existence. And the root of this process is what we are going to examine from every conceivable viewpoint.

One way to prove a theory is to start with the assumption that it is true. If we can then arrive at other observable facts without contradicting our original assumption, we may assume our theory to be sound. This is the course I have taken to establish one fact, as your previous conditioning would undoubtedly have "turned you off," had I opened my remarks with something like "original sin."

But bear with me please. Your problems do have a place of origin. There must have been a first time, at least for you. For you, it was undoubtedly the first time someone hurt you or failed you in some way, and you reacted. And it was the same with your parents and your grandparents and as far back as you can trace your ancestry until you finally arrive at the "original" experience.

Secondly, there must have been a weakness existing in your nature that allowed error to cohabit with you—and once it did, you became weaker and the error got stronger. It happened again and again, and the fault was bound to grow as long as it went uncorrected. What you could not resist once, you could not resist twice, and so on. Thousands of emotional experiences (temptations) later, you have a full-blown problem.

The problem at first may appear to be a small one, but as long as the pulse beat of (bad) emotional experience continues, so will impressions be left behind in mind and flesh to manifest themselves in our behavior and way of life and become parents to the next problem. In this way, cannibals become "good" cannibals, and communists become "good" communists, but never *good* people.

We become like our parents, taking upon ourselves their ways and traditions. If our parents were unreasonable, then we will be too (naturally!). Of course, some children rebel against the takeover of their identities—one of the greatest fears people have is the fear of becoming like their parents. On the other hand, they may not admit to the takeover (due to their weakness), preferring to become proud of their "good" heritage. Either way, the impress of our parents is there, whether we like it or not. Men will either marry their "mother," or a woman who is "apparently" the exact opposite, but the influence of "mother" is an overriding one, making its mark on man born of woman.

Observe the rebellion now going on against the "establishment." You will see in it a pathetic attempt to throw off the yoke of oppression and authority. The first authority a child knows is vested in its parent or guardian, and what this authority proceeds to do to that child is impose its "right" and ways upon him. But if you will look closer, you will see that that authority has no real identity of its own—it simply extends or projects the identity that has been imposed upon it in the same way. The child's psyche is violated by a parent whose psyche was violated by a parent whose psyche was violated, ad infinitum. What I am saying is that identity has a philosophy and tries to make you accept its philosophy, because if you will accept the philosophy, you will accept the spirit behind the philosophy. And children simply do not know how to resist.

As I said earlier, cannibal women have cannibal babies. What our younger generation is rebelling against is this traditional imposition. And if we examine the nature of this rebellion, we see two kinds of rebels. One is searching for real identity and meaning and rebels against the philosophy itself. The other accepts the philosophy but rebels against the dominant spirit behind that philosophy. Many are confused and lost, doing the only thing they know how to do in a desperate attempt to throw off the yoke of advantage the establishment has over them by virtue of having preceded them. Unconsciously, many of them sense that their confusion might be dispelled if only they could destroy, remove, or overcome the authorities. This is a shortsighted viewpoint, of course, but the only one they can know in their confusion. Children react in an unnatural way to unnatural pressures put upon them by the unholy, unnatural, traditional ways of their parents.

If our parents were normal, and if society were normal, we could not possibly have a rebellion or any other such problem in our society at all. Rebellion needs some sort of justification, and the justification is usually found in some injustice. We rebel against authority because there is something about that authority that is just not acceptable in that it is positively destructive to our identity. Yet if we examine that authority, we see that it is vested in one who has gained that position simply by giving up the battle (his own prior rebellion) along with his self-respect. The king is dead; long live the king.

Such people are very guilty indeed for not living their own lives and for their intolerance toward the selfhood of those who will not conform. Every family is composed of rebels and conformists. On rare occasions, we find a family composed entirely of mad or bad ones—or of "good" ones; that is, all have knuckled under to the pressures of the group. Every country perpetuates its own form of traditional insanity, producing rebels and conformists. This has led to the idea that Truth has many forms and that man makes his own brand of Truth. But what we are observing is the utter impossibility of a human being's escaping the impress of his environment. The rebel, not knowing how to rebel, becomes an extension of the evil lurking in the authority that he is rebelling against—on him it looks different, but it's the same evil. Hating evil never makes us good, but it surely makes us more evil.

As he grows up under the influence of his government, each person loses his identity. Some fight the parent group and break off to form new cultures complete with their own nonsense. Some prefer suicide to existence as zombies; a half million people bow out of the world by their own hand annually rather than exist another moment in the agony of their conflict between conforming and rebelling (rebelling actually being another way of conforming to evil).

What we need to realize then is that each one of us is a victim of a *process*, regardless of culture or ethnic background. Each victim of the process in turn is obliged, unconsciously and compulsively, to claim the newborn—he cannot tolerate the innocence of the child. He is compelled to violate it to relieve the pressures of his own anxiety.

If you can see the foregoing to be true, you must be able to accept the concept of an original source, a date lost in antiquity, a place where the original man experienced his traumatic shock and lost his identity to the source of that shock because he accepted a lie, and in accepting the lie, he accepted the spirit behind the lie. In much the same way as animals reflect their environment, so must that first man have begun to take upon himself the nature that violated him in the beginning, and this he has transmitted "faithfully" to his offspring. The history of mankind is one of madness, tyranny, and bloodshed. Claimed by tyrants of many kinds at birth, we all inherit confusion. This is so because we come into the world subject to what has preceded us in the world, and that is precisely the point. Good does not precede us. It is Error that stands there ready to claim us for the traditional ways, to keep us true to the elaborate system of lies and conditioning that assures its perpetuation on earth.

But again, please notice that the pulse beat, the life, of your obedience is assured by your emotional response. Each emotional experience becomes in itself another trauma, identical to the birth trauma, and forming another growth ring to make you more sensitive to outer stimuli. Once established, the fleshly development is slavish in its obedience to the pressures that shape it, and a constant bombardment of lies consoles and keeps you from discovering the Truth that might set you free.

The animal unfolding from the pressures of nature is dependent upon those very pressures to maintain its existing life form. In much the same way, when we develop through emotional stimuli in the way of the beast, we come to crave and be loyal to the stimuli at the roots of our being, completely subject to them; but this is so only if we can be convinced that we are on the "right track," that there is no other way or source of life impulse possible.

Once the human organism begins to respond to

stimulus, it learns to identify with that stimulus, since some of it incorporates itself into his reflexes. Man is made up of many such engramic memories.

If there were only one kind of stimulus to motivate us, we could not have a problem of guilt or deviation. Animals, for instance, know only one obedience, and the changes that are wrought in them as a result of that obedience are natural and proper. But when the same pressures are applied to humans, they appear to displace another possible arrangement.

If you are very aware, you will observe that the aftermath of excitement *of any kind* is guilt, or at the very least, a feeling of anxiety. This cannot be proved by any scientific means, but each one of us can observe it consciously from within himself if he cares to look. What we become physically, as the result of any pressure, recognizes that pressure as its source. That pressure (presence) becomes familiar to us, and we miss it when it is not there, exciting us, tempting us, upsetting, loving, and motivating us. Again, we may discover by observation that persons we need are never really good for us at all; but somehow they exude a familiar presence or philosophy reminiscent of the spirit of the past. In some ancient traumatic shock experience, that same "spirit" motivated our forebears and gave them its identity, displacing the original growth process in order to do so. Eventually our parents appeared and presided over us, dictating our future in the critical formative years, tempting us as they were tempted, loving us as they were "loved."

Now as we grow older and forget the true way that we never actually had a chance to "remember," we are obliged to reach for more of that familiar spirit in other people, the only one we know that can continue to provide the kind of motivating presence we have grown accustomed to need.

When our "familiar spirits" are there in the bodies of our friends and associates, doing their "thing," we develop in a way that is not truly right, so that when they are not present, we feel a kind of guilt or vague uneasiness about the way we are growing. And pride has no tolerance for anything that makes it feel guilty. It is pride, reaching for the services of the evil, that keeps us a bondslave to evil.

Everything that violates you makes you need it, because when you become involved, you are identifying with it engrammatically. You begin to believe that you would be "unnatural" if you didn't respond to its call, that you would be a traitor if you dared to resist the impulse it can so irresistibly produce in you.

As I have indicated, if you were to sit in the silence of solitary confinement, without lies or emotional pressures of any kind, you would feel guilty, lonely, and afraid. And it would be Truth that you feared. The longer you are left alone, the more the entertainment of imagination fades, and you will tend to see in your nature the ugly grotesque form of the power that has laid claim to you. So you reach out for the familiar excitements in order to feel comfortable again, but each experience leaves its mark, its growth ring. Soon we need more and more stimuli to feel secure. Notice that as the excitement emanating from a person or pill or bottle fails, or when we discover what a slave we have become to it, we must either cling more tightly to it, rebel against it in some destructive way, or reach for other things with similar excitement values. And as each new thing excites us to feel secure, we become deeply enslaved to that thing. What violates, enslaves.

Of course, if we had no true identity (nature) to violate, we could not consider any of these hang-ups to be enslavements. Animals cannot be said to be "hung up" with their environment. Whatever form they assume through responding to environment is what they are and what they ought to be; they can depend on it without qualms. We humans, on the other hand, are now what we should not be. What is more, the environment that we represent to our child is very like the first temptation that transformed God's paradise into man's miserable earth.

2

Bewitched, Blinded, and Bewildered

Concealed behind every man's normal sexual need is an abnormal need for woman. A man goes to his woman in the same way that a drunk goes to his bottle; or to put it more aptly, a drunk needs his bottle in precisely the same way that he once needed his woman, because he degenerates to need inanimate things as he begins to fail in his ability to use woman and to get comfort for his ego from her. Unfortunately, by the time he goes to the bottle, his woman has usually developed an abnormal craving for his abnormal need of her, and frustration rules the roost.

People do use each other constantly, but in subtle ways that are not easily detected. Both men and women use the physical presence of the opposite sex to derive a substitute "something" for an inner lack. Neither people nor animals can exist for long without some kind of continuous stimulation. For the animal this stimulation is provided by a wordless communication with the environment, which helps it to unfold and maintain its animal way of life.

People need a life presence, too, but it should not

be one outside the self. Unfortunately, however, most of us are not inwardly related, so we unconsciously substitute people and objects for the turn-on value that we should be finding within ourselves. When we do this, we become hypnotized to a sense of false security and self-importance as a result of the support of that relationship.

The human ego is invariably too proud to face reality, much preferring the pursuance of its selfish goals. But these selfish goals cut it off from a divine purpose and presence that would otherwise provide it with an excitement to live in loving obedience to it. In other words, the love of God is expressed by a desire to respond according to His will and not our own. Then, pleased and stirred by our true desire, the divine Presence stirs in us and stimulates and blesses us with the power to move toward an unseen purpose that we feel as "hope." That movement will always express something of the Nature that has set it in motion. It will reflect the identity in us of Him whom we serve.

Without knowledge or living experience with this inner Presence, we are lethargic. We procrastinate until we discover a substitute motivation, an earthy stimulus capable of serving our self-interest, and we appoint the one who supplies it to be the one to replace the divine essence in our lives. The individual so honored by us is usually an exciting "ego beaver," who inspires in us a kind of slavish dependency that we should call "need," but we don't. We call it "love." Our need for this anointed one places him on a pedestal, a throne, an altar—and the rarefied air of the high place goes to his head. He loves it. In fact, you have just given him "the stuff" his dreams were always made of. He knew he had it in him all the time, but it took you to come along and recognize his worth. He may even let you kiss his ring.

The purring pleasure of the one you have appointed to the place of the "most high" reflects back favorably on you, the worshipper, and gives you a warm feeling of security. His approval becomes a motivation in you, in much the same way that the intuition of God's will would motivate the person who loved God and put Him first; except that this earthly motivation gives power to the egocentric purpose in us that opposed the Divine Will. Our "friendships" and/or other addictions nudge us by imperceptible degrees away from a real purpose in life, in favor of the life sensation and self-indulgence that ends in guilt and despair. Every motion away from our center makes us more desolate and needful, and we cling more frantically to our self-appointed gods, be they persons or things.

This hypnotic process is difficult to explain, but our inordinate craving for approval and love makes easy prey of us all. We must take a good look at the "security" and "love" we gain in this way, for they are completely false, merely illusions to support our pride.

Because we have a consciousness, we must be aware—at least in part—of our failings. No one can escape his conscience (divine presence) forever. The consciousness of man was made to behold that

Divine Presence, to draw power from Him to live and express His purpose; but alas, we have somehow lost contact and allowed ourselves to be drawn away. When we are alone with ourselves, our higher Self pricks us and tries to waken us from our dream; but if we have no tolerance for real purpose, we must deny our true Selves, and so we need the presence of another person to help us fight off the sense of lack and the judgment we feel upon ourselves in the quiet times.

So we are magnetically attracted to another person who, like us, seeks escape from Reality and Truth, and is needful of our Presence, too. And this person becomes our hypnotist, our "god." Unconsciously, he agrees to give us a good image of ourselves, to comfort us, and motivate us, in exchange for our looking up to him. All this is a non-verbal agreement, of course, and such a commonly made one that it must surely be familiar to you if you care to look back over your past relationships. Haven't you noticed how subtly we obtain messages and suggestions from one another, how "like a god" the appointed one appears to you or feels as a result of having been appointed by the worshipper? And then, how much more like a god the worshipper feels in the reflected light of his "god's" approval! At one point, each seems to remember that he himself "created" this "god" *by* his approval, and that he must therefore be the greater (certainly not the lesser) god. With a little doing, our ego soon gets the picture turned around more to its liking—we are no longer the supplicant at the altar, but the god for whom the incense is burning. And it all starts so simply, so innocently. Someone indicates a liking for us, and before we know it, we're in "love."

The whole conflagration starts when a terrible need strikes against a "need to be needed." And when we are caught up in this way, it doesn't matter whether we are the feaster or the feast—all we see is that someone is admiring us and encouraging us to go on doing what we're doing. How we love that person! What a great person he (or she, of course) seems to be! What a marvelous friend!

As long as our ego is being fed mystically, we feel alive. Each new friend or lover gives us a new lease on life, new hope—something that appears to be "happiness at last." All at once, our conflicts, our fears and worries and guilts vanish miraculously— suddenly we really *are* "something," and we're *going* somewhere. We're in "love!"

While we have been speaking of this hypnotic relationship primarily as it concerns the male-female infatuation, the basic principle is at the root of all our hangups, whether we are hung up on one person or thing or hung up on being hung up. Some of us gain our strength from "putting on" many friends.

In any event, the excitement of a love presence (or friends) makes us forget the truth about ourselves, so much so that we cannot possibly view the truth about any facet of the relationship, including the fact that in making our selection we made sure that we had to stoop a little (if not a lot). We fail to see that we have elevated a bum to the throne and that our dependency on the bum is growing. We may even fail to be aware of the secret contempt we have for the person we are using and keeping beneath us by that using.

Of course, as our dependency on "the bum" grows, he is gaining strength and a sense of superiority because of our need of him, which appears to be "love," and which provides him also with support and justification. So much so that occasionally he oversteps, gives himself one "air" too many, threatens our superiority, and even wakes us to the fact that we have the short end of the stick. But even then, we are not at a loss for long. Our ego soon discovers that we can still maintain a false sense of security and worth by judging the wickedness of the bum that "out of the goodness of our heart" we had once elevated to a place of high esteem. He now becomes Satan Incarnate, and our judgment of him supports us in the hypnotic illusion that, by comparison, we are still "god." Oh, what shabby games we mortals play!

You see, our need to be right even when we're wrong creates a need for a presence to lull us into a sense of security because we cannot produce this feeling in ourselves by any effort of will. Alone, we are uncertain of the future and lethargic. We cannot make our dreams come true. So we have need of a "god" to tell us that *we* are "god." This ego need is so great that we are compelled to appoint a nearby ego to this role, a role that our "victim-god" accepts proudly. When he rebels, he becomes Satan, the first fallen son of the spirit subject to "god's" judgment and wrath.

Strangely enough, this setup duplicates quite closely, or is an unreasonable facsimile of, the divine arrangement of Father and Son, God and the Son of God, who does the Father's will—except that in the case of these hypnotic relationships, each puts the other on and makes him feel like a god by falsely donning the mask and playing the role of the Son looking up at the Father, who now can do no wrong! And when the false son tries to reverse the roles and become the Father, he is damned to Hell to the day of repentance when "god" will forgive his transgressions.

You do see, don't you, that the "god" you are using is also using you? Your need makes him feel "right" and "free" in spite of his enslavement to you. He is not "right" because he is using you for his feeling of rightness, and he is not "free" because he needs you to preserve his freedom from the condemnation his own conscience would pronounce on him if you were to let him go back to himself.

You may be just as exciting to that individual as he (or she) is to you, but you are both so excited by the playback of approval ("loving") and judgment (hating) that you cannot observe what is really happening. "Love is blind," they say, but human "love" is a far cry from what *love* really is.

When your earthly lover deserts you, you tend to wake up, to become aware; but you can hardly stand the feelings of anxiety that awareness, unbuffered by your beloved's presence, produces in you. Your need to escape from yourself and the real purpose for your existence becomes unbearable, and you interpret your anxiety to mean that you need another love to do more "loving." So you appoint a new love, and the grim process starts again. Each "frees" the other with power to do all manner of evil that you cannot see you are doing, so blinded are you by the delusions of grandeur created by the hypnotic fascination each of you has for the other through "loving and being loved" or hating and being hated.

We see a similar blindness at work in the man who steals to obtain money for drugs. He sees nothing wrong in his stealing because his attention is focused on the need he has for the drug in order to maintain his ego "high." Whatever helps him to achieve this "high" is "good." And anything he has to do to provide the illusion of being good must also be good. And so it is with the "lovers." We bow and scrape to attract each other's attention, but we don't see what we are doing as "bowing and scraping." We see it as loving-kindness toward our "subject." We will even sell and debase our bodies, but we won't see what we are doing because we can do no wrong. As long as we are pleasing another person and receiving his homage, we, as king slobs, cannot see our faults. So the faults grow, along with a great anxiety that needs constant assuaging by an entourage of friend-fiends. While we are becoming more wrong, we depend more heavily on people (and later, things) to "correct" this anxiety, and, of course, we as king slobs are obliged to commission our friends' egos in the same way.

The need for "love" is an extension of the need

for excitement and to feel secure on the throne, and that need for love is so exciting and glorifying to the person we "put" it on that it puts him on a throne and whets his need for excitement, too. In our ungodly enthusiasm for each other we become willing to see each other in the way each wants to be seen. Each projects a favorable image to the other's mind and is approved by the other for it. Each reflects the glory of the other.

As each person grows more guilty, he must find newer, more extreme ways to demonstrate his "love" to be worthy of support. Each demands that the other "prove" his love, and fearful of losing the relationship, each does more wrong that he cannot see as wrong because he is immediately rewarded for it with more "love." So you give and give and give in order not to lose your "god." You will not look on your devotions as slavery, but as a kind of "divine love" for the Son of God. Even though it may cross your mind from time to time that you had to scrape bottom to find *this* one, you push the thought away quickly and do your best to see him "honestly" as good (synonymous with god), lest you feel guilty for pretending, and inadvertently betray your real assessment of his "qualities," and thereby lose his "love."

So you brainwash yourself until you really see your beloved as "good," knowing that the more genuinely you believe it yourself, the more convincing you will be in your declaration of it, and the greater will be the reflected approval on yourself. The love we bestow on another in this way is tantamount to a license for him to do terrible things to us and to others, but we are afraid to see this, and we *refuse* to see it for fear of losing our beloved (support).

Incidentally, you may now be able to see how people can "tap" the most evil persons for their "love," and in so doing become in part responsible for that evil by making it appear to be divine and right.

The variations of this theme are legion, as the reader can no doubt see for himself. (By now, we have surely lost the readers who refuse to face the Truth and bought the book expecting to be treated to the same old positive thinking hokum they are accustomed to.) The principle is the use of another person to substitute as an inferior Divine Presence. Appointing him to serve us in this way hypnotizes him to hypnotize us back again. Every interpersonal problem we have, every hangup on another person, is based on the hypnotic fascination that one ego has for another ego. The reason it is so difficult for a person under a formal hypnotic suggestion to realize that he is hypnotized is that the rapport with the hypnotist simply duplicates the hypnotic pattern of *all* his associations with people. He behaves like a trained seal for the hypnotist and is applauded and told that he is a good subject, but it is almost impossible to convince him that he is actually hypnotized or acting out a post-hypnotic suggestion. He is absolutely sure, as a rule, that his behavior is his own idea, and that he is as much in control of himself as he ever was. And when it comes to that, he's probably right.

In our hypnotic relationships with others, we are unable to see that what we do for them is triggered by the spell their presence casts over us. We will do *anything* for that presence and see it as love for the person, originating in the goodness of our heart. But in reality, all of our behavior is now triggered by that person's demands, direct or implied, subtle or obvious. We start to lose our identity to that person, and he starts to become us.

What your "lover" wills of you becomes "your" will. Conversely, you see any righteousness he might manifest as the product of your approval of him, the result of *your* divine love operating in him. You liberate each other to do terrible things, fancying them to be original and spontaneous, but once you have fallen under the spell of that substitute divinity, everything that you do is aimed at keeping him near you for security reasons. What seemed originally to be an innocent need for each other's "love" may begin to show an ugly side. You may find your lover wanting you to engage in acts that are not yourself—and you may find yourself unable to resist these demands for fear of losing your divine presence substitute. More and more "free" time will be spent degrading yourself so you can stay high until you see that you can do nothing right.

Indeed, the persons you use in this way can completely possess you. The more wrong you are inside, the more desperate you will be to escape the truth about yourself, and the more you will turn toward the evil and the bizarre for comfort. At every level of the descent, there will be people waiting to be your guide to Hell. When your marriage fails, you will turn to witches, fortune-tellers, advisers of all kinds, and friends of the same sex who will capture you completely and tell you what you "need" to hear. You will gobble up their lies and do anything at all for them in order to feel beautiful, manly, right, high and mighty.

This abnormal need, this ungodly hunger for people to hypnotize us into a sense of well-being and righteousness, all starts with the terrible emptiness we experience in our failure to find and to love Reality. In Truth, we have no identity of our own, our real identity being God's Identity in us; but if we are egocentric, out of touch with Reality, we are unbearably alone in our nothingness.

The egocentric mind, unwilling to be committed to a purpose other than its own, has no vital wish to contact Reality, therefore rejects the offering of true life force. It has an insatiable need for something to live from (or on), and its anguished cry serves as a signal to bring "help" from the environment. That substitute essence is used to "make good" its loss, fill up its lack. Unfortunately, once we invoke this kind of help, we become a subject of the "helper," just as dependent upon him for reassurance as we were for assurance in the beginning and to escape from the knowledge of how weak we have become as a result of that "help." If our ego does not live by the light of Truth and is not aware by His Presence, it is blind, groping in the dark toward anything that will help it come alive to its ego glory. It has no thoughts or life direction of its own because of its unrecognized yearning for an existence separate from God, the Source. It wants to BE God, the Source. Man, however, unlike God, needs to relate to something in order to exist at all. So we reach for something that will assure us that we exist in the way we yearn to delude ourselves that we can exist; and before we realize it (we *can't* realize it in the beginning), we lose our identity to the "helper."

Once we are excited to feel "loved" and important, we become the property of the "worshipper." As I mentioned earlier, a hypnotized person obeys the will of the hypnotist without realizing that he is obeying. The same principle holds true in the case of the ego vampire. The need of that ego mind actually causes it to appoint a hypnotist (inferior god) for itself. It uses the hypnotist (lover, preacher, tyrant, analyst) to engender comfort, well-being, animation, motivation, righteousness—in short, anything and everything the vain soul needs to substitute for the real missing essence, and to inform it that IT is Number One and can do no wrong.

The subject, then, thinks he is god. He cannot see that he is, in fact, a "subject," drawing all the support for his life from his victim-hypnotist-god. One reason that he cannot see this to be true is that it IS true, and if he were a person willing to see Truth, he would be living in a proper relationship to that Truth, depending on it alone as a life presence and fountainhead of virtue. Certainly, he would not be using the presence of another person as an escape. When he does so, he forgets Truth entirely and is blinded by his egocentricity to the power that his substitute life source has over him.

The victim is influenced because of a vital need for influence (something he desperately needs to hear and feel), and that influence duplicates exactly the process of hypnosis. The net result is that the "subject" gains the life support he needs in order to live egotistically without being forced to acknowledge a power greater than himself, but there *is* a greater power over him.

The excitement provided by this hypnotic arrangement gives to the subject, through the power of suggestion, all the values (false) that he lacks within himself because of his egotism. He feels like a righteously motivated, comforted, well-adjusted, secure person (god). He isn't, but he has the impression that he is, and the impression is being supplied to him by his "hypnotist" friend. Each person's delusion does come from a "power" bigger than himself—big enough and strong enough to prevent him from examining what is happening by the light of Truth. His rejection of Truth and his pleasurable sense of security about what he is prevents him from seeing the Truth by the light of Reality. The friendship arrangement, which stimulates his ego to see and feel only what is acceptable to it, is purely a hypnotic arrangement.

Political and religious fanatics are driven insane by the same process. Our idolatry of a guru, leader, priest, saint—whatever—is naturally acceptable to the leader's ego. If he wants to maintain a following, he must convey to his "flock" all the subtle essences aforementioned; then he, in turn, must degenerate to serve their needs. Eventually, both "god" and "subject" degenerate and become conditioned to the demands of Evil in all its forms, and Evil then controls both sets of puppet strings.

People are caught up with cults and political madmen of all kinds because feelings amounting to salvation of the individual ego emanate from the leader of the group whom their own need has appointed. He is under a strong obligation to give off these signals to his followers. At first, his ego may be inspired by reflection to feel very important and rightly motivated, but later he may become aware of his subjects' use of him. Then God help the "subjects!" He will not let on about his discovery but proceed to change them into herds of swine, just as Hitler did in Germany. He gave each man the notion that he was a superman; but to him they were all super pigs, expendable servants of his glory, living testimony to his might and power and divine authority.

Generally speaking, particularly in our one-to-one relationships, the roles of hypnotist and subject are shuffled back and forth a great deal. One moment, one person is the hypnotist, and the next moment, the other one is, in a continual conscious or unconscious jockeying for the upper hand.

At times, we become aware of others using us, and sensing that they are asleep to the principles involved, the tyrant in us takes over and becomes an authority that they cannot escape from or deny. This is because once people allow themselves to get caught in this trap, they cannot admit that they have given up their authority to another. They see their subjugation as "love." A clever hypnotist, seeing the power that his followers have placed in his hands, can use it to keep them asleep to the fact that he is licensing their baser desires to further his own mad ends. This was dramatically evident in the case of Hitler, but if you look closely and objectively at some of your local leaders—doctors, ministers, counselors, etc.—you may see the principle at work on a smaller scale.

Of course, on occasion, the minister or tyrant may remain unaware of the process he has been caught up in. He may not realize that he is being used to license the depravity of his followers. He may spend his entire life working hard and diligently, doing good works, loving and helping his sinful flock, and not realize until the very end of the road that he was being used, and that his "love" and "devotion" were actually a compulsion to serve the evil in his flock in return for the flattering image of himself they mirrored back to him.

Let's admit it—we all live in this hypnotic relationship with one another. We're just too "bewitched" to be aware of it. And the last thing we want to see is the awful truth about ourselves.

Under hypnosis, a man can be made to stand on his head, but only rarely can he be made to understand why he does so. Even the hypnotist is unable to convince him of the real reason behind his foolish behavior. Whenever we are motivated by another person, our pride simply refuses to see that we're not our own boss. No matter how outlandish our behavior is, we cannot relinquish "authorship," so we are forced to fabricate "reasons" for having done what we did.

In reality, we have no life of our own. From the very start, we have entered into hypnotic relationships with the people in our environment, and each has left its mark on us. But we cannot realize this as long as we are playing god, rationalizing, explaining away, rewriting the script as we go along to cast our ego in a better light. We imagine that our security "naturally" depends on the approval of others, so we bow and scrape to get it, and they make us do terrible things to feed *their* feeling of security, even as we make them do terrible things to lull us into forgetfulness of what we have done in the past, and to make us feel secure through their elevating and saving "love." While we are using them, they are using us in exactly the same way. The illusion is flawless. Arm in arm, corrupting each other mutually, for the sake of our proud egos, we march blindly down the broad road to destruction.

When a woman marries a man for this kind of ego security, she cannot accept any correction from him because she is *using* him to maintain her own sense of being right. His presence in her may become so strong, or she may draw on it so avidly, that she may lose her feminine nature entirely—gradually, "she" becomes "he." Then when he criticizes her (for what he has licensed her to do), she does not see that criticism as emanating from or originating in him at all but sees it as her own criticism of him, based on her own original observation of his fault. As long as he worships her, she loves him. In other words, she is secure on her throne. But his slightest criticism of her becomes *her* condemnation of him and justifies her. Her illusions about herself are strengthened by that "divine" judgment.

A man unrelated to the truly Divine Presence is helpless in the hands of such a woman. In "loving" her, he is feeding her some of his own nature, and in judging her, he is arming her with judgment upon him; until she, gorged on his essence and drunk on the power of his judgment, goes out of her mind.

The man who finds Reality does not love a woman in the way that her ego demands, and he then does not hate or judge her. His relationship with the God Presence is intact, and he cannot be used to support illusions nor has he any need to play games. He discerns by the Light of Truth, and when a woman reaches out to him, she is forced to reflect that discernment because she can in no way "absorb" such a man and take title to his identity. And since there is no excitement in discernment, she will become free to see things the way they are. Of course, if she is a proud woman, she may insist on seeing the man's discernment as "judgment" in order to maintain that judgment in herself. But more about this subject in later chapters.

3

The Fall

The human race could have come into existence in one of two probable ways. Man either evolved *from* animal, or he *de*volved from a higher order *to* animal. Either way, we are on the move: on the way up, or on the way down, from an original pair. The process, whether it be devolution or evolution, must be progressive and orderly. The first specimens of the type appear, and others come from them. No creature can set the process in motion; a species does not come into existence spontaneously in different parts of the world, but inherits its place in the scheme from a parent.

No man, whether he be evolving or devolving, can originate. He can only inherit. But what does he inherit? Is it the "innocence" of evolution or the "guilt" of devolution? In other words, as life goes on, are you getting better or worse? In the possibility that we are actually deteriorating, can you also see the possibility of an original sin on the part of the first pair that started us on a downhill course? Or do you still prefer to think that we're on the way up?

As long as the two possibilities exist, an objective

look at the field of human feelings should provide us with some clue as to which theory is more tenable. We seem to have inherited quite a storehouse of feelings, but which ones are "natural" for us? Which of our proclivities have simply "become" natural? For example, let's take the impulse to steal. If it seems natural to us, we will naturally give ourselves over to the impulse, and as we continue to steal, our desire to steal grows progressively stronger. Now, place a restriction on it, and you have an unhealthy repression of "natural" desire, which is still accumulating in a natural way.

It is this writer's contention that although man does inherit a natural body, complete with natural (animal-like) desires, these animalistic desires are not at all natural for man; and that each desire rises out of the untamed one that preceded it and that he gave in to on the grounds of "naturalness." He would ask you to beware of the words: "only natural," because they are keeping you from the discovery of your authentic Self.

When you begin to question, you learn to discern what is natural and what is temporal, transitory, masquerading as permanent, original, and natural. You will also see what it is in the world that is promoting "naturalness" and why.

If we accept the idea of evolution (for man), we must also accept the naturalness of every impulse that arises in us, but just look at what happens when we do! Surely our tendency to do exactly as we please forms the very root of all our troubles. But if we can open our minds to the concept that we are "naturalized" citizens here as the result of an original error until we learn the lesson of error, then we can honestly begin to question our temporal natural feelings and seek for the way to modify them, to see restored in ourselves the bright nature that was lost in the Fall.

The world, of course, is mostly encouraging you along the path of evolution, encouraging you to give way to your feelings. "Live it up," they urge. "Express yourself; be free!"

A soul in search of Truth finds these lies indigestible. He is ever ready to admit the error of his way, whereas the egotist can never be wrong. His vanity impels him to pile sin on sin, desire on desire, fall on fall, like the growth rings of a tree, with emotion supplying the sap.

We are either growing from natural good, refining ourselves, getting better—or we are growing more faulty, repeating over and over again the errors of our forebears. We must either be *e*volving or *de*volving. If we are evolving, going from "good" to "better," the moment of consciousness must be the moment of decision without the factor of deception—we must see clearly the road we are taking. But suppose, then, we were to choose the base or evil? Is there another choice? What covenant could God have made with us or our primitive forebears to assure us of salvation? Looking back on things from the evolutionary point of view, we see that Adam could not have known what he was getting into, but we, being in it, seeing error repeat itself and grow worse with the repetition, should be well aware of what we need to get *out* of. I know that I am. It is the observation of the mess around me, in fact, that makes the entire idea of salvation so fair and beautiful. And I have hope for salvation because I have now become aware within myself that a promise, a covenant, *was* made, even though it was not made to me personally even as the choice was not personally mine to make.

Only a first man could have made that choice from which man has descended. As individuals, here and now, we have something good to look forward to, inasmuch as the worst (the wrong choice) is behind us. If, on the other hand, we're on the way up from ape-hood, we have yet to make that choice as individuals. Either way, the story of man unfolds from that fateful first day. What happened then determines whether we are innocent or guilty at this moment.

The meaning of our presence here on earth is clear to me. Clearly, it is for the spirit of man to learn of the nature of error, of vanity, and the full extent of the love and forgiveness of God, the Creator. We could not learn our lesson in Paradise, which is the place reserved for the perfect, the place where not a single error can be found for us to practice our overcoming on—and until we have learned to overcome the evil, our very presence would corrupt Paradise and hence be intolerable there. But here on earth, we are free to go on duplicating the original theme (the Fall) until we see what there is to be seen and learn what there is to be learned—and fall we must until we do. Or, to take the other viewpoint for a moment, we can go on living in our original innocence, give ourselves over to the pleasures of the world and get high on our "God-given" feelings such as anger, hate, lust and fear. We can say with wide-eyed innocence, "Why, God would not have made us this way if He hadn't intended us to give in to it, would He?" Under this system, it's hard to see how we could have an unnatural desire, in which case all's well with the world and what's to learn?

Inasmuch as I would like to get the theory of evolution out of the way once and for all in order to get on with this book, let's take one more look at it, this time with the idea of dealing it the "coup de grace." Let us assume for the sake of argument that we are indeed on our way up from the ape. When we assume something to be true, and it is not, we cannot go very far before we run into contradictions, situations that cannot possibly square with our theory. For instance, if we were to start with the assumption that 1 plus 1 equals 3, we could not go very far before we discovered that something was radically wrong with our calculations.

Let us assume, then, that we are risen beasts, having descended from apelike progenitors. If this is the case, nothing that man is naturally prompted to do can produce a fault or error in his development. He comes into the world with an original "innocence" as a child of nature. He can commit no injustice because he is not free to stray from nature's course. In fact, such moral considerations as individuality, freedom and purpose, fairness and justice are nonexistent under the law of the jungle, which is simply that the fittest shall survive. In a cold statement of natural fact there is no room for hypothetical idealizing; either it's so or it isn't. If it is the law under which we must exist by nature, we must accept it in the same way we accept the fact that we cannot, by taking thought, change a single hair on our head. All we can say is, "Well, that's just the way it has to be."

So, accepting our animal nature as "natural," we fair children of nature cannot be discontent with our lot in life or our natures or the natures of others. We would all naturally agree with one another under this natural system, even if we should agree to fight someone to the death. We could never fight for our "rights" because everything and everybody would be right just as it existed.

We could have no moral problems, no conscience, no inner conflicts, no emotional disturbances; and without emotional disturbance we would have almost no sickness, no cross-purposes, no conflicts of interest. Our only "purpose" would be the one that nature had decreed for all of us, and we would never have to decide anything for ourselves. We would all be healthy and happy except that we would not know that we were, as we would have no consciousness to give us this awareness. After all, in a naturally perfect world, where we never had to decide anything or control anything, a consciousness would be superfluous; a big brain should do very nicely. (And many a big "brain" would "drink to that!")

Perhaps I've taken the argument far enough. By now it's clear that the state of being I've described bears little resemblance to the world we live in. We do have conflicts, we do have emotional disturbances, and we are extremely sensitive to the injustices of others when they threaten our "rights." Certainly we should not be able to hold our neighbor "guilty" if he is just being his innocent monkey self! But we do. And all our judgments on our fellowman carry in them the tacit assumption that he could have "known better."

Now, before we settle on the theory that man is not a "risen ape" but a "fallen angel," there is one other possibility to examine. Suppose we are indeed rising toward consciousness or union with the Creator, but we just haven't gotten there yet. If that be so, then how far do we have to travel on the evolutionary scale before we experience this? Will it be in our lifetime? Or in the lifetime of some Super-Brain of the future? And what good does that do us as individuals? Or don't you think that *you* are important as an individual? Can you find comfort for the consciousness you don't have yet in the thought that you are just an expendable ancestor to the perfected souls of the future, even as the apes are to us?

Also, if we are rising toward enlightenment, the fact that we have not yet arrived does not reflect in any way on the correctness of our present condition. We must be moving in an orderly way, without choice, from one correct state to another even better correct state. In which case, it doesn't really matter where we find ourselves on the rainbow relative to the pot of gold at the end of it. We're all right where we stand. Are you? Or perhaps, at a very special moment in our lives, we are each to be given a choice, an opportunity to transcend our present state.

But let me ask what it is that prompts you to search for answers to such questions as these? Is it not *problems*? And now that you want to live a better life, should you not be able to make that *choice* to be good? But if you are *evolving* to betterment anyway, why bother? Where is the need for choice or "self"-improvement?

Have you noticed that your life is one big problem, filled with sickness, conflict, guilt? Are you getting better "naturally," or are you naturally getting worse? Of course, you see that you are getting worse, not better. And if you do wake up to the need for a better life, it is because the sheer agony of a faulty present existence drives you to seek the higher ground. Then you discover that although you would like to make a choice to become a better person, you cannot, either because you don't know how or because the ability to do so is simply not available to you.

The reason you can't make that choice is that you were wrong before you knew that you were, as the result of a decision that you obviously could not and did not make, and that is now used up. You simply discovered the error—you don't know how it got there, and you don't know for sure what it is. But if you are wrong and guilty, it must be as the result of a choice, though *you* don't remember having made one; and now you are adding to the guilt by trying to excuse it or make a decision that you lack the authority to make. You are as guilty for trying to be good as you are for not being good and excusing it. There is no guilt without choice; yet when you try to make that choice, you feel the guilt of that foolhardy attempt. Now, if you are an evolving ape and you claim the right to make that decision, go ahead and decide to be a better person by your own efforts. See if you can do it.

What happens is that you start acting like the kind of person you think you ought to be, repressing all the contrary emotions that don't fit your new "role" until finally you can't stand your own hypocrisy—the sweet drivel issuing from your mouth turns your stomach (to paraphrase the good book). So then you might decide to let your hair down and let nature take its course; but if you have any sensitivity at all, you see that it's downhill all the way. And you realize that you were going in a downward direction (devolving) all along, since nothing was really changed by your efforts to improve yourself. Surely your own experience tells you that you cannot choose good from evil—all choices are blind and compulsive in favor of more error. The best you can hope for is salvation from one you did not make, simply because you are *not* an evolving ape but a devolving proud fool that needs to be saved from a choice that has been used up. This sad state of being is your legacy from the past.

You wake up dead wrong already, never knowing Right but partaking of the mystery and misery of the guilt that you share with the entire human race. But how can you be wrong without having chosen the wrong, even though the very "way" or "quality" of life you inherited is wrong? And how could you "choose" it unless you personally had some alternative? No, the fact that you are guilty in the way you exist and that you can't make yourself better indicates that you are under a curse, falling from a point of choice, not rising to a choice. You add fresh guilt on top of the old by your blind proud attempt to improve or excuse your existence, rather than to seek the salvation that has been reserved for that special day of repentance.

If you have not yet discovered that your New Year's resolutions don't work, just keep trying. One day you will see how impossible it is to make a choice; that is, if you don't drop from exhaustion and frustration first. Even though your conscience keeps nagging you about the way you are living, it will nag you just as much for the efforts you make to lift yourself by your own bootstraps.

So, if you are not innocent, you still could not have made the choice because that choice originated the entire human race; and if you are innocent, you are ascending to make the choice, meaning that you are an evolving animal on the way toward the spiritual plane. But the fact is that *you* can't make the choice, the transition, because the only choice has already been made, used up and not by you.

A lie stands in the way of man's salvation, a lie I mean to dispel if you will bear with me awhile. A seeking soul can recognize the truth by referring all that presents itself to him to his conscience, and great is the joy of recognition. But there is an error in man, and as it develops in the course of his fall from grace, it becomes manifest in outward, tangible ways—symptoms. People who have fallen to the same point in the progression of error will share the same kinds of problems, and as this book unfolds, we shall be taking a good long look at some of the worst of those problems. But we shall proceed on the premise that man is, in fact, *falling*, not rising.

4

Hypnosis and Animal Magnetism

. . . For by whatever anyone is made inferior or over-come or worsted, to that (person or thing) he is enslaved. —2 Peter 2:19

A person tends to look for *reassurance*, support, and comfort to the person or thing that has already enslaved him, and whatever he may receive from that source only makes him worse. He becomes weaker, more dependent. A body builds around the core of an original impression and is subject to the cause of the impression, which is the "god" of (and in) the emerging creation. The oak tree builds around the acorn because the image in the seed has not been altered or dislodged by another impression, such as any of the pressures that are brought to bear in an evolutionary process. The forces of good and evil contend for the soul of man amid the continuing pressures of a negatively charged environment.

To the degree that a body responds emotionally, to that degree it learns, develops, and is enslaved to the source and must answer again when called by the "master" who sired the response. We take shape from, and we owe allegiance to, what turns us on, motivates, comforts us. As we become worse and cause others to respond to us, they become worse in turn. Our very presence can be a pitfall to the unwary ones around us, and we become a "master" to them.

The body that responds readily becomes completely vulnerable to subtle inferences, subliminal and verbal suggestions, persuasions, lies, false philosophies. He is easily tricked into wrongdoing by flattery and ego-building lies of all kinds, including excuses and justifications, and he is an easy mark for remedies that are not remedies at all, but temptations that lead to greater dependencies and compulsions.

In the beginning we have the lie that tempts, then the suggestions that "save." The original lie is a matter of choice, but the others arise as a matter of need (if only to save face). For example, if we have been misled, deceived in some way, we draw upon the excuse; or being in a quandary, the idea of having a drink begins to have a stronger appeal to us than it might otherwise. The process is progressive.

Hypnotic suggestion and animal magnetism work hand in hand to keep men and women slaves of the evil that is working its way up through them. The most powerful type of suggestion is an outcrop of animal magnetism, based on emotional excitement or a direct appeal to a person's ego. Suggestions are used to make the victim doubt the truth and embrace the evil. After he has been talked into doing something foolish, he feels bad, so that when he is offered a "remedy," he sees it as "natural" and "reasonable" that he should want to feel good again, and he reaches out for what is offered. Thus he falls into the "remedy" trap where the hope of a cure becomes the compelling sickness. The last stage of suggestibility is reached when a person loses all sense of direction within himself. He is easily excited, and because he is direction-needful, he will respond to almost any suggestion, direction, even demands, without question or ability to resist.

Let's go over the ground again from a slightly different viewpoint. Words without enlightenment, because they are the most sensitive tools available to us for communication, are hypnotic by nature. They can become an acceptable substitute for conscience in a vain or weak person, permitting him to do as he wills. Hypnotic suggestions agree with our ego will, as well as the state of mind that we reach ultimately, wherein we no longer have a will of our own but are compulsively subject to deception. The first half of a person's life is spent doing "his" thing—the last half hiding from the shame of it.

For example, if you can persuade a man to steal, it must be because his ego wanted that "advantage" anyway, and he would have stolen before if he had not been inhibited by his conscience. All you have to do is energize the belief that it is his "divine" right to have. The ego derives energy from the fact that he is inclined in the wrong direction and welcomes the offering, support, and encouragement of the temptation.

Hypnotic persuasion is acceptable and possible

only because: 1) our ego wants to believe the lie, and 2) the excitement behind suggestion provides the motivation to move us in the direction of the intellectualized concept or false ideal. Motivation (evil operating through the force of animal magnetism) is required to create and power a false idea, just as Divine motivation is required to make us know and do what is right. The man in our example must first be motivated by animal force to accept the lie as the Truth, and then he steals.

Now suppose you were the first man on earth, the first to be tempted. What position does this put you in? Surely, separated by the temptation from the ground of your being, you can no longer be in contact with the Power that could motivate you correctly. This is because the false belief, motivated by a vastly different order of stimuli, has separated you from possible future modification of any of your responses under the original system. No longer standing on original ground, you have been pulled over the line (changed) by this spiritual tug-of-war because you lacked the ground to dig your heels into for resistance. From this time on, the war is on the enemy's ground on his terms. The power and the ground for future resistance no longer exists for you.

Life is a continuum. One cannot live wrongly one moment and rightly the next. Many of us think that we can, but we are quite mistaken. Whatever "good" we see in a person is usually only an intellectualized idea motivated by a lie to help us deceive ourselves. Real life is more decisive and permanent.

The weak end up in the enemy's belly and become the life support of the victor. In much the same way, when the lie is believed, a new way of life is conceived, one that supports the victor and assigns the victim's vitality and power over to him.

So lies, suggestions that appeal to the wishful thinking of our ego, pull us off balance in favor of the new order: temptation. Once we give in, we are *bound* to answer to other demands. The pressures of animal magnetism and conditioning claim our responses on a permanent basis. We can no longer resist because we have been completely swallowed up by the environment that introduced us to the lies and support factors for our ego. The order under which we now live is that of the animal. The most powerful combination of suggestion and magnetism is a "polite suggestion" that really covers a demand. Hypnotic suggestion brings us down to being subject to demand.

Our human dilemma is the result of our having been cut away from the true ground of our being, the ground on which we might once have taken our stand to see clearly and resist the tempter. A suggestion that makes our selfish wish or desire appear to be possible is the lie, always exciting, that cleaves us away from what is reasonable and just. Still assuming that this has happened to you, as the first man or woman on earth, you can see how it will be from this point on. The body, with the soul trailing helplessly behind, will continue to answer to similar demands and appeals, with or without suggestion. Once the choice has been made, used up by you, it will not be available again. Mankind forevermore will inherit a choiceless way of life.

Once a person is motivated to act wrongly, that which motivated him to do so becomes the only motivation he knows. It also matches and upholds the only "direction" he knows. What has developed in him owes its existence to what established it there in the beginning. His body becomes obedient and compulsive, answerable to that presence as well as to pressure. He adapts readily to new temptations and pressures that appeal to the same ego fault. He can be made over into a robot instead of a man with an entirely new nature, character and set of values that seems "natural" and "proper" to him. Such a robot enjoys doing the wrong again and again. He feels vital and alive only while he is being motivated by that which made him as he is. If he has been motivated to steal, he gets his "kicks" out of stealing.

Once the body learns to respond to emotional stimulus, any other emotional influence, particularly emotional upset (pressure), will contribute to the development of that animal body. Tension, fear, and guilt will develop as well as beastly cravings and a lust that can never be satisfied. We embrace, or "love," that which stirs "life" in us, so that in effect we are slaves to it, and it is "good" and "god" to us. As the creature adapts to its environment, it becomes totally dependent upon the vibrations and supports emanating from it. When any creature evolves, it embraces the new environment to which it adapts and upon which it now depends.

Animals just naturally steal from each other. Similarly, when we tempt and upset a person—make a monkey out of him in a manner of speaking—we may create in him a desire to steal and act like a monkey. In reacting to us, he deserts his birthright as a human being in favor of the way of the animal. In addition, the animal desire to steal somewhat matches his ego need to claim the godhead, to be master of all that he looks on. "What's yours is mine, and what's mine is mine also" is the philosophy every child seems to have when it comes into this world, already deeply etched in both its ego and animal natures.

As the body continues to decline, respond, and develop, various needs arise that are not actually related to the individual's basic ego selfishness. For instance, a person who has been made nervous by constant nagging may suddenly see the idea of a drink as tremendously attractive. Unloving parental pressures can lead to a veritable parade of unwholesome "needs." One does not have to be very astute to see the pejorative intent (unconscious though it may be) behind such a remark as "You will grow up to be a drunk and a criminal just like your father." Such a remark acts as a powerful suggestion to a person who is already off-center, upset, and resentful. After all, we did not begin life with an ambition to be the world's biggest glutton, dope head, or drunk.

The pressures of animal magnetism create the climate in which the power of suggestion flourishes. Make a man hate anything enough, then put a gun in his hands, and he will kill the first person you point out to him with the suggestion that he is the "enemy." He will rarely turn to kill the source of the suggestion that leads to his ruination because that source is also his "god," the source of his life and motivation.

It is in just that way that evil dictators condition the people to fight so readily for them. By means of unrelenting lies and pressure, they develop an enormous power over their followers. The same technique is used in brainwashing camps, where men are subjected to such continual and unholy pressure that they gradually become dependent on the motivation of their taskmasters—sometimes even learning to love them with an insane "loyalty."

Once you have pressured someone away from his own "center," he becomes so unbalanced, nervous, afraid, and confused, that if you suggest to him that he is going out of his mind, he accepts the suggestion readily. It will seem to be the confirmation of what he already suspects to be true. A "friend" might re-mark unthinkingly, "My, you look terrible today, just like so-and-so did just before he went insane," and such a remark will put the finishing touch on a condition that was set in motion by the insane pres-sures of unloving parents. Here, again, that person did not have insanity as his lifelong ambition.

Once a person is suggestion-prone, certain sug-gestions are irresistible to him because they match the fears, hungers, desires, or anticipations that have already grown up in him as the result of this sort of conditioning. When a man accepts the suggestion that it is natural for him to take up drinking as an answer to his problems, he accepts a lie, a new substitute for his conscience, and his way of life begins to duplicate the "original sin" setup. This time, however, there is no conscious consent to it. The idea trails the compulsiveness or arises from it as a need to excuse it. But see how he clings to that lie and the excitement of indulgence in it until it is no longer enough for him, and he must seek newer and bigger excitements. In obedience to this principle, many churches have grown top-heavy with pomp and ceremony. As the novelty of a ritual fades and it becomes less exciting, new rituals are added to the old ones that are retained for their traditional values. In this way, the faith is revitalized and kept going, and the priestcraft retains its control of the flock.

While preoccupied with the suggestion (what he thinks he needs and loves), a man cannot realize what is going on or come to his senses. His condition is no longer based on an original temptation, but on a thought process (suggestibility) that originated in, and continues to be manipulated by, the processes of animal magnetism. The thoughts that come to him in this state he believes to be originating within himself as a divine original instinct that he associates with a personal (divine) freedom. The hunger arises first, in answer to an ego need, and the appealing idea that comforts, matches, or excuses it comes second and "frees" him to satisfy it.

Whatever excites us makes us crave it as though

it were our own idea. Little children, born without original and true roots of their own, must be carefully guarded. They want everything that excites them as though it were something they had "always wanted," even though they may never have seen such a thing before. When children are loved as they should be, they are not allowed the luxury of these things but are kept from exposure to too much temptation, companionship, and outer conditioning.

Man's responsiveness to the hypnotic power of physical objects (cars, houses, motorboats, gadgets, prestige symbols, ad infinitum) is closely related to his responsiveness to woman, who comes to represent the doorway leading to all the "good" things of the world. She is the familiar ground from which his kind of existence sprang, and she is Super-Object to man in his restless, covetous, ambitious quest for "things." The delicate relationship that exists between the hypnotic power of things and the hypnotic power of woman (from a man's viewpoint, of course) will be dealt with more fully in a later chapter.

If you emotionalize any person sufficiently, you will create a creature-animal that will not only answer to you, its outside maker, but will also make a home in itself for the false spirit of "truth," the unholy spirit that seizes every opportunity to stand in the holy place. Women do this almost instinctively to their men and their children, and few men are able to escape the emotional tyranny of the woman.

Born of orginal sin, all of us are cells in the system

of a gigantic beast (country), and each beast has its own grotesque head or "ministering angel" (in the form of a king, dictator, or elected official). When you respond emotionally, you simply receive and pass on your orders. The "cell" that you represent carries them out insofar as it can, then feeds the impulse to the next cell, so that the original *head* that caused the original response remains god to us all. He finds his emissary in the woman. Through her his way is passed on to her offspring to produce a society in which all are subject to the corruption of the vehicles that preceded them in the form of parents, who are subject in the same way to their parents, back into antiquity. But through it all, it is the "serpent" that holds the reins of our destiny and the pattern of our identity.

Woman has the power to re-create the original misery, or original sin, by a mystique that she does not understand herself. It pushes up in her compulsively, then projects to and takes shape in the man and beckons to her from its new home in him. Her compulsion now takes on added force as she becomes tempted by herself in him. And when her son appears, she transmits something of this same essence to him, so that he is forced to bear the mark of the beast and fall for the "beauty" when he matures.

A man's ego is constantly reaching for something that it should not need in a way that is as faulty as it is traditional. He reaches out to the image of a woman, and the woman herself, for reassurance and support. Her image bears the impress of the original exchange of identities perpetrated by his mother, who violated him and claimed him for the process when he was very small. Men are compelled to keep that image alive because it is the core of their being, upon which their existence rests. Pornography is one of the means popularly employed to support this imagery.

A man must learn to reject the image of woman as an answer, entertainment, support, or comfort to his ego, to suffer the emptiness and anxieties that will assail him in its absence and wait patiently for the unmerited grace of salvation that will break the chains binding him to the process. Until the vacuum is created in the mind, the new answer cannot be drawn into it. The pain of the sincere soul's need calls upon God's invisible presence for salvation from original sin and restoration of its true identity and path of life.

Whatever good is, man cannot decide to be its living embodiment by his own will because an original decision was made that referred him to animal ways, subject to burning for woman. He may refer to this burning as "love," but it is not true love at all. Only a yearning for salvation from the process of "love" can save him from it through an answer of His grace that is never merited but becomes possible only after a man rejects the idea that his ego must have the comfort of woman or material advantages and remedies.

For her part, a woman would do well to recognize that she does not truly have the strong sex drive or desire that man has, but tends to lie about her needs in that area to keep the only security she knows, the deteriorating presence of her lover, on whom her body and soul feed in a vampirish way. Her need is largely for physical presence, while his need is for deception and motivation toward fame—at the very least, for reassurance about the nature he has inherited. He needs her lies and motivation, and she needs his deteriorating body presence or essence.

When a woman is honest about her sexuality, she risks losing her security through waking her husband to the facts; but though she may flounder for a season, the pain of this, too, will call upon God's grace to infuse more new life into her. When she loses the false security of the man's maleness, she is again forced to seek strength in a new way and from a right source. Indeed it is incumbent on both men and women to desire no substitute for Truth, to recognize false needs and values and reject both their image and their emotional support. Only then can they make way for a new answer and life impulse from within.

5

The Tyranny
of Sex

When Truth is not uppermost in the mind of a man, sex is. And as long as it is, he cannot see or find the truth. And as long as he abandons himself to sex, he becomes increasingly addicted to woman. This fixation, of course, is a hypnotic one, a legacy from his mother that he unconsciously transfers to his wife.

A male child in his early years comes under the dominating influence of his mother, and in most cases she is a woman who has never known the loving correction of her parents or her husband. Although she is quite unaware of the effect she is having on her son, her uncorrected presence is a shock to his system. It is a temptation that lights a fire in his nature and sets the pattern of his female-oriented conditioning. She becomes a ''god'' to him and inadvertently prepares him for his ''Eve,'' who, of course, inherits in him, a compulsive woman worshipper.

In the presence of Eve, a man's body comes to ''life,'' and the name of that ''life'' is ''lust.'' This lust she comforts, and in doing so, she provides him with more temptation and more support for a faulty way of life that leads to more lust. So that while a man gains the ego ideals and illusions about himself that he craves, a woman quite often assimilates the entire man, all that he is and all that he has.

As long as she remains uncorrected, "Eve" is obliged and even compelled to take advantage of her "Adam." She is not only tempted by his weakness and the advantages to be gained from playing on it, but she is further excited by the reflection of herself in him; because, as you may remember, he has taken on some of her nature by responding to her. A seeking woman caught up in this compulsion feels twinges of conscience about it, whereas an egocentrically inclined woman feels that she is inheriting a sort of Divine "right" (security). She consolidates her advantage with additional security precautions in the use and development of her power to promote his sex needs or simply comfort him in them.

Sex desire is the evidence of an orginal conditioning coming to full bloom from the seed in the ground that conceived it. It is a man created in the image of a woman, and after her likeness, coming back to "god" to worship her for the sake of his original life, original sin being the source and the support for all false life. That life is an ambitious one, even though the individual man may have no personal desire to be ambitious because he needs the woman's natural support and reassurance, and to get it, he is obliged to be ambitious. And there you have acceptance of suggestion not based on original agreement, but arising from a woman's animal magnetism.

A woman is a man's origin in the way he thinks himself to be a man. If a woman were not present, he could not think of himself as a man; and without the environmental direction, support, and illusions that emanate from her, he would fall apart. Even if he does not want to entertain illusions about himself but would rather seek his true identity (salvation), a man finds that the ground of his being is inherently identified with woman, and he feels obliged to do her pleasure, first, by virtue of his ego deficiency, and second, by virtue of his sex drive, his sensitivity to her magnetism. A woman's "loving" presence is synonymous with ego support to a man, whether he likes it or not; this kind of ego support arouses his animal nature on a compulsive basis. As woman comforts this animal nature and hardens man in the course of his conditioning, she also fills the void in him that would otherwise have caused him to cry inwardly for identity. Her comfort and reassurance arouse his highest animal feelings toward her and cause him to burn for her sexually, over and over again, with each "fulfillment" sowing the seed of greater need, so that the promise of ultimate contentment is never kept.

A woman's uncorrected presence acts as a companion temptation to man, comforting and motivating him in the ancient tradition. So man is sensitive, both to a woman's guile and to a woman's body, through which that guile operates. She is his source, the only one he knows; and as time goes on, she also becomes his identity. An unspoken communication passes between them. In effect, she is saying, "If you want my support, if you want me to help you *be* something, if you want relief for the pain and burning that my presence produces in you, get me the things of the world and/or love me, glorify me."

Men have always felt guilty, lost, hopeless without women. They grow desperate to the point of deteriorating like an animal when it is deprived of its accustomed environment. They feel the threat to the root of their being and will do anything to win back the acceptance and support of the woman. That "anything" includes an increased suggestibility to "her" will and the resumption of the old ambitious role. Thus men continue the lineage of original sin by which man fell in the beginning and to which process man is now a slave.

It pleases the ego of a woman to see a man responding to her like a trained seal, and her acceptance is his excitement, so that he lusts for her like an animal when she seems to withhold it. Some very desperate men become ferocious and try to frighten a woman into submission, forcing her through fear to support their ego. If they succeed in this, it is at the time of the woman's fearful submission that the man derives the greatest ego security and with it the greatest sexual lust.

Conditioned to lust after and to be accepted by his "god," a man will become more and more inadequate and in doing so will make greater demands on his "woman-god" to offset this effect.

The woman, on the other hand, conditioned to accept this man's ego demand that she tempt and delight him in devious and dishonest ways, may grow uneasy and anxious; for not being corrected by him, she is actually being abused by him in a secret subterranean way, and because he himself is not correct, she has no recourse but to use him also.

If each of them should try to become independent, he would lose his ego support, and she would lose the security of the miasma of his deteriorating presence. Without the other, each feels the original (sin) shame and guilt and must escape again and again to the false security of the other's arms.

The principle is the same for every hangup, beginning with marriage. The more a man is conditioned to woman, the more of a woman or beast he becomes, and the more he loses out in the process. Later on, he grows more anxious about the "man" he thinks he is in his brief moment of triumph, so he must return to gain reassurance, only to lose without knowing why. His moment of glory is only an illusion; it is also the very moment of loss—that is why he cannot see it. And one woman may not be enough; and still later, more women will not be enough, so he must go on to the bottle and the wild blue yonder. While our troubles do not begin with marriage or fornication, they certainly mature there.

When women are no longer sufficient to comfort a man's guilty and unsteady ego, he needs something in addition to women. The need created by his failure with women (his fall) is for something to make him feel high (as women do) and to make him forget his conflicts and inadequacies with the opposite sex and soothe the fires of tension and guilt. And almost invariably, the moment a man reaches this advanced stage of dire need, the proverbial snake in the grass shows up in the form of a person who has fallen a notch or two below our protagonist and offers him a drink.

The moment a man accepts drink as his support, he is weaker for having accepted the suggestion. He learns to come back to it again in time of need, just as he did, or perhaps still does, with women. The total personality leans upon thousands of subtle dependencies, temptations and motivations that will be explained in later chapters.

The powers that be now trade on the weakness of the drinker, who is told that drinking is manly, healthful, sociable, necessary, and right. From his *need* viewpoint, it all sounds quite logical because these are the lies (suggestions) that his ego needs to feel secure in his existence apart from Reality, and so the threads that bind him to error grow into a rope.

Separate from the Light in his conscience, he remains subject to the power of animal magnetism, which creates abnormal needs, cravings, and hungers that also produce (independent) ideas (when a person is hungry, he thinks of food). And when he finds another person with the same idea, agreeing with him, he accepts his new "friend's" lie offering, that person and the thing in that person. But the ideas he accepts and the activities he engages in are not based upon his original ego plan. They are based instead upon what the serpent has made him want as though it were his own original idea, and therefore an idea that cannot possibly be wrong, and so his enslavement continues.

A man who is subject to animal magnetism is compelled to do things that are wrong, and when he does so, he needs something, or someone, to "steady" his nerves, to set things back in the "proper" perspective and justify his existence. To achieve this, he usually reaches out for a woman or a drink, whichever physical form or substance agrees with, best fulfills, or is most readily available to match his own. The process starts for all of us close to the time of birth with the trauma caused by our parents' failing presence. They manage somehow to feed on our dependence, seeing it as love, and borrowing from it a sense of power and respectability in themselves. The children who have been most violated in this way grow up shaky, needing people also—a boy in his way, a girl in her way. One of the signs of sickness in our current society is the fact that people can sing and enjoy listening to the song, "People Who Need People," without retching at the thought, without even seeming to be aware of the cannibalistic ways in which we express that unholy "need."

People feel that their loss of identity can be resolved, first, by love (sex), then wine, drugs, games, etc., and each addiction in turn grows to become another problem. Let me remind you again of the basic principle. Whatever tempts or comforts us leaves its mark on us, deposits in us something of its own essence that requires us to identify with it again and again to support the identity that is growing up in us as a result of playing host to the tempter. For this reason, once you have been tempted to do something, you will enjoy doing it again because it has planted its stimulation factor *in* you. It has modified you so that you can now act only out of the stimulation provided by that which now supports the feeling of life in you. In other words, what you have become is revitalized by what made you, or assisted you, in becoming what you have become. The impression that it has made on you needs (loves) the stimulation that made it in the first place, and all who sin are slaves.

The need for woman is a man's misguided need for God, a "god substitute" by displacement. The displacement comes about, of course, as a result of yielding to temptation. Anything that successfully tempts us displaces our true values and replaces the spiritual presence that *should* attend us with a false physical presence that should *not*. Step by step, we give up the (holy) ghost and turn ourselves over to the source of pressure, depending upon it to support us in the kind of life that it compels us to live. We gradually become remolded in the image and likeness of that which we respond to.

Before temptation, a man needs nothing; but after temptation, he begins to need more and more and be affected by everything. Whatever he amounts to originates at that point. If the physical presence in which the temptation resides should absent itself, the victim ceases to exist. For just as nothing can exist without a source (base of support) for it to originate from and stand upon, so the person tempted will cease to exist (and see his error) without the presence of that which tempted it.

A really crafty woman will not worry long over the dishonesty she is bringing to the relationship because she soon sees that it offers her a great variety of pleasurable effects "on the side," as it were. For one thing, the sex act is a great reliever of tensions and anxieties that may have arisen as the result of an argument. If she can induce her husband to forget the fight and love her suddenly, his sudden loving attention provides her with a sudden relief of anxiety that is indeed pleasurable. But it's the kind of "pleasure" a finger feels if it is plunged into a glass of cold water after being burned—if it had never been burned, it could never have known the pleasure of relief. In addition, sex is a great reliever of guilt; that is, she sees her husband's willingness to relate to her sexually as a blanket "pardon" from him for all that she is and has done. And, of course, there is always that vague psychic need for his body essence that she hopes to allay in the sex act. But this is a hunger without ceasing that grows greater with every attempt to satisfy it. If a woman is crafty enough to see *this*, she begins to repent of her craftiness and to long for an honest way of life.

The way back for a woman starts with her willingness to be honest with herself and her husband, regardless of what it may cost her in terms of advantages. She will allow the sex privileges her husband so desperately needs, but she will no longer feel compelled to "match" him in pleasurable reactions that she doesn't really feel. Also, she will be willing to assume her share of the responsibility for her husband's lust and forbear to hate him for it.

In the days and nights of her honesty, a woman will bring to the sexual experience the love and forbearance that were not available to her before by reason of her guile and mixed motivations. Now she will be able to suffer sexual abuse, if need be, without hating her husband for his need to abuse her, and in so doing she will become a correction to him, a shining example of what it is to love "for real."

Just as her dishonesty formerly provided the temptation to feed and perpetuate the problem, the honesty that she now brings to the same experience will undo the problem in her completely and will loosen its hold on her husband over a period of time.

Her new security will be based on the fact that she no longer needs to lie or to tempt—she can be free of guilt. Her husband, of course, is bound to wake up to her guiltlessness sooner or later, and he might not like it at all because, next to it, his own lust will look so lusty. But in the meantime, making love can become a beautiful experience for her, an opportunity to transmit a loving, nonverbal correction to him. And her husband's sexual desires, once overstimulated by her dishonesty, are gradually quietened by her love.

Virtue discourages vice, or to put it the other way around, the default of virtue automatically constitutes a temptation to vice. Before a woman finds love, honesty with her true Self, she plays the role of temptress to keep the man failing and falling. Her love is a lie. It supports him, aids and abets what he *is* as a result of not being true to himself, and so keeps him apart from that Self, so that as an unprincipled swine he cannot correct her either.

By now you may be wondering where a woman is to find the courage it takes to be honest, and where a man can find the courage to accept the possibility that he might not be living up to his highest potential. As far as this writer knows, there is only one answer to these questions: meditation. Love and courage are not qualities we can bestow on ourselves. At most, we can only long to be graced with them, to hunger and thirst after righteousness; and (correct) meditation is the way the sincere seeker of Truth has always employed to express his commitment to Good.

The victim of temptation identifies temptation with love and his life support and is terribly threatened if the temptation is suddenly withdrawn or lost. See how "gallantly" and fervently we fight for our vices, our dictators, and our women; for anything that corrupts us is our master, claiming our first loyalty—at least until the time when we see how we have been used by it. At that time, we may indeed rise up against the tyrant.

But how can a person fight against what has supported him, against what he really needs to exist and feel secure, without replacing it with another support? Unfortunately, the "comforter," the "saviour" that jumps into the breach is usually a more advanced form of temptation in disguise, and it takes us over where the first left off.

Until a person discovers the source of his true Identity (the truth that will set him free from his slavish way of life), he will always reach for an outer presence. Men owe their present dilemma, along with their actual physical existence, to women. What they do not realize is that they have come into being through a woman who has succeeded in demanding the life of a man and has received it to make yet another man to serve her appetite for the male essence. (Women, before you slam this book shut and go screaming into the night, remember that this is an unconscious process for the most part. You might find it helpful at this point to adopt an objective stance by relating yourself to a discarnate life form several planes above the physical body you inhabit—to take a "God's-eye view," as it were.)

As mother was temptation to father, so is she, from the moment of birth, temptation to her son. Hence, the displacement of values we observe in the male craving for support and acceptance from women. By the time the boy grows tall, his fall to woman is complete and her actual physical form is a kind of god to him.

Women are compulsively dishonest with men, and seeking women often see that they are under a compulsion to be dishonest in spite of themselves. They long to find a man strong enough to expose the compulsion for what it is and to insist on an honest relationship; but most men, unfortunately, don't want an honest relationship with an honest woman. Their ego demands that women continue

68

to play this little game with them, and it is a deadly game indeed.

A man's unconscious demand for a woman's dishonesty grows out of his need to deceive himself, and it supports the pride of ambition that is his security. He cannot allow a woman to be honest with him because in order to be honest with him, she would have to refer herself back to the true self that she has not yet experienced, but that she subconsciously *hopes* to be introduced to through her relationship with the man. But it would never occur to a man who is busy trying to *be* God to a woman to assist her in finding Him. Furthermore, society itself is so guilty that it places both men and women under a strong obligation to "play the game" and act out their sex roles "properly," lest they shine the light of truth into the comfortably dark corners.

Until she finds correction or a life force substitute, the "security" that a woman inherits is based on the faulty arrangement with man that now exists. She is "secure" by reason of his blindness to Truth, his insistence on identifying truth with *her*, and she is "superior" by reason of his responsiveness to her. She has power by reason of his needs, beauty by reason of his beastliness and saintliness by reason of his worship. Woman looks to man for the real security that his love would give her; but forced to "make do" with the false security provided by his weakness, she strives to identify it with the real security nevertheless. "It *must* be there," she tells herself, and she continues to test for it, nagging the life out of him in the process. But all that she can accomplish in this way is at the expense of his vital substance and her own illusions. She may go mad with the power that his weakness has turned over to her; or, if she is sensitive, she may fear that power, sensing somehow that it is not she who wields it, but the serpent that lurks secretly within her.

The incorrigible "woman's woman," not wanting to recognize the truth concerning her uncorrected nature, claims this demonic power as her own and proclaims the superiority of women. In doing so, she continues to identify with Satan, who is the woman's god before she is set free by the love of a man or God's love directly. Just as man is slave to woman (first, his mother and then his wife), woman is slave to the serpent, the original corrupting power that lurks inside her.

A man must find the love and the Light in his heart to contend against the evil in the woman, and when he does, he may appear to be fighting against her in the old way, but he will actually be fighting *for* her to free her from the forces of evil. For as long as a woman is a servant of the devil, she drains the life out of a man by demands that she is under a compulsion to make and that he cannot resist as long as he is asleep to this real identity. And as she draws upon his failings, he fails more and falls for her more, and she obtains the substance by which the evil in the world is served and made manifest in her.

In time, most women become manlike because they live on the essence of men. The ectoplasm of his nature that a man yields up in falling collects around the nucleus of the serpent, or evil, that resides in the woman to form a corrupted kind of "manness." At the same time, she is projecting her identity to him, marking him, so that he grows to bear the likeness of the evil that lurks in her.

A solid core of God-relatedness in man could safeguard him against the violation of his nature and enable him to stand as a correction to the woman. From him would emanate a real loving-kindness toward the woman that would ward off the dark forces that traditionally attend her and emancipate her to grow in a new and proper way. But while men base their sense of security on woman, all that they crave and need of her are the lies that come through her to feed their egos. A subtle exchange of identities takes place as the man takes on the guile and cunning of the woman and gradually becomes possessed by the evil spirit that attends her. This exchange is often quite overt, the man growing effeminate, the woman growing masculine, but whether it is plain to be seen or hidden from view, when the woman begins to play the role of the man, Evil is her guiding spirit, and everything is the reverse of the way it was at the beginning.

A man should offer his wife a new kind of security, the security of knowing that he is loyal for loyalty's sake, good for goodness' sake, and that he no longer requires her to exaggerate her interest in sex in order to support his ego. This will free her of the unholy demand men make upon women and leave her free to appreciate and respect what is true in him. And being reminded of Truth through him, she will first doubt and then discard her false self. In time, her contempt for man will change to love through shame. This can come about in marriage—after the smoke of battle has cleared away, that is; for the delicate perceptions of Reality are not easy to point out and share with another person. They can easily be misinterpreted and hotly contested. The astringent quality of true love, for instance, can be easily mistaken for coldness, even hostility, by the self-indulgent egotist, and it very often is.

A woman accepts the idea that she has, or will have when she has fully matured, a sex need that is similar to the man's, because her entire feeling of security is based on it. And in the beginning, she may not mind bluffing a bit and exchanging a salvo of sex for the many advantages she can gain in this way. But eventually, the need to lie begins to trouble her conscience, and the acting becomes burdensome. She may come to dread the sex experience, even though she retains the psychic need for the vibrations of man's deteriorating body presence gained in that manner.

The man, of course, is excited by the woman's pretending. It encourages the sex desire in him as it supports his ego, so he keeps coming back for more, and by doing so, he maintains a false sense of security in her. Most men, unfortunately, have fallen so low in their sexual cravings that the one-to-one relationships normal to human beings no longer satisfy them. They have deteriorated to the level of the herd, so that they require a wife to take the place of many cows.

A man actually "gets away" with this low-level living rather well. His physical body is able to adapt and develop a greater capacity for the activities that the male animal requires of it, and it is greatly aided in this by the fact that conscience rarely enters the picture, thanks to the cooperation of the woman. When it comes to the woman, though, conscience (hence, conflict) does enter the picture, and when it does, her beauty often goes out the window, and she starts to age beyond her years. She, after all, is invariably aware of the underlying "lie," and he is not, thanks to her having supported his ego and kept him comfortable. Her awareness joins hands with her fear of being truthful to create a conflict that threatens her health and well-being.

A woman is essentially monogamous. She finds it difficult to substitute for many cows in order to please her husband, who has become polygamous in his fall from principle, but she knows that in order to hold him and keep him "respectable" by being a good lover to him, she must also be a good liar. Although her ego security rests on his being a male animal, she may begin to have nightmares in which she sees him becoming a herd master and monster, without conscience, while she becomes a sexual slave—or slave-dealer, trading sex privileges for advantages in other areas.

No matter how monstrous a man may become, he likes to surround his sex life with an aura of respectability. He wants his boss and business associates to see him as a good, substantial married man, and his wife can use this need for social approval to increase her power over him for the sake of what she considers to be her own security.

A woman (as any lesbian knows) can learn to enjoy sex like a man or to convince herself at least that she finds some pleasure in the relationship with her husband, but the motivation that impels her to do so is the need to solve the conflict by trying to *be* the creature that she is pretending to be. Either way, her efforts in this direction provide a greater inducement to the male animal in her husband.

6

The Many Faces
of Love

We invariably interpret our need for someone as "love." But in reality, we are using our "loved" one, abusing him to serve an unrecognized, unhealthy purpose in ourselves. Such a "love" makes subtle and dangerous demands upon the victim. It is a love that grows more dependent upon the "beloved" as we force him to yield up vital force to those demands.

When we "love" another person through our need for love from him, we are unable or unwilling to free him to live his own life. We are inclined to weaken that "loved" one so that our own ego can continue to exist in security. Yet, when our "love" is actually "need," and not love at all, we become more needful and insecure at the center of our being, because we know it is morally wrong to indulge ourselves upon that person and use him to serve our vanity. It is wrong for us, humanly speaking, to live by another's support while we violate him, or "put him on" to obtain that support for our ego. The trouble with the world of love today is that it never comes closer to real love than this hypocritical state of "need" that we call "love." Secretly, we violate one another and live at one another's expense in the name of "love." That is, if we don't drive our "lover" off with our hungry demanding nature.

When we have been unfortunate enough to have been "loved" by a parent, we have been used by that parent to fulfill his or her emotional needs with our puppet-like conditioned responses. Very vain victims of this process are afraid to admit to their slavery. They interpret the giving up of their lives to a parent or spouse as "loyalty" and "devotion." Then, when the child-victim grows to become a parent himself, he naturally expects his children to respect him and give up the same something of themselves in the same way, all in the name of "love."

When you are tempted, regardless of who does the tempting, be it parent or friend, you are usually tempted by someone who professes to have your "best interest" at heart, but in that moment of obligation, you move silently away from the Light of Reason and change into an "environment" upon which the beguiler feeds. Once we have given up our true life to a beguiler, we tend to turn around and make good the loss by the same kind of demands on others. We become tyrants to our children, even as our own parents were tyrants to us, and their parents were to them. The identity and the lives of the young are sacrificed to serve the sense of righteousness and respectability in the parents, so that when the young grow to be parents, they think it only "natural" that they be given the same homage.

What can they do? This guilt, this lack of a life to call their own must be made up in some way; so "naturally" they feel it's right to stuff themselves with the same kind of "people-approval," to fill the void of guilt that the approval of people always brings. It is such an urgent, pressing need that they feel that a normal need of their body is being served. They don't realize how they are helping themselves to the lives of others, and they cannot see that they are violating others just as they were violated by others.

When children are ambushed in this way—when the lifeline that connects them to inner reason is broken by a parent's need—they become like dying plants that the fungus of society can prey upon. As the victim responds to the "love bite" of the "loving" vampire, he also becomes a vampire. The victim's life is actually converted into an environmental support by the love bite. Something of the nature of the vampire is transmitted to the bitten person, so that he also requires the life's blood of a weaker victim to exist.

Nature can live on nature with perfect safety, because the natural sequence of nature is based on a cause-effect relationship. Effects grow from causes that are effects of earlier causes, all the way back to the beginning. But the true love of man for woman should not be an effect of nature; nor should the woman's love for a man support the fallen nature in him.

An almost imperceptible change takes place in a man when he is tempted away from, or revolts against, Reason. His consciousness loses all direct life communication with the true authentic Self that would know how to deal honorably with the presence of woman. As a result, he cannot truly command respect, for no respectable woman can respect the indiscretions of a lusty male. She may try to ignore or avoid him, but in a direct confrontation, she has no recourse but to "turn him off" and make him feel embarrassed and ashamed. Under the circumstances, the man who is not yet ready to repent prefers to seek his comfort in the arms of the guileful, untruthful female.

A male who has been stripped of his identity in boyhood by his mother (his father not having been man enough to prevent her doing this to him), grows up with a need for assurance from a woman's environment. So when a woman, younger and more vital than his mother, comes along and "loves" him just the way he is, he seems to get back what he lost to his mother. And of course, he "loves" her for it. He also becomes the same sort of animal or weakling his father was in the process, and he pays for this ego support with the remainder of his life. In other words, when a man draws his ego support from the environment of a woman, he grows more dependent on her for that "security." Without her, he would topple. Meanwhile, the woman's ego is maintained by the soul food he provides in the offering of his body.

True love (whatever that is) strengthens and does not weaken another person. Being fulfilled, it has no need of its own, but corrects another's need. Ideally, man and wife share a common Source of life together. He, loving the purpose for which he was made, stands in the Light of Truth, and she shares that life as it is reflected through him. Such a love operating in man would correct a woman's ego need and prevent her from dominating and using him, while keeping her feminine in the order of grace.

The ego of a young man can be "love" trapped on a low level of existence by a woman who uses her love-support of him to keep him high on an ambitious binge. We honor this form of temptation, of course, and call it "encouragement." We cheer the young man on as he pursues the bait, and it isn't until he is hooked and standing at the altar that we sometimes have the grace to cry—women, especially, as they are considerably more aware than men of what is going on. In any event, the man thus trapped begins to deteriorate and become an unprincipled animal that grows to need his environment: woman. What he does not realize is that he is being used (as she is too, of course) and gradually becoming assimilated into the body of the female. Instead of sharing the life and the Light of God in man, she subsists on man's servitude, which was no real value to her, but only makes her wax fat, powerful, and strong in a parasitic way. This faulty kind of love relationship between man and woman provides a good breeding ground for cancer, which is basically a female disease. Her ego lies to him in the name of "love" to keep him dull and weak enough to live upon, like a mushroom on a decaying plant.

For a long time a man may not realize that he is literally being "loved" to death. If the pain of his dying wakes him up, it is only to the fact of his dying, not to the underlying causes, and he experiences a terrible concern and anxiety over the unfortunate turn that his "love" affair has taken. He may try to restore his life, make good his loss, with other women, but without understanding they will only do the same thing to him. So he persists in seeking and demanding more environmental support in the form of woman, because he has fallen to the order of woman. And that very demand tempts the woman to grow still more powerful.

At a certain point, a man may become aware that his environment no longer serves, but actually threatens him, so he revolts against women or learns to become one. When a man learns to survive in his jungle, it is usually by learning how to put the woman in the place that he once occupied in relation to her. He learns to take over *her* essence and assimilate *her* as a meal in exactly the same way that *she* ingested him originally, but with additional refinements.

As I have stated, cancer is basically a female ego disease in that it involves a negative void or lack that is striving to be filled in a vain and self-defeating way. When a person lives at another's expense, "loving" the life out of him for the advantages that only egotists can appreciate, he is the living representation of cancer in action, on the level of the soul. When a man gets cancer, it is because he has become, basically, a woman, and he begins to feed off

80

the "man" in the feminine form of his spouse.

A typical leukemia victim is the child who is "loved" to death by a doting egotistical life-needful woman. Her "love" is a vampirish need that appears to be genuine concern for her child, but actually weakens him and converts certain of his body cells to serve the needs of his life-hungry mother and answer the demands of the environment rather than the child's bodily needs. The more she loves him, the weaker grows the child.

Malignant tumors occur when a part of the body, the part most abused by the needs of the hungry ego, refuses to give up its life to the hungry ego's demands for life feeling. In order to protect whatever remains of its life against the ego-lust, the plundered component, cell, or gland, will plunder the life of other components that are not healthy enough to resist. These cells serve the malignancy in the same way that the now-malignant part once served the ego, until they reach a saturation point of abuse, rebel, and become malignant themselves. When this happens, they too form a center of resistance. So cancer runs wild in the body components, each part defending itself wildly against the lawless demands of other parts, without any pattern or clear direction, and all is anarchy.

Unless we live from the Light that illuminates reason, and share this light with the body components, we fall to temptation. Our body is changed subtly to give off an animal life force to others, and we then tap others to get it back. Our "love" is only the need we have for people to give us the same kind of support that we are giving to others without realizing we're doing it. The fact is that we cannot truly love another until we are self-sufficient, fulfilled by true love from within, so that we no longer have need of another's life and can no longer be tempted to violate him to get it.

A true love as it would reflect from man to woman would gradually effect an adjustment in her needs. For awhile they might share the same life root until their compatibility brought them to the same level of awareness, where each could switch over to the Light within himself. At that point, each would become a whole person, mature, and full of the kind of life and love that can set others free and can in no way weaken them.

While a good man lives, his good wife shares this Light and obeys him as he obeys God within. And if that man be taken from her, she will feel no real loss, because having obeyed him, having respected the respectable in him, and having cooperated with his proper demands, she has truly obeyed God. Her obedience to her husband has qualified her to remain in contact with Him who informed her husband and rendered him "obeyable," even in his absence.

In contrast, a woman who has never been properly loved by her husband is utterly lost in his absence. She flounders, and even curses her lover for leaving or dying, even to the point of pursuing him beyond the grave for this unearthly support, calling on a medium to deliver up his ectoplasm in a seance, or simply re-creating the past over and over again in her imagination.

We can "love" the life out of a person by our need; or we can impart life *to* a person by our love. When you cuddle a baby, your embrace can rob it of vitality, or it can impart a mysterious something *to* the child. A needful person is a taker, a psychic vampire, and children are more sensitive than adults to the demands such a person makes on the vitality of others. They often cry out in fear when someone approaches them with this kind of "love." They know instinctively that this is not "love" at all, but "need," a psychic craving of the ego for physical substance and security.

A person with an emotional need for "love" will never be satisfied with the quality of "love" he extracts from another person, but will use it to power his physical progress and spirtual self-deception, in a way that is detrimental both to himself and his "beloved."

It is true that people do have a capacity for love. But if we hurt the one we "love," how can we call our feeling "love"? We can not really love anyone as long as our ego insists on playing god, and as long as we believe that we can originate love, or that we are entitled to the love and homage of another as though we are indeed a god.

Quite often we use our approval to dub a person "Sir Knight," expecting him to glow with glorious adoration for us, the "King." Instead of falling into our trap, however, he seizes on our approval as an absolution from guilt and uses it to justify just about anything he wants to get away with.

When we have not found God's love within ourselves, we need the worshipful "love" of another to remind us that all is well, to give us the power to do wrong without losing our sense of security. Every wrong action on our part restimulates our need for reassurance in the form of our beloved's emotional embrace. We prefer his apparent opinion of us to our own, and we seek to escape self-condemnation by appointing him custodian of our conscience.

This is the classic male-female relationship: a man demands and gets from a woman "love" and acceptance for what he is. But let's take a closer look at that "love." In the first place, where does it originate? And who should "love" whom first? Should a man love a woman first, or should she be the first to love? And where does it come from, this "love" that we "love" with? If we can originate it ourselves, why should we ever need another person's love? And if we have it to give, why should we want it returned by another? What kind of giving is that? And how can we call it "love" if no real giving is involved in it?

Obviously, we cannot originate love. If we could, we would be gods, needing no other god, or god-man or god-woman, for support and reassurance. But the fact remains that the kind of "love" we crave is the kind that supports the notion in us that *we are god*. Now, how can we be so needful and still be god?

Can we obtain love from another person? If so, where did he get it to give us? From still another person? If so, he'd better not let us catch him "filling up!"

It is a fact that before we can love anyone else, we must be loved ourselves. But now we are speaking of real love, not the kind that seems to originate in another person, or within ourselves *for* another person. We know that we cannot be the source of real love. All that we can originate with another person is the little game that we call "love," in which each glorifies and justifies the other just the way he is. The longer we play this deadly game, the greater and more terrible grows our need. When we promote another person to keep us supplied with love, like a cow in a pasture, and we continue to accept this love as our due for liking him, we are denying the love of the Divine Presence within us, and it is this that makes us guilty.

Unfortunately, we rarely become aware of the wrongness of our "love" relationships until we lose our earthy, earthly "lover." In the absence of the beloved who made us feel secure, we discover our emptiness, desperation, and anguish. We see, if we are willing to see, how far from Love and Truth we have traveled by following our ego-feeding notions of what was loving and good.

The desperate need for human "love" signifies that the ego is rejecting God's Love, His Purpose, in favor of the "human" variety of "love" that encourages us toward our vain goals and dreams, and consoles us in our wrongdoing. An ego so afflicted puts down his guilts and anxieties by reaching out frantically for human sympathy whenever he is threatened by the light of self-knowledge that would show him how badly he is using and being used by others. And for a while, the pacifier of human sympathy and homage can soften the harsh outlines of Truth and convince us that all's right with the world.

Men have always been ambitious, but as you know, either from searching or from experience, it is wrong to be ambitious. There is one thing worse than not having what *you* want, and that is having it. It is the place of man to seek and be guided by Truth and Principle and Honor, so that he can reflect the Higher Glory and Purpose of his Divine Maker and not his own will.

Nevertheless, man is ambitious; and his "accessory after the fact" and scapegoat has always been woman. He needs her not only to build up his ego and give him the confidence to do what he shouldn't be doing, but to reassure him after he has done it. Traditionally, men demand that women love them just as they are—lock, stock, and barrel—even though they are unspiritual, unprincipled animals, insecure, vile, violent, and cunning in satisfying their desperate need for ego security. Most women understand this male ego need which men call "love," and they are anxious to play their proper role in life by being good helpmates, but men prefer playmates.

Men who have not experienced the mystical love of Truth, and have not known the purging of guilts and needs as a result of that love, are not truly men in the real sense of the word. They are still ravening beasts, trailing an anxiety-ridden soul behind them, as they go their willful way. These are the men who need the "love" of a woman, and to whom the pursuit of that "love" becomes the most important "loving" thing in the world. As it does so, sex becomes their greatest pride and joy, and also their greatest source of guilt.

Man's "love" is the great pretender, because while it should be correcting Eve, by virtue of its first allegiance to the Higher Love, it is being used only to serve his own vanity. Ego-sexually, his need actually encourages "Eve" to lie and forces her to support him and approve of him just the way he is. Woman, the "beloved temptress," in time becomes "woman, the accursed scapegoat." "Good old Eve" becomes "Evil Eve." Man, starting with Adam, blames all his mistakes on Eve. "It wasn't my fault," he says, "Eve made me do it!" After "loving" her for the sake of his naughty games, and egging her on with a great show of approval, he gradually weakens her to need his approval and to base her entire feeling of self-worth upon it. As she degrades herself for the sake of that "kingly" approval, she becomes worse as a person, but she may not realize it because he is showering her with attention, approval, gifts, and rewards. So her need for him grows too. Now, he can either bless her or curse her for the "demands" she makes on him. If he chooses to escape from her "loving demands," he will curse her and use her demands as an excuse for moving on to another love—sometimes with the "loot," the fruit of his ambition, but mostly without it. If he manages to take it with him, it is only to yield it up to the new "Eve."

The demands that we make on others in the name of love can be regarded two ways. They can be seen as a sign of acceptance, and therefore elevating to the ego, or they can be seen as over-demanding, and therefore unfair, a breach of contract.

Can you see that man's need for love is a need for woman to deceive him about what he is as a soul? And to accept the animal body that houses that fallen soul? And when she accepts the lust of that man, she excuses the soul that produces it; so he becomes worse, less of a man, and she, less of a woman for playing that game. But then she hides her wrong behind his, even as he had done with her originally, and she begins to find a false sense of security in degrading herself for his pleasure and sick love.

As a woman is tempted to play this dangerous game, she becomes more wrong for the sake of the man's "right." But she is justified in this by the male's lusty encouragement, and her ego soon learns to need that encouraging pat on the bottom, lest she be forced to face the disgrace of her degradation. It is as though Adam, having become an animal by Eve's temptation, is trying to get even with her by pulling her down to a level that is even lower than his own. When he succeeds, his male ego looks upon his success as "conquest."

It is difficult for a woman to give up a male's love-lust for her because of the justification and power that accrue to her as a result of it. But if she does try to be honest with a man, if she refuses to play the game of "spiritual Russian Roulette" with him, her reward is his scorn and disapproval. She may even lose her unprincipled lover to another "more worthy" of him and his lust.

It is hard for a woman to lose everything that her ego life is built upon, like sex and/or money. Even though she has built on a faulty foundation, it is painful to have to face the truth of her lifelong error and emptiness. In the beginning, it did seem that she had found her purpose in making that man happy. How marvelous it had been for her ego to be the "sun" that his world revolved around, the giver of love, life, and happiness. How beautiful she had felt as a woman, how glorious. But now, in her lover's absence, through death or earthly departure, she must face the facts of her whorish bargain and see what a mess she made of her own life and his by going along with him, and how, drunk with power—and later on, madness, anger, frustration— she ruined the lives of her own children.

It is not a woman's place to love a man; it is the male responsibility to love the woman. There is a fine line of difference here, though, between love and need. His inhuman need can pose as love, though it is only a need urging the evil in her to support his ego, demanding it again and again to serve his male vanity. "And with all that need for love, and so many women willing to service it, how can he be so bad?" he might ask himself.

As a man matures, he slowly loses his needs, because *all* his physical needs have grown out of his lack of spiritual identity. But when a man is young, his ego does not like to admit its failings, and he must see everything that he becomes as a result of those failings as right, never wrong. If he finds a woman who will help him to become a pig, he will enjoy being a pig in preference to facing himself. And when a woman pretends to love sex, he seizes on her lie as a stamp of approval for what he is.

Please don't misunderstand me. I am not saying that sex is wrong. What I am saying is that no body organ should be abused to make us feel right when we are not.

If a man wants to enjoy doing what pigs do, he needs a female pig to do it with, and that growing need becomes identified with greater "love" and thus a justification for a lifelong preoccupation with sex and pleasure. Men put women on a pedestal of glory, but in them shines the dark light of purgatory that shows man in a goodly light.

It is men who should occupy the place of respect, men who are truly enlightened, made whole and just by the light of Truth. The bright nature that was in Adam should illumine the love that today's Adam extends to his Eve, to correct her and countermand the demands that he made on her in the dark night of his soul. This is not a case of mutual worship, but a hierarchy with God at the top. Touched by His Love, man can touch woman with that love, and she, the children.

We are changed by the company we keep, or by the spirit that overshadows our lives, and so it is that when a man embraces the spirit of Truth, and grace flowers in him, he can begin to embrace his wife with more real love and less lust. He can hold her as one would a child, and feel contentment, loving life into her as we should love life into our children.

But how is it presently with you, sir? Holding her, you feel life stirring in your ego, and then in your genitalia. You love the life out of her for the sake of your need. If sex is your problem, then your "love" is an evil need and no good will come of it. A woman can find life from a man, or through him. And when it is not through him, it is from his substance, and that is the start of tragedy.

7

The Mystery of Our Lost Identity

Although some of the message of the scriptures has been omitted or lost, the remnant of the story of Eden finds a warm place in this writer's heart, almost as though he had a personal genetic memory of the way it was, something to check the accuracy of the story against.

It is written that God created man in His image and then created woman out of man. If this be true, then the quality of life that a woman (who does not love the Truth) can hope to find as a wife, good or evil, and all that will befall her, will be through the character, or because of the fall from character, of her husband.

The original ruination of man was in Paradise, Evil having got to him through woman. Today our ruination as individuals begins at the moment of birth, through the presence of an inadequate, love-hungry woman who needs more "man" than her husband provides. Each male child is violated by a mother who has unconsciously grown male, but is still hungry for male "essence" and male love.

Every eager woman since the first ambitious

woman appeared on this earth has been dependent upon a mystical substance derived from a male. However, if she is allowed to get away with this substance, she becomes hungrier for it and less satisfied with it as time goes by. In some parts of the world, less sophisticated women and girls have been known to develop an insatiable appetite for clay. This can be regarded as a way of satisfying symbolically the need for the substance out of which man was made.

Every woman hates her husband. She rarely marries him out of love, but because her ego needs his substance. (And he thought she wanted sex!) She feels contempt for him because she is using him, and she hates him because she is unable to use him successfully. She looks on her male child as a new source of maleness that she can train and condition to serve her ego with male devotion. A veil of delusion covers her eyes, so that she cannot see that her love is not really love, that she never really loved her husband, but needed him, and interpreted that need as love.

A proud soul cannot truthfully admit to having a need, because to need is to be inferior, so that if a woman does concede to the fact that she has a need, she will make it acceptable to the man by implying that it is a sex need. (Breathe in his ear, and he'll follow you anywhere.) From her frame of reference, her "love" is the kind of love that God has for His children, but in reality, it is the kind of love a lion has for its prey, or a fungus for a dying plant, in which one life is served by the death of another.

A "smother" love is usually a child's first traumatic experience. Mother does not see the harm she is doing. She could project a protective mantle of true love around her child, and she might be glad to do so—that is, if she knew what true love was. But few women know of that love, never having experienced the correcting influence of a real man in the form of a father or husband. Both have failed her, each in his own classic, traditional way, even as the first man failed his Eve when she tempted him for that same love. By failing to love her properly, man gives woman a terrible power that is first an ecstasy, and later an agony to her, an agony that can be relieved only by more of the same ecstasy.

Man, in his rightful place, should be the woman's authority. Sara loved her husband Abraham and called him Lord. Today's man is most certainly not worthy of such a title, but ideally, he would be and should be. In an ideal marriage, the presence of God in man and the love of God in man would become the way of a man with his wife. But men, true to the fallen nature they inherited from the first man who failed his wife willfully, now fail their wives compulsively. They simply cannot love them because they don't know what love is. And they don't know what love is because their mothers, powered by their inherited contempt for mankind and needful of their sons' love substance, have ravaged them from the moment of their birth.

Women sometimes pride themselves on making men out of their husbands and male children; but the kind of man that is "made" by this means is no man at all. He is simply a person whose weakness serves a woman's ego with a *sense* of correctness; his mother has drained him of the power he might have had really to correct a woman. He invariably chooses a wife in the image of his mother, and this strong wife picks up where mother left off—in the name of "love," of course.

When Adam allowed the exciting tempting presence of his mate to cut him off from the presence and power of God, he lost his loving authority over Eve. When he responded to her temptation, he disobeyed the "voice" of his own conscience and lost his power to correct her; which is to say that he lost his power to love her. The strange hunger for woman that he calls love is merely the frustration his ego feels for trying to reassure and replenish itself from the wrong source. For truly, unless man loves God *more*, he cannot love woman at all. Or, for that matter, his neighbor or himself.

When a person is not firmly grounded in Reality, excitement has the power to topple, or violate, him; and when it does, he automatically reaches for and clings to the very thing that excited him off balance in the first place. Violations, usually of an appealing, tempting nature, are stimulating to us. Because our egos are deficient in the love of God, they are easily excited, and they welcome anything or anyone that offers support and comfort. As the ego leans toward temptation, it moves further away from its true identity, until finally it becomes dependent upon the excitement of each new temptation for its motivation and life support.

You see the same principle at work in a lost puppy dog—feed it once and it will follow you everywhere, loyal for the sake of that meal, which it is now unable to get for itself. Some animals are so easily violated that they will die when deprived of their owner's presence. A chimpanzee, for instance, will often withdraw and die without the environmental presence of its trainer to which it has adapted.

So when the first man was violated—and the fault was his own—he lost his identity. He was separated from his real nature so that he could no longer function independently as a man without the presence of a woman, whose support he now required. From this point on, he could not correct his wife because he needed her too much just the way she was. Man was no longer the man that God had created in His own image. He was a "god" in ruins, a male superior to Eve only by virtue of his strength, male only by virtue of the virility that burned in him for his woman. With all this need, of course, man could not truly love and correct his woman, for we cannot correct those whom our "bad" ego needs in a "bad" way. And as long as the original beguiler lurks in her ego mind, ambitious Eve welcomes Adam's state of need and dependency (called "love") upon her. Conversely, man's ego is excited by a woman who makes him welcome, for it is a tempting support to his pride. But man soon becomes afraid of a woman who "loves" him too much, who "welcomes" his sexuality with such intensity that she excites him beyond his capacity—even to the point of madness or impotency.

In many respects, man is the weaker sex. When his frustration, loss of life substance, with woman reaches its lowest ebb, he is seized by anger and fear. In a panic, he seeks to escape from the mysterious stranglehold that his "loving" demanding wife has on him. At first, he may even escape to other women, but before long he finds himself in the "loving" trap. At this point, he may either go on to another sex trap or hit the bottle.

Man's attempts to whittle his hangup with women down to more comfortable proportions lead him to become dependent in varying degrees on numerous devices and habits that promise to recoup his loss of real life values and spirit. It's all a series of variations on the original theme: anything that excites immediately becomes a support, then a crutch, then a way of life. Every life support (dope, drink, gambling, etc.) is either an escape from woman or an attempt to make good the loss of life feelings to her.

At first, woman appears to give, but in reality, she takes away. Drink seems to give a man something, too, but it also weakens him into dependency on it. Once a man starts "table hopping" with his dependency needs, he becomes addicted to each new support in turn, "loving" it until he becomes frightened of it.

Music can gain ascendancy over a man's mind in much the same way. Once the body begins to sway to the substitute life rhythm and his feet begin to tap all by themselves, a man begins to need the music. No matter how obnoxious it may be, he gets accustomed to its "charming" presence and feels lost without its soothing "in" sound.

When wine, women and song are absent, man feels lonely. His life is empty. He is lost. He has nothing to which he can refer. He feels the way he did as a child, afraid, alone in a big world, looking for identity. He feels the anguish of this loneliness in his nothingness. His inadequacies haunt him. As he matures, his ego identifies woman as the "god" associated with his birth trauma. His agony forces him to reach out for a vital mother substitute, and the substitute violates him still more. His first comfort is his second loss at the hands of the woman he "falls" for. It is his second traumatic experience, the comfort and the violation being one and the same. What comforts also violates because it has no business *being* a comfort and substituting for the true Comforter, the Divine Presence of God.

The man-child is born into a climate of intrigue. On one hand, he has a weak egotistical father who needs his wife (and by this time he may need someone else's wife, too, with a bottle of whiskey thrown in), or perhaps he is not even around anymore, having escaped to another temptress. On the other hand, he has his demanding mother, trying to save the love of her man child for herself. All that she is is fashioned out of a man's dying remains.

The female child is usually rejected by her greedy mother. Or perhaps the mother will try to make the girl into a boy, convert the child to love her as a male would. Quite often a daughter, sensing mother's rejection, will do her best to be a boy to draw mother's approval, which the child's disturbed ego needs, since it is not loved. The child might even be showered with a great show of false affection because the mother is ashamed of rejecting her daughter and has to make up for it or disguise it.

If a female child rebels against her mother's demands, she may begin to compensate and become more of a woman than her mother; but mother, sensing this, will often use this rebellion and promote the child to become even more of a temptress than she herself is in order to get revenge on mankind for its failure to satisfy her ego, or better yet, *correct* it. On the other hand, she may offer the child up as a kind of sacrifice to Dad, for Dad to use and play with and debase, and thus take the pressure off herself. Then, when Dad starts giving all his attention to the child and none to mother, she will be jealous of her daughter, and daughter will be driven off to look for a "Dad" of her own to use. And there is another Eve, created from Adam, going to her own Adam; and the conscience of the parents is "saved" by the sedition of the child who has been trained to perpetuate sin and so can never shame them by her correctness.

If everything were as it should be in the family, the mother, having received the seed from father, would acknowledge his authority to correct the child. She would be mindful of his power and respectful of his true authority. But the selfish mother needs the child too much for her own ego's sake, and considering the father to be only a beast or a fool, she feels justified in keeping the child for herself if it is a male, and if it is a female child, either making it over into a male or "letting" the father take the child over in a way that will assure herself a maximum of self-righteous martyrdom when things work out badly.

The male child, along with his father before him, is mother's possession. At this point, the father may still think that he is in love with his wife, as he may still be in the stage of giving her the world in exchange for her support of his ego. But the time will come, of course, when he will either rebel or give up completely to her authority, deriving what comfort he can from her mistakes.

The female child comes into the world with a great deal of encouragement to be what she is. If she develops severe masculine tendencies as a result of her mother's mishandling of her, she may become a lesbian; but if her tendencies in this direction are not too severe, she may try to counteract them by seeking out a man to love her back into being a woman. When she does, she unwittingly goes too far. She becomes overly willing, in her effort to achieve womanhood, to serve a man as a Super-Eve ego support for the sake of her own feminine image—and there we go again. The man is delighted by all this willingness, and he has neither the power nor the wit to love or correct her, so he just makes a bigger pig of her to serve his ego. And now she becomes more masculine than ever and/or a frustrated mother. She may look for other men or for the mother (in men or women) she never had as a child, a loving mother who will let her in on the mystery of what it is to be a woman, the secret knowledge that should have been her birthright. If she were wise, of course, she would forget both men and women, and meditate to find her own identity under God. But we all come into the world under the curse of original sin, blind to the mystery of our suffering, our confusion, our wars and unhappiness.

Man is born weak, and he is weakened even more by the animal presence of his hateful and hungry mother, who often appears to love him. And when he escapes from his mother's clutches, it is only to be caught by the female that his mother, unconsciously perhaps but through her own need, prepared him for. So the soul of man continues to identify his loss with the woman.

Women are awake to the weakness of man. They trade with his weakness, as a matter of fact, and never with his reason, which they would rather see him asleep to. So they never leave him alone but nag him or love him constantly. Comparatively speaking, man's blindness is a woman's awareness. She is aware of her righteousness and power, and she derives her security from this awareness. But while she is excited and secure, she cannot see the truth of her real place with man and God, the place that her ego secretly despises and rejects.

When there is no God in man, God having left a long time ago, man is left alone with woman who provides him with illusions of his own grandeur. The substance of her own illusions is provided by the foolishness of the man her praise has blinded.

All that she can be, whether good or evil—in the married state, at least—is through him. Without him or some substitute or facsimile, her ego feels helpless and hopeless. Men need answer only to God, but married women should answer also to their men. It is perhaps for this reason that women sometimes find it more difficult to accept Reality than men. A woman will often be seen clawing at a man to keep him off balance so that she can maintain "first" place with him secretly. His deteriorating physical presence becomes first an hypnotic fascination and then a terrible animal need. Yet, even in this secret state of superiority to man, all that she hopes to be egowise must still come from him. So while she controls him in one sense, she is still dependent upon his giving her his strength.

Now here is the mystery of the Divine Presence substitute of man to woman. Woman needs man's fallen presence and cannot tolerate his corrected presence, for his corrected presence would take the glow off her maternal drunk and sober her up. She would then be forced to see Reality and face herself in its Light. She would also be forced to acknowledge his true authority and relinquish her domination and ambitious dreams. Unless she is a seeking woman, she can only be horrified if her mate should suddenly discover the truth about himself and his Divine obligations. For in the light of this truth, he would have to put Principle before her presence and unreasonable demands, and this would disable her from going her own way, even to the point of showing her that it was never really her way at all.

Under these conditions, you see, a woman cannot continue to use a man's carcass for her hallucinations and daydreams, and for those glorious self-righteous, narcissistic feelings that her erstwhile beast inspired in her either with his "love" or his abuse. The egotistical woman uses the "remains" of man to uphold an hypnotic illusion about herself, and she does this to all men, whether she wants to or not, because she is under a compulsion to do so. Until the light of real love gets through to her and corrects her, until she is honestly loved by her husband or finds the Truth by her independent seeking, the serpent still guides her consciousness.

A woman knows that she has a desperate, but non-sexual, need for the presence of a man. In the words of a once-popular song, "It's so nice to have a man around the house . . ." She uses her body to hold that man captive and weakens him through the sexual experience. Sex can be a proper experience, of course, but it rarely is.

Excitement that the male exudes as he is weakened by the woman (as a result of his need for her) excites her to do all this to him, and both begin to react compulsively and hypnotically. The interaction produces in the female ego mind a perfect illusion of security. The excitement is so intense that she is disabled from seeing the reality of anything other than her "holiness" and "omnipotence," provided by his compulsiveness toward her that she cannot understand because of the excitement and power she feels.

The presence of man somehow suggests to the woman that he has planted his authority in her, even his own intelligence and identity, and when she adds this to her own cunning, she feels that she has the power of good and evil. She does develop great skill at interposing herself between her man and the God that he should be putting first, in order to keep him obedient to her own selfish purposes. Women are extremely aware, awake as it were, to the blindness of men to the nature of their falling. And a woman is quick to pull the cover of darkness over the eyes of her sleeping giant should he show signs of waking. Her skill feeds her vanity, and her vanity sharpens her skill.

We all learn to use the presence and company of others to make us feel alive and acceptable to ourselves. Most of our friendships duplicate this pattern. A friend is a substitute presence of God. For man, it is a woman. For woman, it is usually a man that she "regurgitates" to the godhead, after having cunningly ingested him and processed him within her own ego.

For the most part, people prefer the company of members of the opposite sex, but they often have satisfactory substitute relationships with members of their own sex. These relationships are basically homosexual in nature, even though they may not be overtly so. We often see a weak effeminate boy in the company of a stronger, even overmasculine one, and a weak woman with a strong woman. The "weak" one needs, and the "strong" one needs the assurance of that need. Each in his own way presents the other with a lack that challenges and inspires the other's ability to fill it.

But to return to the battle between the sexes, the unholy ego of woman standing in the place of the holy, uses the miasmic energy of the male presence to fortify her body and invest her own mind with the attributes of Reality, God. She experiences a flow of thought and feeling that she believes to be originating within herself as the fountainhead of Truth and love. What she actually feels, however, is the power that she has appropriated from the man to make herself feel supremely beautiful and infallible.

Every human being who lives is hypnotized by the presence of other human beings. Indeed, we develop our personalities with an eye to impressing others so that they are obliged to feed us back a favorable impression. Little do we realize that we are destroying them, and also ourselves, with our needfulness that masquerades as friendship or love.

What looks like a friendship is often a situation in which one ego is building on another's weakness, using friendliness to feed the other person's ego and keep him weak and dependent, ever-present for the friendly giant you are to feed off. People *fall* to liking you because of the feeling you give them. You shock them with your instant approval, and they come to depend on it for a good image of themselves. Then you've got them! If you like someone, it is because he has done something to build your ego—you return the favor by liking him back and feeding his ego—he thrives on it, and then you become dependent upon each other.

For a while, you have what seems to be a friendship. Each is delightfully deluded by the other's presence and lulled into a false sense of security about himself. You fail to see how you are using your friend. You only know that you like-need-love him and want him to be always around in what seems to be an innocent way. But how lonely, desperate, and empty we feel when our "love," "friend," "idol," "god" is not there. Do you see how our instant acceptance of a person keeps him around for us to feed from and how he comes to depend more and more on our continued acceptance?

Now, this need also seems innocent enough. "We *love* people," we exclaim, but we're lying. We need their deteriorating presence at the inner sanctum, to worship our ego and to offer themselves up as living sacrifices at the altar of our soul. When they are with us, they are *in* us. When we are with them, we are *in* them. Our individual identities become blurred as we shuffle them together in one another. Jesus spoke of the Father as being in him, and of himself as being in the Father, of his disciples as being in him, the Christ, and of himself as being in them. But he spoke of a divine relationship that we try to duplicate in an unholy way.

Each person feels ego security, as god No. 1, only when the presence of another human being makes him forgetful of his conscience and of his relationship and obligation to the Divine Presence. When we forget the Truth about ourselves, we are high, as though we ourselves were the Truth, and as though we existed for the sake of ourselves alone.

By extension, what we are, as well as what we think we are, emanates from a "superior" source. We are not independent at all, but we think we are, and the excitement of thinking that we are makes us forget the Truth, which could show us that we are not. Our ego simply cannot see or admit that this is so. We receive praise, not as a compliment originating in another person, but as a confirmation of what we have always known about ourselves. "At last," we think, "we've found a kindred soul with the wit to see us as we really are!"

Under hypnosis, a subject will play back or act out hypnotic commands. Yet he is not able to concede that those suggestions have not originated within himself. He must believe that he is doing what he is doing, no matter how outlandish the action may be, of his own free will. His pride can't "stomach" the knowledge that someone else is controlling him. Under hypnosis, the conscious mind is pulled away from its relationship with Truth and loses its ability to see objectively where its thoughts are coming from. We all feel that the ideas that arise in us are the product of our own unique way of thinking. The nature of the ego is to consider itself godly and to preserve the notion that it is original and independent. Good salesmen know how to take advantage of this fact of human nature by "allowing" the customer to think that his desire for the product is his own idea. Witch doctors know how to plant a death wish in a person in such a way that he believes it to be the edict of his own divinity.

Under the spell of hypnosis, a person's mind feeds

on direction just as it does in everyday life. It has no direction or selfhood of its own but acts out the commands and motivations that it needs in order to act at all. This need for direction is what makes a person a "good" subject. And this is the way we are borrowing motivation and a sense of divinity and direction from one another all the time. We are without lives of our own, but it might take us a lifetime to discover this fact. Our need appoints a hypnotist to impress and excite us with feelings of omnipotence. Then we, as subject-"kings," believe the feeling to be originating within ourselves.

We are constantly seeking out people who will excite us by their presence and whom we can serve and excite into wanting to be in our presence. We are completely at the mercy of those who know how to create a good image of themselves in us and to mirror back to us a good image of ourselves. Our entire "life" depends upon what others think of us. We all reach out for people, win our way into their hearts and live on what radiates back to us. We promote them to think about us in a certain way, not realizing that our behavior is based on a compulsive desire to please them. You identify with whatever gives you your image of yourself. You are that, and that is you. When someone dents your fender, you feel as though he has broken your arm. When death threatens a loved one, it threatens you because that loved one is your whole life. When the witch doctor sticks a pin in the effigy that you identify yourself with, it is as though he were sticking a sword through your heart, and you can die as a result of this action.

The compulsion to take over the identity of a "loved" one often makes it impossible for a woman to accept criticism from her husband. She is he, so that what she is is coming from him. She is using his love to feed her illusions, so whether she likes it or not, he, in her, is the source of her being. When he criticizes her, her identification with him is so perfect that she sees his judgment of her not as a judgment emanating from him but one that is upon him. He is not looking down on her. It is she who is originating a judgment on him.

The human male egocentric cannot really tolerate his conscience, his memory of a divine presence and commitment. And the female ego is glad that he is as he is, for if he lived from his conscience, he would threaten the "serpent" in her, the one that beguiled her in the garden, the one with which she still identifies, believing it to be her own true self. For this reason, sensitive, sincere men are not popular with most women. Ambitious women go for earthy ambitious men who are malleable clay in their hands, and the serpent is still around to teach her, through her intuition, how to obtain glory from them. But the glory she gets is not hers, but the devil's very own.

Before salvation, a woman is helpless before this power operating in her, which she believes to be her true self speaking to her. And before her, or in her clutches, the worldly man is equally helpless. Both are bondslaves of evil. And so it goes, from generation to generation, until the dawning of

Truth—or the final catastrophe.

While a woman remains determined and obstinate, she demands from her male his life substance, loving him like a leech, draining him by a terrible and mysterious demand that she makes on him and that he does not recognize because of the hypnotic fascination it has for him. And again, because the human egocentric wishes itself to be the supreme consciousness, it must avail itself of the help it needs to maintain this lofty position, and to that it is enslaved.

Alone, we feel guilt. We fear and tremble in the Divine Presence, which we resent and seek continuously to escape. Alone, we are terrified and not really alone, lonely for that which made us feel secure, no longer second, no longer wrong, in the condition that we imagined to be our "aloneness." The Truth that taps on our awareness when we are truly alone threatens the mysterious presence that has made us feel egocentrically secure in ignoring the Truth, and that has disabled us from seeing things as they really are—as we would have seen them if we had not feared to look at them by truth's light. We cry out for the dark savior, so dear to our flesh, to "save" us from our soul's true salvation.

These words are true, but there would be no point in trying to hang onto them by learning them, for they have no purpose or value other than to lift the veil so that the light of Truth can shine into your mind, even for a moment, and dispel false knowledge. Before that light, all the ghouls of the earth tremble and crumble helplessly to dust. And by this same light of understanding that destroys evil and illusions, Eve is set free by Adam, and Adam is set free by Eve. And so they may rise, each mutually correcting and forbearing to corrupt the other. Only in this light may they live happily ever after.

8

Our Hypnotic Relationships

Under an hypnotic trance, a person can remember experiences that he has forgotten, that have long been unavailable to his conscious mind. And when he is wakened from the trance, he may well forget again what he has just recalled from his past. It is as though his memory had not returned for that brief time at all, as though he had never even been hypnotized. Since the hypnotic state is rarely one of complete unconsciousness, this phenomenon is fascinating and puzzling.

The writer has been preoccupied with this mystery for many years, sensing that it held the key to a hidden value for life, and wishes now to share his discovery with the seeker for whatever it may be worth to his own growth and development toward being a better human being.

Because of our sensitivity to animal magnetism, we are all born under a "curse," in a manner of speaking. We are under an irresistible magic spell, subject to the subliminal suggestion and influences of our negative environment. And the people who form this environment have also been unable to resist the negative environment that overshadows them. We are all subject to an hypnotic compulsion, obliged to influence even as we have been influenced. And most of us are not even aware of our compulsive behavior and the effect that it has on the people around us. There is a peculiar "twist" to our conscious mind that will not allow us to see ourselves in an unfavorable light. This conscious blindness is dictated by an egocentric will.

Some people, of course, truly wish to find the reason for their existence. They desire to face Reality. As a result, they may be privileged to witness their own compulsiveness, and even find the way to be relieved of it in time. But for the most part, people wish only to continue on a selfish course. They refuse to face the light of Truth that reveals the falseness of their direction and what they have become as a result of going in that direction.

The egocentric mind does not want to see its own wrong. It will not allow the light that could save it to be beamed upon its faults, but seeks the comfort of the lies that "people" the darkness. Fortunately for humanity, however, it is not easy to blot out that light forever. It is always close at hand, even for those who make a lifetime preoccupation of denying its existence.

The entire function of our conscious mind is to be aware by the Light that illumines it, to discern by this light what is good, and what is evil, what is wise, and what is unwise. This quality of mind, or consciousness, is peculiar to humanity. It is the one quality that can separate us from the programming of lower-order influences.

As I have indicated, some people are not ready to avail themselves of this Light for selfish reasons. They close their minds to understanding—not only their own minds, but the minds of others if they can manage it. They do not want seeking people to attain to clear perception, because the light shining through the others on the outside would tend to remind them of their own inner light, the one they have been trying so desperately to "put out." Such a proud selfish soul, detecting awareness in you, will make a frantic attempt to upset you away from it. He will threaten you, accuse you, confront you with past mistakes; in short, he will do anything to confuse you and cut you off from your true perception. If he succeeds, as he often does, he will feel immensely relieved, as though some divine good had been served by his whittling you down to size.

Please understand that the selfish soul cannot realize its wrongs because it does not want to realize. If it succeeds in keeping itself blind, it remains subject to the forces that overshadow it. To the degree that a person wishes to exist solely for himself, to that degree must he remain blind to the Truth, unconsciously and mechanically motivated by the influences that make his "own way" seem possible. Of course, there is no "own way," only a need for what makes the illusion of power and grandeur possible. And while a person has this need, he has no stomach for Truth.

Now, even though you may not be perfect yourself, your attitude of questioning awareness can have a terrifying effect on the egocentric people around you, as it tends to force them to question and be aware of their own failings. Many will feel that your goodness, however latent, is their enemy—the saint in you is a sinner as far as they are concerned. Some of these people can become extremely paranoid and dangerous, and will kill the righteous to preserve their own sense of self-righteousness. Sirhan Sirhan saw Robert Kennedy as a saint, and so felt compelled to kill him for that very reason. Kennedy's example was a torment to his self-seeking soul. Martin Luther King, Mahatma Gandhi, President Kennedy, Socrates, Jesus Christ, John the Baptist, were all killed by people who could not tolerate the light in varying degrees that shone through them.

To come back to the point, all of us are born under an overwhelming compulsion to act irrationally. The forces that compel you to obey them also justify you in the way of life that they compel you to follow. The credits, comforts, philosophies, excuses—the devices, such as drink, dope, pills, panaceas of all kinds—become both the religions and the rewards of the Devil. Our false philosophies endow the comforting lie with the force of suggestion and convince us that we are going right while we are going wrong. They appeal to our egos and enslave us, and we are blind to the truth that we are slaves because our egos have blinded us to all truth.

Yet, even for the self-righteous ones, the truth is never far off; its haunting presence is ever at hand. They can never completely escape the understanding that illuminates the consciousness of man. At best, they can evade it for awhile by misinterpreting its message through elaborate rationalizations; and while they are engaged in this activity they cannot see their cruelty. When they manage to upset their victims out of their common sense, they thereby "create" their own enemy, blind even as they are blind, cruel as they are cruel. For a brief time, they feel relief and righteousness through having put out the light in their adversary. Their maneuvers have bought them more time to remain in the dark, unaware of their guilt, preoccupied with brooding over the wrongs of others. Yet they must keep on doing it, putting out lights and sowing evil, lest the haunting presence of Truth catch up with them and reveal their responsibility for those wrongs.

The mind of the living ghoul must be reaching out constantly for ego support, and in order to get it, it must reject, cripple, or destroy the awareness of those who would otherwise unmask and incriminate it. It attracts only those people and those experiences with people that entertain it with exquisite torture and distract it from its own failings, that justify and encourage it in its selfish goals. Such a soul cannot exist without the presence of "friends" to substitute for conscience.

The subconscious mind is the memory bank for all our experiences. The conscious mind can draw from that stockpile of information according to its desire or need. But a soul that is sick does not want to see its own failings. A person who has been made to respond badly—and all of us have been claimed and scarred in this way from birth—dares not look too closely at the impressions left on his subconscious mind, for they would tend to show up the ego in a bad light.

When the ego-heart is hardened, it is not willing to view the truth, even though it might understand consciously that it cannot be held responsible for what it has become at the hands of others. As long as it is egocentrically inclined, it will reject the Truth, salvation, in favor of its selfish hopes that are inextricably involved with its problems. It does seem that we come into the world with the cards stacked against us. All of us have reacted badly to the claims of our forbears, from generation to generation, since the beginning of time.

The secret of salvation lies in the inclination of the ego consciousness. Some people are willing to face the truth about themselves early in life, and the pain that their observation causes them stimulates them to seek the right kind of relief from the right source.

Other people relieve themselves by obliterating the knowledge that their problem exists, and one way they do this is by creating greater problems than their own in the people around them. They sit back and enjoy their judgment on their neighbors' faults, while repressing their own from their "in-sight."

Since it is almost impossible to put out the light that illuminates a human being, we are forced to find some way to escape from it when we are unwilling to live by it. One way is to antagonize others, dramatize ourselves through them, and make them brutish, a blind extension of the forces that are acting on them so that they are the problem, not us.

Another way is to reject the information in the subconscious mind that the light tends to outline for us. The ego mind is not a thinking mind. It can accept the truth that illuminates it from "behind," in the form of an intuitive "knowing" that can and should guide the thought processes. Such higher thinking does not offer to bring us our heart's desire, neither does it suffer us to dream ambitiously. It merely makes us narrow and "good." Such a way is boring and objectionable to the ego mind, which seeks only the way to its own glory.

The egocentric conscious mind has the power either to accept what is right or to accept what makes it *seem* right. When it does not accept the right way, what it does accept has the effect of helping it to maintain its separate and selfish existence, and a compulsive slavishness that it is powerless to perceive. It accepts the suggestions that appeal to the ego, as well as the familiar motivating forces of animal magnetism.

Remember the important qualities of the conscious mind. Ideally, it is an objective observer, totally open one way or another, dependent on the light that will show it what it needs to know in the moment of its need to take action. Actually, it is highly selective, one way or the other, in its inclination. It is open to reason, meaningful observation, or it is open to whatever it is that lies as though it were gospel truth. The ambitious egocentric mind suffers from lethargy and needs the motivation of animal magnetism to which it is enslaved—and of which it is an extension—and which it cannot see, because it can *not*, because it won't, because it is egocentric. What appeals to our ego, alas, is never right. And when we respond to its urging, we take shape from it. It gets into us and leaves its mark on us. In other words, what lies to us "saves" us from the truth; what excites us takes shape in us and possesses us. Later, we may observe the newer impression left behind in us by the experience, but when we do, we reach out quickly for another impression.

Whenever we react wrongly, the memory of our wrong response becomes impressed in our reflexes, emotions, and minds. The light of truth tends to outline the situation for us, but when we reject that light, we are left uncorrected and unprotected, compulsively obedient to outer demands, hungry for the presence of other evil bodies and lies. If we were to face the truth, as truth, we could change. But there is a special way of doing this that only a true seeker can understand. The egotist may face himself when forced to do so by a showdown, but he does so in anger. He fights his failing, tries vainly to change it, and almost goes out of his mind trying to make his thoughts behave.

Most people prefer to remain oblivious to their errors. Their egocentric minds refuse to recall negative thoughts. Instead, they direct their appeals to the subconscious mind, forcing it by need and sheer insistence, to bring before them the good impressions that pass as "thinking." Good opinions rarely "happen into" our minds on their own, but arrive by way of experiences with the "right" people. The wrong people motivate us in a wrong way, though we may look on them and their ways as "right" for us at the time. Then, when the truth dawns on us, we quickly fall back on experiences with people who make us feel "right" and groovy again. We have fun with these "nice" people, but while we are having fun with them in order to escape from ourselves, they are leading us astray.

First, there is the exciting adventure, romance, or whatever. Then, there is the instant replay in the mind's eye. The egocentric mind bathes itself constantly in this type of thought stuff. It is completely preoccupied with the ideas that pander to its delusions of grandeur. The heat of emotion that rises from animal magnetism infuses these ideas and causes them to glow until they blind the mind's eye to reality. The more wrong we become, the more frantic grow our hallucinations. These impressions can become so intense that they actually interfere with our vision, and we literally cannot see where we are going.

In other words, we become so intensely involved with what we draw upon to look at that it becomes a world of reality to us, like a powerful movie. The distraction of these thoughts as they rise swiftly from our unconscious minds prevents us from seeing where we are going, and we may become involved in serious accidents. We curse whatever it is that we bump into, as though we had a natural-born, built-in "right" to the right of way, and we judge people for their bad reactions to us, completely oblivious to our own part in the misadventure. Now we can get high on our judgment of the other driver. We curse his stupidity, clumsiness, and general malevolence. It doesn't take much of this heady stuff to make us forget that we were daydreaming "to our ego's content" at the time of the accident.

It *is* possible for a person to see his thoughts by the light of Reality, but the conscious mind rejects any "inside" information that reflects badly on the ego; and it does this so promptly and violently— almost reflexively—that many people have degenerated to the point of not being able to see their thoughts at all.

When our thoughts become so horrible that we just can't manage them ego-wise—that is, we can't fit them into our self-image—we repress and disclaim them. That is, we try to, but as long as a vestige of the human condition clings to us, we cannot succeed in this completely. We inevitably betray the fact that we have some degree of consciousness of those bad thoughts by our instant recognition of them when we see them in others and by the alacrity with which we pounce on those bad thoughts in self-righteous judgment. If we did not know how bad they are, we could not judge them. And we cannot know how bad they are unless we have entertained them at some time, however briefly, ourselves.

The ego of man loves to pretend that all the evil and trouble are "out there" somewhere and not within the ego-consciousness itself. We are constantly becoming involved in emotional experiences

122

with other people in order to build up a stockpile of memories, favorable to ourselves, to draw on later. Our lives are made up of "bad" and "good" experiences, the "bad" experiences being largely those in which somebody encouraged us to "take" and wound up "taking" *us* instead—or those experiences that have left us with an aftertaste of guilt. The "good" experiences, of course, are those that flatter us and counteract the bad ones, so that we can draw upon them later as source material for the hallucinations, daydreams, and fantasies that we use to distract ourselves from our own sins and failings.

Dwelling on our pleasant memories, a process that we often refer to as "accentuating the positive," does not contribute one thing toward making us "good," but it entertains our pride and gives it a false sense of security. So we keep the chorus line of pleasant memories dancing across the screen of our mind—or we ennoble ourselves with the worry, analysis, and rationale that we refer to as "thinking." In either case, we are impelled by one desire: to become oblivious to our sins.

The knowledge of good and evil is available only to a consciousness. A lower animal, because he has no consciousness, can know nothing of right and wrong. But many of us deny ourselves the joy of consciousness in favor of the way of the animal by stuffing our minds so full of distractions that we become oblivious not only to our own evil, but to the evil of those who assist us in the fabrication of that dream stuff. We are caught up with, and fascinated by, the wrong people—those who will swallow the lies we dish up to them and serve us back the lies that are acceptable to our own palates.

Now, if the Devil played one role only—if he always appeared in his long red underwear with his pointed ears and his pointed tail—it would be relatively easy for us to catch on to his ways and come to our senses. But he is a master of camouflage and deceit. In fact, he hardly ever looks *bad* to us because he is doing such a *good* job of helping us to feel good and forget our mistakes. In fact, as long as we are egocentric, we tend to lean on him rather heavily because we need him, both to enable us to live as we please (so we think) and to love us for it.

The conscious mind cannot press the button that will bring the error about itself to light. It *cannot* only because it *will* not. And as long as it wills not, it remains "innocent" in regard to its error, but the error is still there, masquerading as the self and controlling it. As a result, we are never "saved" from the error but saved from the knowledge of what we are becoming under its overshadowing influence.

Every child that is born into the world becomes the extension of an original conspiracy against good, victimized by the establishment, and claimed by an outside compulsion that it falsely assumed to be its own true identity. Selfish deluded parents compel the child to commit its first wrong, unconsciously using the principles of hypnotic suggestion and the excitement of animal magnetism to do so, and the child's own egocentric proclivity keeps him chained to the process from that point on.

When a state of hypnotic rapport exists between

two people, the operator-hypnotist (father, mother, friend, entertainer, teacher, etc.) can act in the place of the subject's own conscious mind and press his memory buttons. The subject steps aside, as it were, and gives the "operator" a direct pipeline to his subconscious mind. When the operator says "remember," the command goes directly to the subject's subconscious mind, bypassing his conscious mind completely, and he finds himself reliving the experience. Therein lies the key to our problems with certain people, the ones who know how to push our conscious, civilized selves aside and get *in* to us—*all the way in*, to the dusty files labeled "Things I'd like to forget ever happened."

Indeed, some wicked people take a fiendish delight in pressing our most sensitive "memory buttons." "We *can* forget," we keep telling ourselves, "but not when these idiots keep reminding us!" So we resent them, and in doing so we give ourselves something more to forget and to feel guilty about. We get to the point that we dread the sight of these people. Now these *are* wicked people, of course. Let's make no mistake about that. And they are a great deal more conscious of what they are doing to us than they pretend to be. Furthermore, they are often as skilled in their use of the hypnotic techniques as any professional hypnotist or psychoanalyst, even though we think of them as "that meddling old witch" or "that lazy good-for-nothing bore who never sees the good side of anything." When our desperation finally drives us to look for ways of placating them, they know that they have us in their power. They may even throw us the bone of a kind word or a change of subject or whatever it is that they see us grovelling in the dirt for.*

As in the laboratory, so in life. Have you ever thought of being hypnotized? Well, let me ask you this: Have you never been the victim of the hypnotic process that I have just outlined above? Answer honestly now. All right. Now what makes you so sure that you have not lived your entire life under hypnosis, the pawn of one "operator" after another? Think about it. Your answer could be your first step *up* in consciousness.

As in the laboratory, so in life. When you, the subject, are awakened (laboratory), or when you stop arguing (life), you quickly return to the secret entertainments of your consciousness and forget what you said and did under the spell of hypnosis, pressure, excitement, and temptation. You were never really asleep, of course; you just did not *want* to be aware of what you were doing or what you were. You insist on your idealized version of yourself, and that's that—you forget or rationalize. No matter how ridiculous your actions may be under post-hypnotic conditioning (laboratory), you must remain stubbornly blind to the fact that anyone can control you against your own egocentric will or that you are wrong, even though your insistence drives you to concoct outlandish reasons for your "will-

*When a secretary corrected Winston Churchill for ending a sentence with a preposition, he retorted, "That is the kind of arrant pedantry up with which I will not put!" We go along with that.

ing" to be so foolish. This is a real-life phenomenon, of course, and the laboratory technique of post-hypnotic suggestion merely brings it into sharper focus for us. The next time you find yourself building an excuse or a rationalization of your behavior, you might find it enlightening to ask yourself what made you do it, whatever it was, in the first place. Who took over the driver's seat after you pushed your conscience, your true identity, off of it? Your answer to this question could be your *next step up* in consciousness.

As I have shown, "hypnosis" is merely the scientific name for a real-life process that has been operating in human beings ever since Eve persuaded Adam to bite into the apple. Our minds and bodies have never been our own. We are caught up with everyone and everything in an hypnotic way. We use people and objects to promote a sense of well-being and delusions of grandeur in ourselves. We say that we are "giving" ourselves, or "of" ourselves, to people, but actually we are using them, even as they are using us; and the use that we put one another to is the building of our conceit and a feeling of self-confidence that has no foundation in reality. We lull one another to sleep and so prepare the way for newer and bigger errors in judgment.

As in the laboratory, so in life. The careful hypnotist, before waking his subject, tries to relieve him of any bad aftereffects by assuring him that the trauma will be forgotten and everything is going to be all right, just the way it was before, when he wakes up. In the same way, the "friend" who has been amusing himself by pressing your "wrong" buttons and teasing you away from your common sense will allow the friendship to be "restored" back to what it was, after you have obliged him with the "right" response for his ego. And when you respond to him, you add the trauma of that "right" response to the trauma of the "wrong" response that enabled him to "get to" you in the first place.

The excitement of our hypnotic relationships with one another opens the door of our subconscious mind. When we allow a person to anger us, our secret feelings about him may come tumbling out. And we can turn the tables on him and needle him into betraying what he secretly thinks of us. Each person stands in the place of the other's conscious mind and gains control of the other's subconscious mind, in exactly the same way that a hypnotist can gain control of our conscious mind and cause us to dig up "lost" information, or to reverse the process and "lose" information.

Because we are all caught up in these hypnotic interrelationships, it is sometimes difficult to sort out the thread of our responsibility for our actions. Somebody presses one of our "buttons," and up pops a reaction, quite beyond our ability to control it. Nevertheless, our compulsiveness betrays our guilt and bears witness to our weakness. Our body inherits a weakness that the weakness of our spirit, called Pride, will not admit to. We are under a compulsion to serve Evil, but our pride will not let us admit that we have an allegiance to anything at all. Just as we are forced to invent "reasons" for the silly behavior that the hypnotist compels us to engage in post-hypnotically, rather than admit that he has control over us, we are compelled to refuse to see the truth about our "real-life" behavior, but find "innocent" reasons for it. We simply *must* keep up the illusion that we are the masters of our fate and the captains of our soul, until this position is just *too* untenable. At this point, we still refuse to face the whole truth. We may refuse to remember anything at all about the incident in question. We plead innocent on the basis of having no memory of our compulsive hypnotic behavior. But the excuse always trails along behind the compulsion, and sets itself up as the truth in our eyes. It saves face for us and allows us the luxury of continuing in our proud ways a little longer, and a little longer, and a little longer. When the lie comes to save us and soothe us, what it saves us from is the necessity of facing Truth, or Reality. It frees us to serve Evil, and "saves" us from the knowledge that that's precisely what we are doing.

Most people are oblivious to their own faults. They are unaware of what is wrong with them because their ego needs lies and illusions, memories, distractions, and entertainments in order to feel secure in the world. We do not *choose* to react badly, but we are *compelled* to react badly by the hypnotic nature of our experiences. We can not help ourselves in the first place, but when we find ourselves serving Evil in the second place, that is just too much! What we *want* to serve is our own self-interest, and although we can not really do this, we must cling to the idea that we *can* in order to bear up under life at all. The point is that we had no real choice of allegiances because we were too young to choose at the time of our first "programming." We were victims of our environment. Right; "Yes," you say, "aren't we all?" But then, what are all those excuses doing up in your mind?

We all find it difficult to realize that thoughts do not originate in our minds. We are as "closed" to this idea as the hypnotized person is to the idea that his actions are not under his own control. In plain English, we simply cannot realize that we do not originate thought or action. When people like us, for instance, our good thoughts about them seem to be originating in our own minds. Thus we remain original and right and originally right. And when you make a mistake, and then make an excuse for the mistake, you are doing the same thing. By egocentrically preserving your innocence, you preserve your rightness.

Yet if you concede to having made an error, can you suppose it to be your own original error? No, because to do so would imply that you had access to all the facts and were free to make a better choice of alternatives, that somehow you might have known better and yet you did not bother to use that knowledge as a basis for your choice. But the fact is that you did not know better, you never did know better, and you were not *tempted* into the error either, for the simple reason that you never really had any choice in the matter. And what we are left with when we take out the element of choice is compulsion. The original error, the choice, was made and used up long before your time, but because you are a "chip off the old block," you are still reaching for the forbidden, the lie, and maintaining your innocence by an elaborate system of excuses and rationalizations. Of course, it is more than likely that had you stood in the place of the original man, and had you been given the same choice between good and evil, you would have made the same choice. Otherwise, you would not keep yourself so busy reasserting that "choice," excusing, defending, and justifying it, and rejecting salvation *from* it.

The original fall to temptation has brought man down to the order of Compulsion, and as long as we remain unrepentant, the compulsion that drives our ego keeps us in need of the excuse and in bondage to the lie. That is where we stand as individuals today. Kept from salvation, the path of Light, by our bondage to Evil, maintaining our innocence of a failing that we did not initiate, and therefore cannot be held responsible for, and seeing it as a good thing anyway, we swing from compulsion to excuse to more excuse to more compulsion, ad infinitum—like monkeys swinging from tree to tree by their long prehensile tails. We chatter like monkeys too, keeping the air shrill with our lies, noise, and excitement, distractions, more noise, more lies, more excitement—never daring to face a moment of quiet, knowing that we might lash out at Him who made us if He should require us, even for a moment, to face the facts of our condition. Somehow, we know that in spite of all our excuses, we should not be trying to go the way of the monkey. It is not seemly that man should still be trying to whine his way out of the moment of reckoning with such words as: "Eve did it! The woman you gave me to be a helpmate—she gave me of the fruit, and I did eat."

9

The
Marriage Gamble

The entire world system is based on a lie, the lie
that the relationship between man and woman is
one of "love." In reality, this so-called "love" is
nothing but an animal need that is abnormal for
mankind. The animal need that man calls "love" is
the result of his fall from what love really is. As
long as he insists on calling it "love," he strengthens the hold that his compulsive fixation has on
him and it becomes the breeding ground of terror,
violence, and trouble and woe of every description.

To most men, women—even more than money—
are the root of all evil. They like to think this, of
course, because it constitutes a handy excuse for
their own weakness. But the more they think along
these lines, the more fixated on women they become. And the weaker they become as they loosen
their contact with Him who charged Adam to love
and correct Eve. To this day, Adam uses Eve to support his rebellion against the Creator, and he needs
her so badly in this respect that he grows ever more
fixated to her, ravaging and plundering her for all
she has, needing her but certainly not loving her.

Love, whatever *that* is, he has long forgotten. All he knows now is the kind of "love" that makes the world go 'round.

Marriage should be a holy institution, but it is not. A terrible and wordless intrigue is playing itself out relentlessly and is quietly concealed under the lines and gestures of the actors playing "mother" and "father."

Life *could* be a joyful game, of course, played correctly with love and honor under God; but something has gone wrong. The actors in the marriage game are as phony in their way as the hypocrites of the pulpit are in theirs. Dimly aware that this is so (by that Light that refuses to be put out completely), we throw ourselves into our parts with great zest. The better we play our roles, the more we are admired and applauded by the friends who are caught in the same trap, and we all draw comfort in the thought that "the play's the thing!" What you *are* no longer matters. It's how you play the part that counts. Actors on the stage are greatly admired for their ability to portray courage and virtue. As long as we are observing reasonable facsimiles in the framework of make-believe, we're all for them, and we root for the "good guys." Real virtue, in the framework of real life expression, frightens us, however. Just as we give lip service to religious principles at the "right" time and in the "right" place; i.e., on Sunday in Church, yet the physical presence of the Prince of Peace or any *real* person embodying these principles in his lifestyle would make us tremble in our boots. He would unmask our hypocrisy simply by being himself.

Our reason for playing games is quite simple. It is one of the ways our vain nature chooses in order to avoid and distract itself from an earnest commitment to God. Games can be won. They are a challenge to our pride. But who could be proud of being good, when to *be* good is to give up pride?

So we play the role of being right, and graciously accept the "respect" of those who are taken in by our play-acting. And by a kind of gentlemen's agreement we accord the same respect to other actors. But under this blanket of respect we continue to play our dirty little games, feeding the pride of others in exchange for the "respectability" they offer us, doing our own thing and licensing others to do their own thing, with never a trace of guilt.

A young mother can accept glory for her accomplishment only because she is proud. The praise she receives makes her feel secure in her vanity. But she cannot be honestly good because if she were, she could not then accept the praise that her ego craves for its glorification. Furthermore, we are all dimly aware of the contempt any hint of real goodness would arouse in those from whom we solicit applause. So the young mother soon learns that "the play is the thing," and playing it, she becomes lost in a web of self-deception.

When we *play* at being good, we receive the acceptance we crave—we never have to experience the humiliation of facing up to our mistakes. And so it is that under cover of the applause our pride receives for its hypocrisy, it gets the support it needs to do the things that nobody could condone if they were done openly. (And seen clearly, of course, by a true light—but who's to see?)

Friends who play craps together are not really friends. They seem to be friends because they encourage and justify one another, but secretly each is maneuvering for the big advantage. Each person's desire for advantage justifies the same desire for advantage in others; and that's how "buddies" are born. The wrong you decide is all right for you to engage in is invariably justified by the people who take pleasure in joining you in it; the shared wrong shows you to be of one mind concerning a philosophy of life. If you are a band of cheats, your only use for an honest man is to cheat him—the thought of his joining the club is something else, too odious to contemplate.

Suppose you decide, as a woman, to make full use of your beautiful body in order to gain certain advantages from men. Now, the men who are drawn to you will not see what it is you stand to gain from them, as they will be too preoccupied with the pleasant prospect of all they expect to gain from you. As long as each has hope of gain, the illusion of sweetness and light is practically perfect. Each takes the other at "face value" and tacitly agrees to overlook the secret maneuvering that is going on on both sides. In fact, we are so good at overlooking our own skullduggery that when something goes wrong, all we can see is the other person's part of the blame. When we get away with something, our very success proves us right; but when we fail, it's because that "dirty so-and-so" tricked us. *His* injustice is immediately obvious to us—not so, our own.

Whether we look at gamblers or at lovers, we can see the same principle in action. Each justifies the other's larceny, each is fair game, and each seems to like the other just the way he is. But then the battle is joined, and the winner emerges feeling glorious and perfectly justified in his victory, while the loser burns with the judgment he pronounces on the winner. Neither sees his own mistakes, and therefore, can learn nothing from them. The winner feels encouraged to win again, and the loser burns to get even. Neither sees that in the game for selfish advantage, the stakes are really health, sanity, and life itself, and that the winner is also perforce the loser.

Wherever we encounter this uncorrected desire for power or selfish gain, to be acquired through "love" or money, we also encounter a blind spot in respect to our "friends," the people we become entangled with. The problems we all encounter in life are evidence of the fact that we all have this blind spot, and until we learn our lesson, trouble and woe will follow us the rest of our days.

All the intrigue in the world originates in the close "friendship" of man and woman. In the delirium of this relationship we learn tricks that run the gamut of all that a sick, fevered mind can conceive of. From the day we are violated, the day of our birth, we are seeking to get even at the expense of the unwary. In marriage we find our best, and bloodiest, battleground. Many men, frustrated to find that they are losing their lives and advantage to their wives, become enraged and begin to cheat their fellowmen, if only to win favor with their powerful wives. They justify the game they start to play on the basis of getting even—like the man who feels justified in stealing because he himself has been victimized by a thief. The prevalence of this attitude may account for the apathy of most citizens toward the law. They don't really want honest law, or law enforcement, because it would force everybody to be honest, and that would spoil their own little games.

To get back to marriage, the game we are playing (whether we know it or not) for an empty jackpot called "despair," could it be that we are married to the right person for the right reason? Theoretically, it could be, but chances are against it. For one thing, you don't really want a "right" person, because a right person would hold a mirror to your real motives and expose you for what you are. No, you need someone to make you feel right the way you are, complete with the uncorrected selfish ego that you brought into this world, and that counterpart must be just like you, philosophically speaking.

Many women enter into marriage with great ideals as to the sanctity of marriage, and soon they are to be seen wringing their hands and wailing, "How could I have been so blind? I thought he was such a wonderful man who would make a fine father for my children, and now I see that all he was interested in was *sex*." Now, depending on the turn their false idealism takes, they will either stick to their bargain and play the part of "good wife," or they will run, clamping the lid shut on the past by saying, "I loved you once, but it's all over now. It wouldn't be fair to hold you back, so goodbye." Of course, this attitude reveals the fact that they had no love to begin with, for love "suffereth long," is patient, endures all things, and after everything else is gone, still stands. In other words, love is *not* a "sometime" thing. But our idealistic woman magnanimously frees the man to marry again, causing him to commit the sin of adultery and making sure that she will not have to suffer the guilt of doing it first—all in the name of "love."

The fact is that a truly honest man or woman can not possibly be deceived by another human being. You don't find an honest man in crap games or in false churches. There is nothing in those places to appeal to him. He already has the "advantage" he needs, and he is not seeking to take it from anyone else. He simply cannot become involved with dishonest people. You cannot cheat an honest man.

From your own personal pedestal of camouflaged dishonesty, you may often have observed the foibles of others and wondered how they could have been so blind as to get caught up in their unsavory involvements. From your vantage point, you can see how stupid they are, but they can't see anything, because they have been blinded by the "romance" of the prospect of "getting." You may try to warn them, but they won't listen, and when you try to help them they only take advantage of you. They sense, perhaps, that you are seeking the advantage of the glory of "saving" them, and this observation justifies them and hardens them in their course. The only advice people seem to listen to is the advice that will show them how to get even with their sparring partners. But what kind of person is it that will give that kind of advice? Only a person seeking his own advantage, if only to justify the follies of his own miserable existence by making you as wrong as he is.

My dear idealistic friend, that contemptible man in your life was just what the doctor ordered to wake you from your self-deception. Your life is not ruined—your virginity, perhaps—but not your life.

Every person comes into this world egotistical and vain, and each of us must discover for himself the meaning of egotism, and come to repent of that egotistical nature that we cannot of ourselves change. When you were a child, your father did not love and correct you properly. Perhaps he "loved you too much," spoiled you to need the things he needed, and built up your ego, so that now you must find a man to sustain the distorted image you have of yourself, and justify the things you want. But your ego will still be dodging real love, real correction—for the love you will receive will be for being what you are—neatly justifying what he wants out of life.

Or perhaps you had a mean, contemptible father whom you secretly hated, so you set about to find a man who could "love back into you" the image of a woman that you lost by hating your father. Or you may determine to remain pure, to differentiate yourself from the unprincipled parent you hated, but cannot admit to having hated for fear of marring the image you have of yourself.

However you arrived at your worldly ideals, you were impelled by the desire to maintain a sense of original purity that a doting parent, needing your approval, imparted to you, or to regain the sense of purity that you lost at the hands of a man as the result of a proud ambition that made you vulnerable. You did such a beautiful job of looking like an angel from Heaven, and a man pleaser, that you managed to frighten away all the honest men. And the love (lost advantage) you needed so badly "perfectly" justified the sinner you got involved with. He did seem to be a wonderful person—otherwise, you would not have married him—but so did you. The "advantage" he gained from you went to his head—it frightened and frustrated him and made him do foolish things. The criteria you used in picking your man were all based on superficial prejudice and unconscious need, the need you had to use another person to lift your spirits or maintain the illusions you had about yourself. And when you saw the one you needed, the kind of "love" you had to give him, unmodified by the presence of God, helped to make him into the pig he gradually became. If you are still married to one after forty years, you may still not realize what a big nothing he is. He has appeared great only because your "love" has supported him and made him into a "good" man—to you, but a good-for-nothing in the eyes of Reality. When death claims him, your life

141

will be a big, bottomless hole, and in that hole you will go around muttering about what a good man he was (could you admit otherwise?), and friends will nod their wooden heads in agreement. And all the while, the grave is waiting for you also. Take care that you do not enter it as self-deceived as ever, having paid for the false consolation of friends with a wasted life.

Marriage has become a giant "put-on." Of course, we all want to believe that there is nothing in this life but boys and girls: girls for the boys, and boys for the girls. If we did not believe this and encourage one another along these lines, we would find ourselves alone with the truth that every ego seeks to avoid; namely, that there is something in life other than boys and girls playing games together. We just don't want to know about it.

All we want to do, perhaps subconsciously, is to make life serve "our" purposes, "our" goals. People who pride themselves on their rational approach to life are fond of saying that there is no purpose or aim in life unless we make it ourselves and then strive toward it. But then, to have the incentive to do so, boys need the needling of girls, and girls need the strong backs of boys. So, willfully or unwittingly, we all join the crap game of life in the time-honored tradition of "boy meets girl." High on the ambition we generate in one another, we claim to be "working together" for a "better world," but actually each is trying to outwit and use the other, and we are not really as unconscious of what we are doing as we like to pretend. Challenged, we're right there with the excuse: "Why not? He would have done it to me! That's the way you play the game, isn't it?"

For both sexes, it would appear that the game is everything, but there is something about the way a woman plays it that is hard for a man to understand. Women are certainly a mystery, but part of the reason men cannot understand them is that women have managed to keep the men asleep, perhaps compulsively, prompted by that secret drive in women that has never been fully explained. It seems reasonable to assume, at least, that women are more aware than men, as they are more prone to guilt and anxiety feelings than men.

Most women understand the games they are all playing with the menfolk, even though they never discuss the subject with one another openly—and certainly not with men. A guileful woman's "security" and "advantage" lie in keeping her mouth shut and playing her cards close to her chest. And she might as well, because if she were to hand the truth to most men on a silver platter, they would prefer not to believe it, and their own kind of women would back them up in their denial of truth.

Fortunately, a small minority of men and women, by virtue of their true desire, do not engage in the unspoken conspiracy of the game-playing multitude, but they sense the difference between themselves and the vast majority of people. As a result, they often suffer a kind of compulsive curiosity on the subject of that difference. They cannot be so hypocritical as to join "the opposition," but they are acutely aware of the loneliness of their position. These are the people who are going to be greatly relieved by my letting the cat out of the bag once and for all. When they see me saying what they have really always known, they will be able to take a firmer grip on the courage of their convictions, realize that they have not been left out of anything really worthwhile, and proceed with the business of living happily ever after. For them, the war of the sexes will be over. And let me assure you, until the war of the sexes *is* over, man will be at enmity with God.

Now, let us explore some of the dangerous psychophysiological "misconceptions" current among men, such as 1) sex is love, 2) sex is manly, and 3) women like sex, too.

We may start by asking what a woman is to a man. Is she the object of his love? If she is, then what is "love?" Is love "sex?" If love is sex, then monkeys are better lovers than men. To most men, a good woman (actually, a bad one) is "cooperative." From her he may draw ego reassurance, relief, stimulation, pleasure. She will do anything to keep him "happy," and when he makes a mistake, she will be his scapegoat. She is servant to his lust and cheerleader to his ambition. She is the necessary evil that his male ego thrives on, but he will "love" her only as long as she continues to play her part and follow the script.

At the risk of laboring the point, I must repeat that a man's "love" is not love at all, but a demand that a woman be evil as a prerequisite to being "loved." If she does "well" in his eyes, he "loves" (needs) her again. Meanwhile, his male need "justifies" her existence as a fellow egotist, and if she fails to see through the charade, she may become dependent on his being the way he is.

A man's claim to "love" arises from one central need: the need to remain asleep to the Truth. He is a veritable drug addict, dependent on Eve, "the pusher," his source of supply. When a vain woman sees his ego helplessness and his strong back—well, the "pusher" sees that she has a "push*over*" and she gives him the needle. His sexual overeagerness betrays his spiritual weakness, and his spiritual weakness is just what she needs to make her dreams come true and give security to her failing as an uncorrected person.

That is a fairly clear picture, at last, of the way ambitious women look at ambitious men. They cheer the men on from the sidelines while the men go out and do the dirty work ambition demands of them. The women derive a great feeling of security from this arrangement, and they feel like queens as they bless their subjects and nod their approval. They are the aristocracy, and the men are the peasants who serve them in the fields and on the battlegrounds, bringing back the fruits of their labor and the spoils of war and placing them in their lily white hands. For this, the men are dubbed "super patriots," which, freely translated, means "demented nothings who will do anything at all to be considered important somethings."

But just let something go wrong or get out of

hand, and the adoring subject does a "double take." Suddenly, the beautiful queen becomes the wicked queen and gets all the blame. Little children are especially familiar with this type of relationship. Their friends are great pals while they are providing them with the motivation to do something naughty, but if they get caught in the act, they put all the blame on the erstwhile friend. "It's all *his* fault; he made me do it," they scream.

Of course, it does take two to tango. Eve didn't hand Adam the fruit of desire (ambition) because she thought it would be good for his health, but Adam "bit" because he interpreted her act as a form of consideration for the condition of his soul. In other words, he had already tempted her in a subtle way to light a fire under him. He did not correct her when she did, and she knew that he would not. She knew he wanted and needed to bite into the apple when she offered it to him. And to this very day men tempt women to tempt them by signaling their animal needs, except that now they do it to *maintain* (not to originate) their pride. Like Snow White, Adam fell asleep as a result of the evil queen's charms, and his sons, having inherited his stupor, will sleep on until they are awakened by Love's first kiss. There is quite a difference between the kiss of love and the kiss of death, or eternal sleep, the one that is most familiar to us.

When the first man fell from Love, he literally lost control over his mind and body. The woman, on the other hand, gained power through the increased physical influence of her attractive body.

The guileful woman is instinctively aware of this power and makes the utmost use of it. If man were sufficiently awake and aware to see how the woman is using sex to control him, he would be literally turned off by her ugliness and her antics, but as long as he needs woman's support for his ego, the last thing he wants to be is awake and aware, so he tacitly insists that she continue to play her quiet little games with him and never drop the bomb of an honest word that would shatter the serenity of his "slumber room."

And yet, though man appears to give woman the upper hand by insisting that she keep pulling the wool over his eyes, she would do well to remember that the pride she feeds as a puppy will grow into a vicious dog that will not hesitate to bite the hand that feeds it.

Occasionally, a woman comes along who seems to have been left out of Eve's secret, who is relatively guileless, and yet manages to attract a man by the sheer beauty of her body. Starry-eyed and romantic, she sees her own ego need as a large white canvas on which her man will paint a stunningly beautiful picture, warm and rich in exquisite detail. What she gets, of course, is simple uncomplicated sex, and this may be something of a shock to her. The realization of what *he* had in mind all along comes to her slowly, like falling downstairs a bump at a time until she hits bottom and discovers that, to Prince Charming, love is sex.

If you happen to be one of these "innocent" women, let me point out to you before you allow yourself to get carried away with self-pity that you were not really "innocent" enough. Had you been filled by the Light of God, you would not have been carrying around that void, that ego need, that large white canvas waiting to be completed. You would not have been right there to guide Adam, the sleep-walker, back to bed so gently that wakefulness never for a moment threatened to overtake him! It does behoove you not to hate Adam for taking away the innocence that you never really had.

Usually, woman inherits a power over man that she is powerless to give up, but is driven to exert compulsively, even as man is driven to give her that power and is powerless to prevent her having it until he himself falls under the power of the saving grace of God—in other words, gets off her hook and begins to look to his Creator for the impetus to live. Until that time, the power Eve has makes her feel either beautiful or ugly, depending on the degree of her guile. If she is egocentric, ambitious, and full of guile, the sexual needs of an ambitious male will excite her to tempt him, and to feel like a million dollars while she does it (and before she becomes aware how ugly she has become, she finds herself temporizing the beast).

A seductive woman *broad*casts two ideas: 1) Keep trying, and 2) Don't worry about sex—it's great. That is the image of woman that advertisers use to sell everything from soup to speedboats. It's the woman's form you see on the billboards, but it's the men that put them there—and without much objection from women. Generally speaking, women identify with that high place of glory, whether it's a magazine ad, a poster, a billboard, or neon lights against the night sky. All symbolize her omnipotence, her power, and superiority over men. The men, however, see the picture from a different vantage point. They are delighted, stirred to life, encouraged to strive in the ancient way of proud men, by the vision of beautiful women they surround themselves with. Then too, they are the power behind the throne; they can learn to "manage" women in their various roles of seduction and reap profits from other men who need women.

Tyrants use the same principle when they see to it that their masses are surrounded by blown-up portraits of themselves, like an environment, to justify the people in their failings and keep them in line. And of course, tyrants are basically "female" in their orientation toward, and dependency on, their subjects. But men do not really look up to the dictator with love and respect any more than they really look up to the women that they surround themselves with, much as tyrants and women would like to believe otherwise. In reality, they are engaged in a giant put-on. Hitler, like a larcenous female, made his countrymen feel like supermen and superwomen on a grand scale; and as I mentioned above, dictators are always female-exchanged males, men who have acquired and evolved the guile and the ways of woman, usually their mother.

Sex, initially the springboard for man's ambition, eventually produces violence in him, because the more a man is supported in his ambitions, the less human he becomes, until he degenerates into a frustrated, frightened, wild animal.

Behind every "successful" man there is a "loving," demanding, female counterpart, a Queen of Sheba egging him on and "loving" him, rewarding him for his ambition. Even when she pleads for him to stop working so hard, she doesn't really mean it. It's just that when he is away so much making money—the "love" may not be much good, but then, the money isn't a very good substitute for it either. Now, he interprets her demand for companionship to suit his ego. He may work all the harder "for the sake of his loving, unselfish wife," or he may prefer to see her demand as an unloving one and escape to another woman. She will be miserable regardless of what he does. Even if he were to stay home, he could not possibly give her enough companionship to drive away the guilt she feels for her part in his "success." Her diamond bracelets and fur coats begin to be more of a pain than a comfort to her, representing as they do the spoils of a war that should never have been undertaken in the first place.

Still and all, ambitious men could never succeed without the subtle stirring of their morale by some female who is well aware of the part she must play. Seeing herself as the real power behind the throne, the one who will receive the tribute in the end, she is all too willing to offer her "loving cooperation." She is the beauty, and he is the beast—at least in the beginning. In time, entire nations can become so corrupt that they will demand a dictator god, a combination woman-in-beast, who will free both men and women from their conscience and direct their attention away from their personal failings and toward a common enemy.

Mass chaos and anarchy set in on a grand scale when each person within the borders of a nation develops a conscience factor that he egocentrically refuses to acknowledge to be an inner judgment upon himself. When people are guilty for any reason whatsoever, guilt feelings arise in them, and when they are too proud to accept them for what they are, they see them as a kind of outside presence, a person or group of persons secretly spying on them and judging them. If you have ever done anything wrong, then suddenly had the feeling you were being observed, you know the embarrassing, eerie feeling I am alluding to. When an entire nation develops this tendency toward paranoia, the people open their arms to the tyrant who can offer them a scapegoat.

The innocent and the relatively innocent are always chosen as scapegoats, because the presence of either one emphasizes the sinner's inner sense of guilt and makes him feel bad. He naturally refuses to believe that he can be judging himself—he cannot be bad in his own eyes—so he concludes that anything that makes him feel bad IS the bad itself. So he sets out to prove that the innocent ones are evil. If he succeeds in destroying his victim, his conscience begins to haunt him again, and again he will look for a scapegoat, this time among the relatively innocent. Do you remember my speaking of the ego transference between husband and wife that makes it difficult for him to correct her? She immediately seizes on his judgment of her, and turns it around so that it becomes her own judgment on him.

Our guilt often appears to us as a feeling of persecution, because the incorrigible ego would rather feel that someone is following it around and spying on it than admit that it has weighed itself in the balance and found itself wanting. It must constantly distract itself from the evil within by attacking the evil "out there." Hating wrong makes us feel right, but hating wrong is not the same as loving right. Hating wrong, or for that matter, loving it as though it were good, does not in any way make us right. It just makes us think that we are, and it makes others *think* they are better too, as a result of judging our judgment or loving us for it.

The conscience, or oversoul, our own personal link with the Creator, is so close in shape, form, and identity to the human presence that it is easily mistaken to be "someone out there." When a nation becomes obsessed with its guilt feelings, a "smart" leader provides the people with a common enemy to unite against. In this phenomenon we see the principle of real salvation duplicated in a wrong way.

Hitler, a god, gives people a christ or scapegoat to which they can transfer their sins, and they get drunk on their blood lust. But since their egos have only been saved from salvation (conscience), they must go on and on to bigger and better "enemies."

The total corruption and eventual destruction of a nation, or the world, begins with the family unit: husband and wife. Animal love leads to sex, sex leads to frustration and violence, violence leads to guilt and bestiality that craves more "loving," and the process repeats itself. Through his growing need for sex, a man's attention is "grounded," hypnotically fixated, on the woman who both made him what he is and excuses him for it, so that he is distracted away from any possibility of discovering true love by the ever-presence of sexual stimulation. To get the sex he craves, he must please his wife, and she in turn must accommodate her husband's growing appetite in order to maintain her own ego security. Eventually, man becomes a frustrated malcontent, a decadent, angry, fearful, suspicious, rabid dog. An animal person needs (tempts) other people to be animals, to provide the comfort his fallen nature *demands*.

The faulty relationship between the sexes lies at the root of all war. The slogans read, "Make Love, Not War," but it's the way we "make love" that demoralizes and leads to war. It is the underlying cause of all conflict, starting with individuals and ending with nations. The frustration that grows up in us as the result of our wrong sexual relationships is controlled and exploited by effeminate, devil-possessed tyrants and demagogues.

"Men" who are "loved" into a sense of judgment by their love-hungry wives develop a passion for war, because it is the only so-called "human" activity in which each man automatically becomes "superman," judge, jury, and executioner of his fellowman. The blood lust that he developed in bed is blessed on the field of battle, sanctioned without limit, so that he may whoop with delight as he administers that ultimate and final judgment on the man who is his brother in the eyes of Him who created all men in His likeness. Give a man a uniform and what does it do to him? It gives him back a sense of power.

A soldier with a gun does not see himself as a pawn in a game that is beyond his control, but as a super-patriot who has been given the power and responsibility for passing final judgment. Suddenly, he finds himself elected to the place of the most high, and *his*, not God's, is "the power and the glory." On the battlefield he recaptures the glory that he had originally sought to gain in his love affairs. In the violence of war he can unleash his frustrations and avenge himself for the defeats he has suffered in the boudoir. So we have wars, and millions perish. Then we have peace, and the "love" that leads us back to war.

What makes our "love" so sick is the fact that we insist on using it to support our own egocentric pride and ambition, to *make* respectable all that our true consciousness tells us is *not* respectable. A woman gets married in many cases because she is lonely and feels the need of love. What she fails to recognize is that her loneliness is simply the symptom of her apartness from God. The ego failing that makes her blind to the true nature of her loneliness also keeps her from realizing what she is getting into when she seeks to "cure" her loneliness by fulfilling the needs of an amorous man. The kind of deliberation with which a woman can make this decision in favor of a man's carnal nature as the means of curing her loneliness betrays moreover that her source of motivation is not the same as a man's. Where man's weakness expresses itself in a craving for sex, woman's weakness expresses itself in her craving for Love (worship by way of his sexual needs).

When their different needs drive a man and woman together, each tries desperately to see the attraction as a perfect fit, a perfect meshing of hungers and satisfactions, a "marriage made in heaven," and each tries valiantly, at least in the first flush of romance, to look at the scene through the other's sunglasses. The woman tries to see sex as the real source of her hunger to be filled by a male presence, and the man tries to soften the harsh outlines of his sexual drive with the drapings of his wife's romantic notions about love. Unfortunately, their very efforts to accommodate themselves to one another and to see everything in a false light for each other's sake, carry them further from their true source and their only hope for true fulfillment. The man, accepted for the animal he is, becomes a bigger animal, and the woman, because she is partially aware of what is going on, begins to feel guilty for substituting the man's presence for the Real Presence and tries to overcome her guilt by magnifying her need of the man and becoming more dependent on him than she was before. Thus they are caught in an unholy embrace and tumble into the abyss together. The sad part is that they don't know they are falling. In their mutual comforting and reassuring of each other they have created an almost-perfect illusion of stability and security. They are safe and snug in their little nest, and all's well with the world.

Both are guilty of loving what is wrong, and of accepting the love of what is wrong to give them the illusion that they are right. The man is guilty for offering the woman a false love, but because she accepts it as "love," he is unaware of his guilt, and she is guilty for having accepted that "love" as true love. Both men and women exist under a strong compulsion to need, crave, respect, and embrace whatever is wrong in the other. And so, instead of seeing the principle of mutual love; i.e., mutual correction, we see the principle of mutual corruption at work in their relationships with each other.

We are all born with an inherited need to be loved, as a god is supposed to be loved, and that need, until it is corrected, keeps us developing apart from good, like animals. In man, this is an aggressive need, but when he finds a woman who can appreciate it and accept it as "love," he bestows it upon her as though it were a divine favor. She, never having known Love through man or God, allows her emptiness to be filled in a wrong way, because of her ego ignorance, until she is awakened by the sheer agony of her marriage.

The more we are "loved" by what is wrong, the more wrong we become, and the more dependent upon being loved into a sense of righteousness. At the same time, our appreciation of our lover is energizing and weakening him in the same way. Sooner or later, the monster in us will emerge to kill or get even with its "loving" Frankenstein, unless it is distracted by some other "enemy."

A husband and wife may get along beautifully as animals; that is, they fight and make up, and a direct relationship exists between the violence of the fight and the ecstasy of the making up; but they never get along well as people. As long as each one is motivated by ambition, neither is anxious to correct, or bring out the spirtual, human side in the other. Once a man settles on sex as the symbol of his masculinity, he will go to his grave through woman rather than face the Truth; and once a woman learns to equate her "goodness" with acceptance by The Man, she will not give up looking for that "ideal." By turning away from their Creator and toward each other for their "righteousness," they make certain that their lives will be filled with frustration, hatred, and tragedy.

An egocentric man prefers a woman's acceptance of his haughty spirit to the love of God for his humility. As a result, he is grounded and caught in a vicious circle, with Vanity, the ringmaster, cracking the whip over his head. The lovers exist in a world of fantasy. With all their "loving" and "being loved," they are deceiving and being deceived, and locking themselves out of the world that God has prepared for those who love Him and put Him first.

To seek and need the love of people first, before the love of God, is to be guilty of an inner failing. All who go this way will find that the sweets they pop into their mouths will grow bitter and indigestible in their bellies. We must learn to see the needful "love" of, and for, others for what it is. We must stop seeing it as a sign of our worthiness, and accept it insofar as we are capable of accepting it, as a sign of our common weakness.

Needless to say, the person who decides that he can no longer go the way of the animal, but must put Truth first, runs the risk of losing his spouse. By now, that should be obvious. But once you decide to give in to Reality and be honest with yourself, you really have no alternative. You can no longer be dishonest with anyone, even if your life depends on it. You now know what it means to be prepared to lose your life in order to gain it.

Your honesty, particularly if you are a woman, will strike your husband's passion like a bucket of cold water; and it will be a terrible shock, accustomed as he is to the hot water of your sexual acceptance of him and the value it has had for his ego. And if you are a man, your honesty will wrest the whip from you wife's hand and leave her feeling defenseless, half-naked, and frustrated, accustomed as she is to the homage you have shown her and the security you have given her "for value received."

Either way, whoever you are, you will become the enemy for a season, and you will be labeled "unfriendly," "freakish," "insane," "cold," "evil." You will be accused of every fault your spouse has ever had. You may be sure also that an attempt will be made to make you so angry that the only way you will be able to atone for the resulting guilt and relieve the pressure of your own hatred will be to "love" the one you hate, resorting to the old "making up" procedures that worked so well in the days of your animal-like sensitivity to each other.

Your apparent coldness—at least, your lack of animal heat—may be met by a reciprocal, but phony, coldness that has only one object in mind, namely, to irritate you back into the old ways. As just about anybody knows, once you have come to depend on the support of another person for your ego, and he suddenly withdraws that support, your first reaction will be to try to buy it back by offering him the support that his own ego craves. Your spouse is well aware of this principle, and will pull out all the stops and try every trick in the book to make you "shape up" and come to terms in the old way, and when you do—as God forbid, you might, in the first days of your "testing,"—he, or she, will reward you by "loving" you back into your old sense of security. But to you it will never be the same again.

Once you have chosen to seek and love God, and you are in the process of becoming a whole person, you cease playing games and you no longer want (even if you still need) people in the same old way. You stop using them, and in so doing, you stop justifying them in their use of you. In your new honesty, you begin to see more clearly what the people around you are up to, and you are not so easily beguiled anymore, particularly by the person that you yourself once beguiled into marrying you.

In the beginning, of course, it will be impossible for your spouse to believe that you have changed so completely and that the good old days are gone forever. He (or she) will convince himself that you will be "coming to your senses" one of these days, and while he is waiting for that to happen, he may possibly come to his own. Now that he is no longer being supported in his illusions by your lies, his conscience has a chance to wake up and catch him in his own lies—or he may see himself reflected in the surface of your now-loving and patient eyes and repent of the games he has been playing with you and requiring you to play with him. His guilt will grow to unbearable proportions, particularly if he rejects the truthful way of life that you now represent. His hatred of you will only cause him to hate himself more fiercely, and for this his conscience will haunt him. He will be persecuting you for your righteousness, and insofar as you represent the Truth that is in his own conscience, he will not be able to escape completely the knowledge of what he is doing.

The switch-over in identification, though still positively wrong, might now show a more positive side. That is, your spouse, finding all your "angry" buttons out of order, might now decide that you *are* the good that his conscience has been telling him about. Now he begins putting you on in a new way—on a pedestal—and great will be his show of humility as he proceeds to bow and scrape for your approval, which he sees as the means of escaping from his guilt. And putting it back on you, of course; for if you allow yourself to be tricked into playing god, you will indeed be guilty, and becoming guilty, you might find yourself turning back to your beloved in the old ways for the old comforts. This is quite a crafty game, one that you cannot win if you have a shred of arrogance or pride left in you. And while I refer to the player of it as "he," inasmuch as either sex can play it, it is a game that is probably played most often and most devastatingly by women. Of course, ladies, the social structure itself would account for some of the disparity between the sexes in this respect, and now that "unisex" is closing in on us, we might raise a small cheer of *"Vive la difference"* while there is still a *"difference."* Please bear with me now while I address the next few paragraphs to my fellowmen.

You may suddenly find, sir, that your wife is much nicer to "god" than you, "god," are to her. Now, if you are not on firm ground ego-wise, you may easily fall to "loving" her in the old way and resuming the old patterns of your existence together. If you are not standing firm, you might begin to feel guilty for having judged her so harshly—and off you'll go again. Actually, you should be grateful that your wife is playing this wicked game of worship on you, for it will provide the acid test of your virtue and detachment, and it will help to reveal you to yourself. If your aloofness has been based, not on a waking hunger for righteousness, but on the smoldering ashes of an old resentment, or judgment, then you will surely feel the guilt of this judgment and be driven to "make up" again, to excuse your wife's false way of life by way of atonement, and to smooth over the knowledge of your own hypocrisy with the balm of her appreciation for your capitulation to the old charade. Once again you will become dependent on "playing the game," because your conscience will be bigger than it was before, and you will have to fall deeper into the love-hate relationship than ever to derive anything like the old sense of security that the relationship gave you.

If you are sufficiently centered in your true identity to pass the test of worship, you must be prepared for the test of hate, the sudden withdrawal of "love" and approval. Most women know that one of the quickest ways to get the attention of the male ego is to pull the rug out from under it abruptly and without provocation. Again, if you are centered in your true identity, and not vain or needful of "pride food," you will be able to see this gambit for what it is, *without resenting it*. But if you are still dependent to any degree on your wife's approval for your sense of security, she will see the tremendous advantage she has over you and will proceed to "needle" you and nibble away at the self-control that she sees you don't really have until she succeeds in making you mad. If you get mad, of course, you lose the game, because a madman becomes a "don't-give-a-damn" beast or a frustrated and guilty beast; and either kind of beast must turn for comfort to the Beauty who had the power to make him into a beast.

Once a woman succeeds in angering a man into a rapacious hunger for sex, she finds a great sense of security in his need for her, and she sees it as a glorious escape route from her secret guilts. But alas! The conscience knows that atonement for guilt is not so easily bought, and no woman can derive any real security from turning a man into a beast to "love" her. In the calm after the storm of passion, she finds that she is guiltier than she was before and possessed of an even greater need for his attention. She has no recourse but to start all over again. Prodded by the fear that is the handmaiden of guilt, she must needle him into becoming a bigger beast than ever so that she may enjoy another moment of glory as she rewards him for his beastly antics. Little wonder that men who live under the influence of guilty, demanding wives, are often driven to commit unspeakable atrocities.

You do see, of course, that the behavior of both men and women is compulsive, and even when they see themselves hurtling closer to the gates of Hell, they are powerless to loosen the death grip they have on each other. Short of the shock of Truth, the Love of Truth, and the embrace of Truth, there is no way out of the dilemma. Men become violent and impotent; women become fearful and frigid—it's just a matter of which one is going to crack up first. Do you think you have it "made," that you have a perfect marriage, that with a wife (or husband or lover) like yours, who needs Truth? Well, wait. Just wait. God is not mocked, and sooner or later you will either have to face the facts, or spend your vitality on holding your blinders in place.

No matter what words you find to describe it, or conceal it, the number one cause of divorce is sex. One partner wants more than the other can give, or can't begin to cope with the demands being made in this area by the needful one.

A woman will often become frigid when she sees that her husband has somehow managed to get the upper hand. She had looked forward to being the privileged character and using him, but suddenly she sees that he is using her as an old bag, without so much as a "Thank you, ma'am." It is as though he had spattered her image with mud, stripped her of beauty, and turned her into a whore. Her instinctive resentment of such treatment grows to intense hatred, and soon her whole body is repulsed by him. He, of course, will think at first that she is just playing the old trick of pulling the rug out to get his attention—and in a sense, that is the underlying motivation for her compulsion. The "right" kind of attention from a "right" and loving man, could, after all, save the day; but a man is rarely graced with "rightness" at this point. He is more likely to react so violently to her coldness that he will break down the door to get into her room. In reverse gear now, she is incapable of appreciating his need or deriving any glory for herself from it. She sees herself being ground further into the dirt as she submits to the demands that she is afraid to resist. She knows all too well that her fear is exciting the beast in him to a heightened sense of supremacy and

164

virility, and the most she can hope for is that he will spend himself without having to kill her. Or that her fear will not drive her to kill him. These are the raw emotions behind the front-page headlines. Occasionally, the man kills the woman for having made him into the frustrated, enraged beast that he is; then, unable to escape his conscience, turns the gun on himself. Or on the children, "to save them from the rotten world," and then on himself.

Of course, most marriages don't end with the ultimate judgment. Pride and vanity usually drive people to make some kind of adjustment short of that. The frightened, frigid woman, for instance, might discover that she can "save face" and glow with self-righteousness by comparing her fragile beauty with her husband's beastliness, and in her contempt for him, she can drive him to seek out another woman. She may then discover, belatedly, that even though she despises the sex act, she has become dependent on his performing it to sustain her illusions about her own beauty.

A woman faced with the loss of her man, her "security," will often redouble her efforts to enjoy, or pretend to enjoy, sex; but the harder she tries, the more she promotes the beast in her husband and the more frightened and dirty she will feel, and the more frigid she will become. Naturally, she may begin to think that there is something wrong with her. When she locks her husband out of her own gates of heaven, or when she knows that he is enjoying another woman's heaven, she begins to feel tormented by the classic anxiety of all the Eves that have ever lived—with men, they become guilty, but without men, they know they are guilty, so they seek to relieve their guilt in the age-old way that has never worked. It is truly a mistake for a woman to try to overcome her frigidity with drugs, treatment, a change of diet, or a change of men, psychiatry, or exercise. All that she could hope to achieve by any of these means is a state that will create a greater guilt in her. If she were actually to succeed in overcoming her frigidity, she would find herself gradually changing roles with her husband. She would become more aggressive, and he would become more passive, until finally he would become the woman, with the problem of frigidity.

Sex always gives power to a woman. At the very least, it helps to support her romantic fantasies. Each time she experiences sex, she feels herself to be a superior, loving, divine being. The stimulation provided by the man's "love" for her uncorrected ego energizes her and makes her feel secure. Her feeling of security then empowers her to take certain liberties, to assume for instance that she has a right to spend some of her husband's money.

When an ambitious man sees his wife helping herself to his money he becomes enraged, and when he becomes enraged he becomes passionate. Before he knows it, he is setting up the same pins in the same alley, repeating the conditions that are going to tempt his wife to think that she has the right to take what he thinks of as "liberties" with him or his money. It's the old familiar pattern, like the drunk who drinks to feel good, and is liberated by the drink to do something unwise that will call for another drink, and so on and on. Each "high" leads him to a new "low."

In much the same way, a man's sex drive, his need passing as love, excuses and enlarges the error in a woman. She begins to feel so right and secure, so much above the law, that she does something mean and petty. When he gets mad and the beast comes out in him, they kiss and make up, but then she gets "drunk" on his love again, makes him mad, and the bell rings for another round.

Here is a variation on the theme: *Her* need passing as love encourages the unprincipled beast in him. He can do no wrong, so he does that wrong, and she jumps all over him in a way that angers him into doing it again. Or she may try to bribe him into being good by "loving" him above and beyond the call of duty or good sense, and he seizes on that love again as a sanction for his beastliness.

As long as a man allows his sexual need to be promoted and to grow unchecked, he will be in a highly irrational state of mind, unable to see clearly or act wisely. His burning for a woman tempts her to put him in the place of her conscience (subconsciously—of course) and to consider that as long as she is "doing her duty" by his burning, she is perfectly free to do as she pleases in other areas. If she is vain and ambitious, what she "pleases" to do may be to take advantage of him. The man may see through the steam of his need that this is what she is doing, but as long as his need is so great and urgent, he cannot object too strongly to what his

167

wife is doing, nor can he correct her. His need has given her the upper hand and placed him in the inferior bargaining position. Each copulation that gratifies the fallen beast diminishes the man as a corrective authority, even as it serves to strengthen and preserve his ego illusions.

Men rarely, if ever, marry a good woman; and women rarely, if ever, marry a good man. Each, for the sake of his uncorrected desire, unconsciously avoids the quality of goodness when selecting a mate. In marriage, however, both find the opportunity to acknowledge their failings and work them out together. Marriage is an institution, both legal and moral, that should not be taken lightly. Those who seek to escape the bonds of holy matrimony by running from flower to flower may never see what they have done to what they were supposed to have loved. When two people marry, however, and stay together, each begins to see the effect of his "love" upon his spouse, and to feel his vengeance for it—enough sometimes to cause him to question and seek out the true meaning of love.

A worldly man is exciting to a female. He does not have to be handsome, just a highly seasoned woman's man (meaning weak) or prosperous. The prospect of money warms women sexually (at least to lukewarm) because it inspires their ambitious ego natures. A fat man is a sensuous overly-ambitious man, one who will entertain a woman's vanity well with fantasy. An older, wealthy male, often past his usefulness, can buy a certain kind of female. She will be genuinely excited menta-sexually by the idea of money and jewels. Of course, he thinks that *he* is the source of her excitement, and she lets him think it. These men will do and give anything to experience a little fire under their dying virility. But a woman is not usually as aroused by "pure" sensuality as a man. A male body is not nearly as exciting to a woman as his weakness and money are. She knows, however, that most men have learned to identify sex with manhood and would feel that they were nothing without it. For a price, she will assuage the man's fears and help him to feel secure. And in any given case, it could well be that the woman is sexually aroused more by the man's money and the security he offers her than by the man himself.

And so they both die. Man, killed by the woman he never learned to love by the Light of God; woman, killed by the man she did not love enough to forbear to use as a means of getting her own way.

The "love" affair between the sexes can be so exciting to the participants that they can exist on this "love" (in the wrong way) for some time without realizing it. But eventually the error results in pain, which is the evidence of something amiss. The ego can acknowledge this evidence and thus orient itself toward salvation, or it can reject it and continue on its proud "loving" way to damnation.

As long as man dreams ambitiously, that long will he be tormented by lust. And as long as he lusts, he will need women to get the lust out of the way and off his mind so that he can get down to the business of achieving.

169

While all of this is going on, his conscious mind is separated from Reality, involved in worldly things, making money, pleasing his wife, and he can not find his true identity. On a desert island, man thinks of his "saviour," woman. He has used her so long as an escape from reality that in moments of loneliness and despair, his ego turns to her for comfort. And when he is about to do a "great" or foolish thing he ennobles it by doing it for the woman he "loves." And the woman who tempts him to folly is the woman who comforts him in that folly, just as the drink that comforts leads to the drink that comforts.

On this earthly plane, women actually have the dominant position, even though they don't have the obvious material advantages or positions. It is a terrifying power for most of them, but they are motivated by some force that compels them to keep men blind, and to use men's blindness even though it sickens them to do so.

As I have already pointed out, a minority of women are potentially idealistic. Occasionally, we find one who hopes to find in a husband the missing something that her father neglected to give her, but all she gets is sex. So she sits down and weeps, often after only a few weeks of marriage. Nevertheless, through her bitter experience, she is discovering the inner emptiness and wrong kind of ego hunger that she very much needed to discover. Again, she does not "lose" innocence, as though she had always had it, but she is awakened to her failing. At this point she may repent or go on to become "that" kind of woman, to take her revenge out on men or to "love" them to death for the love that never satisfies.

Navajo Indian women kept the establishment going by teasing the male child with her nipple when feeding him. This practice insured his frustration, hostility, and violence—qualities that he would be needing as an animalistic "brave." The squaws, although they were mistreated by men, secretly felt superior to the male beast. Women of all cultures, incidentally, employ variations of this teasing technique to keep themselves superior to their beastly husbands.

Sexual desires arise in man before he understands anything about woman's nature. They seem to arise at odd moments as a result of being overstimulated in some other area. Male children are sexually aroused by such petty adventures as stealing cookies from the pantry. And when a man dreams of material wealth, or when his mind wanders aimlessly, becoming mischievous, even though he may be deliberately excluding women from his reveries, he may suddenly experience an erection and be puzzled by it. Then he finds that he can no longer hold onto the thread of his dream, as the erection interposes in his mind the image of woman that he associates with the erection. His dream can end in involvement or violence, depending on the factors of acceptance or rejection present in his environment.

Society is ambition-sex-violence oriented, and its basic symbol is the form of woman, which is found everywhere, beginning with mother. Mothers promote their sons to be ambitious for "love" or money, and thereby stir the animal in them. The son-animal serves as a substitute husband, a new source of glory and financial security. Nurtured by his mother's use of him to feed her own fancies, he is gradually prepared to become a tasty meal for his wife-to-be, or for the army.

Men do not understand their own nature. They see only the evidence of their soul's failing, not the underlying reason for it. This failing appears in puberty, mostly as a "natural" urge to cohabit. In their sleepy state of being, and because their ego proclivity does not allow them to admit to anything wrong within themselves, they cannot interpret the meaning of their need correctly, but associate it with the giggling females who suddenly befriend them. Such is the nature of the human ego until it is awakened by the pain of its own follies.

Regardless of the circumstances we inherit— ethnic, religious, or cultural—our ego will justify whatever we become as a result of those pressures. A "god" simply can't be wrong in his own eyes. So it is with the male ego. The same mysterious forces that were brought to bear on him to make him into the naked ape that he is will also cause his ego to excuse his present state of being and seek out the mother-wife combination. The "mother" is now the wife he needs for the sake of original identity and life support, and the wife he "loves" for the sake of his sexual burning.

Man's lust is the bloom, the ultimate development, of the seed that was planted in him by the original female violation. If you remember, whatever violates us also causes us to become dependent upon it. It brings our nature down from a higher to a lower level. As a result, man never realizes his spiritual potential but gravitates "naturally" to woman, and his inability to correct her empowers her to perpetuate the process into the next generation.

Man born of woman needs always to refer back to woman because of her original violation of his nature. And each time he refers to woman as though she were the answer to his physical and psychic need, his nature is subtly conditioned to need her more. This same conditioning of his nature gives woman the power, whether she realizes it or not, to arouse him at will in the future. He is unable to perceive his gradual enslavement because the animal lust that is growing up in him blinds him to his "mother" dependency, so that it appears to him only as masculine love. But there is quite a difference between the animal love we call "human" and the real manly love that we could call "divine." The burning we feel is not "love," but the result of love's falling.

If a man burns badly enough he will do anything for satisfaction. He is like the dope fiend who can cheat and steal, utterly without qualms, in order to bring about the gratification of his needs. He unthinkingly accepts as "right" whatever it is that he feels forced to do in order to *feel* right.

When a man is wrong and will not admit to it, he will do anything to feel right again and to justify what he presently is. What is "right" to him is whatever it is that makes him feel right just the way he is. I can not emphasize this point enough. In most men, sex is the drive that assures them of their manhood. It represents to them the fact that they are men—and of course a "good man" simply has to have a woman in order to prove his manliness.

But please notice that men do unreasonable things for sex, things that take them farther than ever from Truth and put the torch to the "natural" lust that will cause them to sink to still lower levels of dependency, each stage worse than the preceding one. From women, they may turn to cigarettes, then liquor or dope, gambling, politics, even murder—but it all started with sex as the symbol of their manhood and power.

The origin of our problems goes undetected because we use the excitement of the present moment to distract us from the memory of our past failures. The urgency of any immediate problem, and our preoccupation with relieving or solving it, helps to distract us from whatever it was that caused it. Overeating is an example. In the beginning we may fancy ourselves as lovers of life, with a hearty appreciation for all that is good. Then, as our craving increases and we find ourselves bulging out of our clothes and endangering our health, we fight overweight as though that were the problem. So it is also with our sexual gluttony that we come to identify as a "woman problem."

10

Who Pulls the Strings?

A man sees his physical desire for a woman as his own idea, but in reality it is her desire for him manifesting itself within his person. Acting in accordance with her "nature," she capitalizes on the void of his soul, his ancient yearning and burning need for illusion and identity, over all of which she has inherited great power. In a similar way, if his will is so inclined, a man's desire for God is not his own idea, but God's divine will operating in him and drawing him nigh.

No man or woman can originate or create thought. Both feelings and thought originate elsewhere, either within or without, as the result of a stimulus or influence, which is spiritual or animal in origin. By the inclination of his mind, a man can avail himself of either source of knowledge and animation.

In either case, two wills, two hearts, beat as one. Either the Divine Will operates in place of his conscious will—for in reality, man's only power to "will" is to will His Will, or to set himself pridefully against it—in which case he inclines toward woman, and she operates in him as his source of life and poses as him. In other words, our original emptiness can be filled with an identity for whichever source we incline toward, and to love one is to reject the other. But whereas the Divine Will operates in man to show him the falseness of other wills that attempt to claim him as their own, woman's will always seems to him to be his own will, his very own original "love" for her, arising within himself and radiating toward her. And of course, the longer he clings to this proud position, the guiltier he grows, and the less able to see his own self-deception.

Does the little boy's craving for the candy bar arise within himself, or does his hunger originate in the candy store itself, with its attractive assortment of glittering wrappers and sweet aromas? The child is not able to determine exactly whose idea it is, but he will mistake both the idea and the "natural hunger" as his very own and will throw a tantrum in favor of the temptation against his parent's objection to it.

When a lie is accepted as a truth, it becomes truth to us, and as we defend it, we become wrongly related to it as a source of stimulus, a source of truth. Soon the lie that we accepted as true needs reinforcing with a new lie that tells us that the lie we accepted in the first place was indeed true, and when we accept the new lie we become still more wrong and need another, ad infinitum. That is why it is so difficult to persuade man to "go easy" on the candies. He thinks that his desires originate within himself and that his reaching for the candy is perfectly legitimate and natural.

To be sure, there is an "imperfectly" natural hunger for something to eat, but we must not confuse it with an abnormal, unnatural appetite, one that is entirely dependent upon another, supported and stimulated by those who appear to have our best interests at heart. These appetite originators will never let us discover the truth of the matter, but will always be tempting us with little morsels, as though they loved us; but underneath they harbor a terrible contempt for us and make us the butt of private jokes and private exploitation. Of course, a naturally empty belly will cause us to think of a natural solution to the problem, and here we are not adding sin to sin. But we do see people eating when they are not really hungry and drinking when they are not really thirsty. Seeing this, it should not be too difficult for us to understand that the craving for sex is not always a natural one.

The principle is easy to see in the case of a natural appetite, where the idea arises as a body demand. But man is much more than mind and body. He is also spirit, and when this spirit is void and does not incline the mind to seek a true and proper filling, then it tends to reject that inner filling, because it does not as yet wish to be committed to a purpose other than its own. Now, there is only one other possible source of motivation and support adjacent to him, and that is his environment, the people and things around him. These he can convert to fill his ego cavity and support his ego craving. And to a man, the most immediate source is woman—she must be converted to his use as a user. His inner need demands this. Thus his psychic cry is pacified by animal emotional support, which makes him still more of an animal, demanding that she become more accommodating in this regard as time goes by.

A woman is not as "fallen," comparatively speaking, as a man. Man fell through and into woman. When he failed in his responsibility, he defaulted to woman, but he was the first to fall, and he has been trying to get even ever since by bringing her down beneath his level.

Technically speaking, woman is not quite as animal as man; that is, her sexual desire is not as great as his. It is not her natural mating need that arouses him, but her uncorrected guile that excites him and encourages his pride and causes him to burn for "sweet mates" in a way that he has come to equate with "life" and "living." He likes to see her as an attractive animal who needs him in the same lusty way that he needs her, but the truth is that she rarely needs him at all sexually. She merely lets him believe the lie that puts the seal of approval on his lust and excites him to new lows in his craving for her.

Man is more than an animal, however. He is also soul, and the soul must be filled, or quickened, before the body can receive its proper animation. But when the concupiscent soul reaches for its filling in the wrong way, the idea that races to meet his ego need is the image of woman. Even if he had never seen a girl in his life, his inherited need would impel him to conceive of her.

The principle behind all addiction is basically the same, in that the reaching of our sick soul is always comforted by the only support it knows before it knows God. With a man, the thought that races to comfort the soul in the time of loneliness and insecurity is the female form, and that form in turn stimulates him sensually. (In much the same manner, thinking of food makes us hungry.) Man is not so much in heat sexually as he is ego-needful for woman. And man, unlike the animal, must satisfy this craving. Even dogs can cool off quickly in the absence of a mate, but man burns and will commit atrocious acts in order to gratify that psycho-sexual need.

Once he is gratified, in receipt of his "divine dues," he is encouraged. He learns that that way is right, and because of this, he actually becomes more wrong and more demanding. Alone, he becomes aware of that wrong, and again he escapes from the knowledge of his wrong by hiding behind the image of the woman, which his ego need calls up for duty. Again, he is hot and ready for her in the flesh. Any hangup that makes a man high contains this underlying need, and is only a variation of the same theme.

The idea that is associated with the answer to a psychic need (which could be correctly answered only by God) is the idea that produces the sensual craving or feeling in favor of it. It becomes "god," and stands unholy in the place of the holy in the mind. It corrupts and conditions the nature of man and woman by degrees to need and answer slavishly.

As each answer produces more guilt, it places us on the threshold of the need for newer ideas. Then the snake in the grass comes around in the form of a friend, a wife, a scientist, a doctor, minister, or politician, to show us newer answers and condition us to need them and to think of them as an answer. Soon we cannot live without them—we love them and would defend them with our last breath. They are "god" to us; but each of us falsely believes that *he* is the King, served by *it*, "good" beyond measure to be deserving of such loyalty and support. Men and women are both victims of their "own" thinking.

In time, of course, woman comes to need man also. As you may remember, her ego is supported by his deteriorating body presence. In a little while, when she feels "blue," her soul's emptiness will call up the image of her beastly male companion, and her need will excite him to be beastly, and with that beastliness the "honored sir" will serve some of himself up to her.

Do you see how the image of the woman becomes implanted in the mind of men? And how the image of the male is implanted in the mind of the woman? And how they draw upon each other's presence, each other's nature and identity until man becomes woman, and woman becomes man? Do you also see the terrible impact this has upon their offspring?

You cannot correct your child because of the falseness of your love. That which has, in an evil way, displaced the *real you*, is now busy translating itself into your child. What is living through you— the error, that is—is attempting to live through your child as well and make a new home for itself there, as it has from generation to generation since the beginning of time. What you are is his shining example and is becoming manifest in him. You are he, and you cannot correct him because he cannot help being the extension of what is lurking in that ominous self that passes as "you." Your "love" for that child is your egocentric need to be respected and adored as a god. So, as "god," you proceed to love that child in a way that will turn his head and uplift his spirits—adoringly, in your direction. But you fail to see that when you love in a way that tempts and supports another's ego, offering the kind of love that you need yourself in the hope of getting it back, you actually pass on, or incarnate again, your "god" identity to that other person. You are supporting him, motivating him, animating his being—so he becomes you, and he refuses to see the "greater" Light, by virtue of the same ego that brought him into being. He remains true to ego tradition, the rebellious son who tries to refuse to acknowledge and worship God (you).

Most of us are unable to see that what we have become is wrong, that we are the wrong extensions of what was wrong in our parents, even as they were the extension of their parents. We cannot look back at our "creator," nor can we admit that we were put together with the wrong set of plans and motives for purposes that were neither our own nor good.

As we mature, we all seek support for what we have become—first from our mate and then from our children. But in the battle over the children, father usually loses out to the shining presence of mother, who has been working quietly in his absence to get their "respect." She sees herself as god incarnate creating little gods—all "good," of course, for if she is good, they must be good. She cannot correct them, because she is not correct herself, but is unconsciously tempting and using them to supply her with a sense of her own correctness. Needless to say, in order to give it, the children must become as false as the mother who is demanding their "respect" without being respectable. If the son were graced with real love and identity, she could not tolerate his light. She would be compelled to put it out and to insist that he glorify her from the never-never land of darkness she has wrapped him in. She would shut out all intruders, gobbling up the tender shoots of his ego-soul, quickly, lest they be observed by others—and on these she would maintain herself until mother and son were one. "The King is dead—long live the King."

Who is *not* wrong, and proud of what he is, and seeking loyal supporters, and sucking the life out of them?

Just as the plant can in no way become the light that made it, no matter how brightly it may burn when set afire, so man cannot become God, his Creator, no matter how fiercely the fire of hell may burn in him. He cannot *be* the Great Light, even though he return in his understanding to the Source of Light, to the beginning, when the Word was with God and the Word was God. If he *were* the Light, he could not be illumined by it; if he were the Fire, he could not be warmed by it. But by the light on his path and the warmth that radiates in his soul, he can know Him who said "Let there be . . .," and there *was*, from the least to the greatest of created things, even to the sun itself.

In the manifest world man can see God only in man, who was created in His image and likeness, and then only if that man be turned dutifully toward the Soul-ar Light to reflect it purely and thus bear witness to the eternal and invisible presence of the Creator. If he turns his face away from the Light that created him, he withers like a tree deprived of sunlight, and like the dying tree, he signals his weakness and thus invites all manner of "guests" to lie in his failing shade or minister to him in the name of "love." But the sick love of sycophants can never restore the Love that man forfeited by his own inclination toward the darkness. Yet even as the tree that seemed dead in winter will put forth new leaves in the sunlight of spring, so man can know the joy of Eternal Life by fasting from the ways of Evil, acknowledging his failings, and turning hungrily, humbly, yet patiently toward the one true Source for his filling.

To know Reality man must make room for Him in his heart by giving up his ambition or personal gain in favor of discovering his true purpose on earth. Only then will he see clearly how he has allowed the wills of others to pose as him and to operate in him and rob him of his true identity. Only then will he be able to distinguish Reality from the lie, and as a whole man, shine a light on the path of his wife Eve so that she too may see how she has been controlled by the dark will of Satan in the world around her. And only when man and woman are one in Truth will they prevail over the forces of darkness.

Until we sincerely desire to know God and to perceive by His light, we can discern nothing for what it really is, and men and women both continue merrily on their foolish way, each believing himself to be doing just as he pleases with what he considers to be his "own" life. When we feel the emotion we call "love" welling up in us, we believe it to be our own original emotion, our own benevolent love; but what we actually feel is the fruit of the suggestion that the "loved one" has willed us to feel—*his* will (or *her* will) in us. On closer examination, we would see that "love" as a weakness, a dependency upon a power outside ourselves that we had imagined to be our own power, and we would see how we try to blot out the fear and guilt that arise as a result of our seeing, by drawing closer and closer to the shelter of our beloved.

In this way Satan incarnates himself in modern Eve, but she too sees the devil's idea as her own idea—to give Adam "ideas." And Adam seizes the idea of woman as his own, and the unholy chain of dependencies creates the kingdom of Hell on earth. In the process a changeover of identities takes place: man becomes the woman, and woman becomes the man, with the spirit of evil in the place of God operating through them both.

The homing instinct of the salmon closely resembles the back-to-the-womb compulsion of man. To the salmon fry "mother" is simply a place he remembers, the presence that provided the first impetus for his growth. It is a kind of "engram," which as you may remember, is the permanent impression left on protoplasm as a result of stress. Any exciting or emotional experience will incorporate something of itself into the cells and reflexes of the creature and remain with it as a kind of unconscious memory.

No doubt the reader is familiar with the sudden reexperiencing of some long-forgotten memory, a momentary flashback of an old thought, sound, odor, sight, or taste—or whatever. Sometimes it is just a wispy encounter, a "something" brushing by the fingertips of consciousness with a vaguely familiar ghostly presence. Then, of course, there is the more obvious residue from more recent encounters, such as the hostility left by a lover's quarrel. You will think you are entirely absorbed in other matters, but suddenly you become aware that the reliving of your anger has taken over and crowded everything else out of your mind.

An exciting presence not only changes the identity of a living thing, but it also maintains its course of growth (and pulls the strings), so that the offspring can fulfill itself only by following the original pattern, by being unconsciously attracted to the same kinds of experiences and boundaries as those that mother provided for it in the beginning. Even though we cannot consciously remember those intrauterine and postuterine experiences that turned us on, they are still influencing us, attracting

185

us to certain kinds of experiences and people, and predestining our "chance" meetings. Fallen men are links in a chain, passing on the orders and penalties of an ancient curse.

If the father or mother that turned us on was subject to Sin, then we are going to be naturally attracted to sinful experiences and grow up to become mature sinners. But if we are turned on by Faith to look to God who created us as our father, mother, and only true source, in earth as in heaven, then our nature will change in subtle ways to draw us toward the experiences that best fit the pattern He had in mind for us at the time He created man "in His image and likeness."

Because he sinned, the animal body of the first human contained the engram of that first experience with sin, and because Adam did not obtain salvation he was obliged to pass his sin-modified nature on to his seed, who became the extension of his fallen nature. Ever since that time, man born of woman is not reasonable as an animal is in his course of development, but is sensitive to every temptation.

Our bodies are houses built on a wrong foundation. Inherent in the cells of that foundation is the secret knowledge of the kind of experiences those bodies will need. So we are all drawn mysteriously to the kind of environment that will provide the turn-on value we crave.

We have forgotten most of our early turn-on experiences, largely because our egos do not wish to see clearly the changes they have wrought in us. It would be painful to note the difference between what we have become as a result of our experiences and what we should be in the light of Reality, so we excuse ourselves from that knowledge by simply not observing what we are. We continue to reach for the experiences that will provide us with both the "progress" and the rationale for it.

The Kingdom of Hell is spread upon the earth, and all of us are caught up in it. As each person "arrives," he becomes an experience for others. And every person we experience has in store for us that glorious stimulation our egos and body cells crave. Each person is a highly developed environmental factor with the power to provide us with the experiences that we are growing to need increasingly and learning to recognize with ever greater acuity.

We are all environments to one another, tempting others as we are being tempted by others, exciting as we are being excited. Exciting people provide us with the motivation to go the wrong way, then other exciting people come with new excitements to help us forget the way we went. We come to need excitement in order to go on forgetting, and all the time we grow more wrong. Yet that excitement does seem so right and natural to us, as though it were the perfect fulfillment for some predestined purpose. And it is. But it is a wrong purpose, though it may take us a lifetime to discover this fact. We don't ordinarily make that discovery until we have experienced the "natural" to the dregs and to the fullest extent of our "fishy" capacity. At that point we may be ready to stop rationalizing our so-called natural acts because we have actually gone way beyond the natural and are beginning to feel the pangs of terror, guilt, and darkness, that our excuse-making has brought upon us.

Once you have learned to fear another person, your reaction to him will be fearful every time he appears on the scene whether or not there seems to be any basis for alarm at that time. It's much the same with the identity we have inherited through the experiences provided by our parents. They have "set" our sensitivity to temptation like a thermostat and have thereby predestined our obedience as well as our need for it. We cease to exist in a right way, but develop wrongly with a "natural" need for that wrong experience.

We are attracted to temptation in all its subtle forms because temptation is the root of our genetic identity and it represents our animal support and egocentric security. Without it, we cease to exist as the good, purposeful people we fancy ourselves to be. Fear, anger, and animal excitement are a "must" if we are to grow to fulfill our inherited identity. Needless to say, it is a wrong identity, but our pride insists that we are right as we are. Therefore, the natural way automatically becomes the right way for us and we take our stand on it.

The world is full of sinister people all going down the same broad road to destruction, each one a partially-formed personification of evil, developed only to the degree that you cannot immediately recognize him as a devil's advocate. It might even be a sweet young "only natural"—that is, uncorrected of guile—girlfriend. Or it might be an older, more obvious, friend or "fiend" in need. In any event, each in turn becomes easier to detect once we are willing to see truly. But to see truly we must first be willing to see what we ourselves have become as a result of our experiences with the fiends we have called "friends," who have encouraged us to feel comfortable in our proud, egocentric ways. Of course, if our ego wishes to avoid this confrontation with ourselves, we must go on to another friend, another fiend, and work harder than ever with our conscious minds to make every wrong thing seem right and acceptable to us.

Do you see now why you are so easily led into and deceived by temptation? Why you are so sensitive to people and things that remind you of the good old days of your formative years, and why you are drawn to the people who awaken and support your sensuous nature? Even the situations that you hated and feared as a child have a kind of fascination for you now, for what you have become as a result of fearing and hating now needs fear and hate, and the same kind of fear and hate, to continue on its "natural" downhill course.

The young salmon leaves mama's pond to begin its long journey downstream to the ocean, and though he has not been there before, every flip of his fin along the way is guided by a built-in memory of the experiences he needs for his growth. Mama and papa were there before him and cast into his cells the need to follow in their fin flips. This little drama is enacted and reenacted millions of times in the course of evolution, and these creatures develop an amazing sensitivity to the course they must follow and a stubbornness regarding it, despite whatever obstacles they find in their path. For one salmon any change in that course would involve a change in his identity and form, and his offspring would have to include that change in their course.

Once we have found our way to a strange place— to a new friend's house in our automobile, for instance—it is no longer so strange. Even though a great deal of time may elapse before we go that way again, we can do so without undergoing any great mental strain. And so it is with the salmon on its way back to mama's pond. When it is full-grown it is overcome by a strong impulse to go home, and it sets out with confidence that what has supported its growth to this point will continue to support it yet awhile. Each new place along the way brings into view the "memory" of the next one that lies just around the bend. Each one points the way to the next one as it becomes more exciting because it is closer to home. Each milestone represents reassurance and support, and when it is milked of its support, it points the way to the one beyond, all the way back to the beginning. And each experience is more exciting and more vital than the last because the end is drawing close and death waits at the end of the homeward journey.

It isn't so very much different with man. He, too, has a cellular sensitivity, a similar need to experience and to reexperience, to "go home" again. It is what causes him to become charmed or excited by a member of the opposite sex who resembles his mother closely enough to take her place as his unconscious support for what he has become as a result of her support. At first we may not recognize mother in our choice of a wife, but she always lurks there somewhere. You may not see that this is so until you have developed enough to see that your own needs are impelling you to encourage your wife to become more mother than wife to you.

As far as man is concerned, the "natural" always precedes any spiritual growth, whether it is in the direction of evil or of good; but without knowledge of salvation, we are headed for a face-to-face confrontation with the power that made us what we are today—namely, Mother. To say that we come into being through mother simply means that we come through a natural way via the sin of our parents, and we grow up to return to the scene of the crime in a natural cycle. To return to the scene, we "naturally" pick a wife—but wife *is* mother—and mother without the love of God in her is Satan's personal representative on this earth.

"Mother" is not the Principle we should be serving, but as males, rather than men, we need to convert our wives into mothers to serve our fallen animal nature. We need them to preserve the evil male identity we inherited from our natural mothers. Then we must procreate the race until that natural life is spent, and the little ones grow up in woman's "loving" care, under her "protective" influence, to become natural children set on the same course to purgatory.

Meanwhile, papa undergoes a metamorphosis, a sought-after spiritual rebirth, in that he becomes transformed in the presence of woman from "son of a woman" to "son of a bitch." If he leans on her long enough, he may even become a real, live devil.

The allure of a woman is so exciting to a male that her rejection of him would be devastating, unthinkable. The mere thought of it acts like a boulder in the river that makes the salmon leap harder in its determination to get home. For a woman to turn cold on him would literally knock the props out from under his fishy being. At the first hint of such a possibility, he must work harder to get her support—and if he does not get it, he loses hope and feels that his life has been spent, as though he were dying without having fulfilled his divine destiny, the highest culmination of which is the sex act. He can think of nothing else. But what he does now to get her support makes him less of a human being, and because he is not a fish he can not get away with acting like one. His natural form slowly begins to deteriorate and take on the likeness of his spiritual father, the Evil in Eve, because he has used the life force in her as his means of support. The Evil in Eve goads him on and draws on him for a glory and power that do not properly belong to her, but as long as he needs her, she will use his eagerness to make him work for "her."

Men often grow to fear women as they slowly become aware of what is transpiring in them as a result of their need. They cannot exist without women, nor can they stand what they themselves become as a result of cleaving to them.

Men have been violated psychically by the essence that is now represented in their wives. Their physical and psychic needs draw them inexorably to females in something like the fascination of a nightmare or a snake, a spell that can't be broken. They may know that they are hypnotized, yet they know that their very existence depends upon that hypnosis, the fear, anger, and excitement that constitute the life blood of their compulsion. The same is true of almost everything we need. At first we call the fascination "love"; then, as we see it destroying us, we come to be afraid of its effect upon us, but at the same time we are afraid to be without it, and so it lures us on. It is the torment of the insatiable desire and its built-in frustration.

We have all known people who are sex oriented. Everything reminds them of sex because sex has become a center of attention and they see everything in relation to the sex god that serves their ego. As they "grow home" to this god, they become more and more excited, like the salmon nearing its goal. For the season that sex is man's epicenter, the support of his sense of malehood and identity, his appreciation of sex (and the woman behind its promise) grows, until he sees more and more things in relation to and in terms of sex. Then, suddenly, he may go one step beyond and see the evil as it is represented in the woman. Then he may go still another step beyond that and see the Evil itself, beckoning to him, laughing, frightening, angering, tormenting, teasing—providing him all he needs for his total personality. There is his "god"—he is "home at last"—and what a hideous god it is.

Sometimes, in a desperate attempt to escape this kind of reality, men will kill themselves, or they will kill the mother or wife whom they identify as the evil itself, and they will therefore think that they are doing a good and valiant thing; but they can never kill the evil because it is spirit and cannot be killed by destroying bodies. By dealing out such a last ego judgment, a man only tricks himself into experiencing a sense of ultimate glory; and when the forces of evil have tempted us to think that destroying evil makes us good, they take a tighter grip on our minds and bodies and force us into greater conflict with our true selves.

We have come from a world of sin as children, and to it we return in maturity as we pass our inheritance on to our children by comforting them with our unchanged animal natures. The path to heaven or hell (if only on earth) is back through our present animal state. From that state with our wives, mother, or women, we either rise or fall still lower, and most of us fall much lower before we realize that something is radically wrong with our natural existence and the quality of life we inherit. Giving in to our natural impulses, we go the rest of the way down, step by step, impulse by impulse, excuse by excuse. I suppose it would be perfectly natural if our hunger were based strictly on a genuine need for one another's support and services as animals. But behind every human physical need there lies an ego need for reassurance.

In our need for ego support, we are like the science fiction men from other planets whose bodies are unstable in our world. To maintain their human appearance and accomplish their mission here, they must return each day to a glass cylinder to be recharged. Similarly, our egos have assumed animal form, and with this animal body our egos strive to accomplish their impossible dreams, but those bodies will simply disintegrate if they are deprived of their daily charge of excitement and support. Now as long as we are highly charged, the ego feels hopeful and the body feels secure and stable. And as long as we wish this kind of selfish existence, we will go to great lengths to preserve this kind of body-oriented identity, and because men are the way they are because of women, they must, therefore, keep women trained as slaves to serve this need. For man and his dreams, women are the key to everything, anything they want without experiencing guilt.

Husbands literally fashion mothers out of their wives by requiring them to replace the ''worn-out'' mother unit. And many women yield gladly to this requirement because they know that the male existence and dream depend upon them. They have the power for which men will do anything. If a man's ego is not ready to face reality, he will require his wife to play that traditional part. Both his ego and genetic needs demand that she remain dishonest, just the way she came into being. If anything, she must become even more of a temptress to help him remain asleep to his conscience and to give him the false sense of security men feel when they have placed the responsibility for what they have become on women. And of course this implies that the woman must always be getting a little worse as she degrades herself for the sake of that false sense of security in him that serves also to support her own false sense of power and security.

Men force their women to represent to them "Eve," which means literally "life, or living." And in order to draw life from a wrong source, they must, of course, be tempted and violated by it. From this arises their sense of maleness. From that developed maleness arises in turn the need for femaleness, but the need of man goes deeper than erotica. His entire sense of identity and righteousness depends on temptation, and temptation is the spirit of his mother. So men require their wives to be their mothers, to represent to them the same identity in the flesh as well as in the spirit presence.

This kind of man requires everything that is tempting and fleshly and is attracted to the bad in everything he encounters. An honest woman is anathema to his soul and leaves him cold. He tries to plunder everything of its excitement value, and he winds up being as hung-up on the things he uses to serve his vanity as he is on women. A tempting dish, a tempting woman, a tempting cause, a tempting drink—you can't sell a man an automobile unless it subtly supports his maleness and vanity. His car and his boat are his mistress substitutes. His food, his smoke, his drink—sometimes even his work—must endow him with feelings of masculinity and an aura of respectability about his maleness. He must be a male even if it kills him, and it does.

Perhaps you can see why men take pride in seeing their wives seductively dressed. They do not want to see them as persons, only as females backed up by the spirit of temptation that keeps them female, tempting and exciting men away from the knowledge of their shame by the greater shame of being a female. Feminine lures, such as perfume and makeup, are pleasing to these earthy males because they are reminiscent of "mother" and signal the female's willingness to cater to his needs as a male. When such a man sees a woman all dressed up like a dog's dinner for him, it drives him wild, and that is like being free.

When a couple make love, a sequence of causes and effects reverberates back and forth between them. He is aroused by her signals. The temptation in the female appeals to male pride and promptly brings out his animal, and that animal lust excites her to feelings of power. Now, her excitement over his weakness is taken as a personal compliment and as his ego becomes more excited, out pops more of the beast, burning for her more fiercely than ever, and this excites her again. Soon their total existence depends upon the ritual of making love and abusing the flesh of the partner, promoting it to the level of animal to gratify instantly that full-grown animal need.

It is very difficult for a male ego to relate properly to sex. He uses it as he eventually does pot and alcohol, to get high on it, but that high always brings him to a new low. In the time of need, just before he runs out of "gas," his anxiety about what he really is drives him to need a drink or a woman to build up his morale.

Quite often the alcoholic does not see that he is addicted. He claims that he simply loves his drinks—it's that simple. But to give up drinking he would have to give up his self-righteous illusions and face reality to some degree.

In the journey back to the truth about ourselves, sex will be the last frontier we'll have to conquer. To give up *using* sex and women is to come as close to reality as this earth plane will allow. While it is the last frontier—also the last crutch and excuse— on the way back, it was the original one coming forward to our present confusion of hangups and suffering. Beyond that physical milestone we can deal with temptation face-to-face, without ever faltering or falling again. Each sexual experience is like a drunkard's drink. We cannot give it up because our total identity is rooted in it and nourished by it.

Sex is the last problem. We should not attempt to deal with it until we become aware of all those other "loves" and likes and needs that we have been depending on to prevent that original fault from coming to light. When we realize the underlying significance of our hangups, such as smoking and drinking, and why we need them so desperately, we can come to grips with that problem in its turn. We need these things, of course, to maintain a sense of well-being, and when we are not yet ready to face ourselves we need our temptations in a bad way. The longer we have to go without our support, the more we yearn for it. Observe how smokers often fondle their cigarettes affectionately, almost sexually—especially in times of greatest need—as though they could derive additional benefit from the cigarette by feeling it before lighting it.

Everything that is sold is sold on the basis of sex, because that original approach makes everything that is sold acceptable and right for a man to have. Sexuality is the first evidence of an inner failing and it comes full circle; that is, man ends by using the female presence that he first used to make him into the wrong ambitious male that he is.

When mother's corrupting presence overshadowed the child at birth, that child received an ego need identical to that of every other ego that has come into the world, beginning with Adam, and should that baby ego be given the opportunity to do the scene over again, it would still elect to use Eve in the same way.

Man, born of a spoiled woman, is guaranteed corruption at birth, for there is no more original sin, only an inherited one. The young male ego uses mother for its development, even as father is using her. On the other hand, she encourages what is wrong to grow up in that child, hoping its beastly form will remain subservient to her will.

So man leaves his mother and promptly begins to use his wife as his father did his mother. A male's entire sense of well-being depends upon maintaining this arrangement with his wife, and all communication with her is to this end, to oblige her to play that part well. Have you seen what happens to a man when a woman makes eyes at him? It drives him right up the wall with excitement. He needs her like a drink to make him feel secure, and he will love her and need her even more as he becomes a bigger fool. That's how his father fell to his mother, and his mother is the temptress in his own background that violated him when he was a child. That is, she rocked him off his foundation through her guilt, ego need, and frustration.

Quite often a mother will create a carbon copy of herself in her daughter through extreme cruelty, and it is interesting to note that the daughter can appear to love and serve that mother through their shared contempt for the weak father of the house. In this we see a familiar principle at work—mother, being wrong, must tempt her daughter to embrace the same wrong in order to justify herself. She must see to it that the child's larceny and contempt for men be preserved uncorrected and projected into her future relationships. Thus, the child grows up feeling perfectly justified in the role of seductress with men. Her behavior has been modeled on her mother's, backed by her encouragement, and hardened by the contempt they both feel for the head of the family.

In an earlier chapter I mentioned that the femininity of a child is often rejected by her male-hungry mother, who converts her into a male substitute to serve her ambition for worldly things. Many women grow up with masculine ways as a result of such mothering and seek to compensate for their lack of femininity by relating to what appears to be a dominating male, but is in reality an emasculated male who is trying to compensate for the loss of his identity to his mother. Now, by "making" him the boss, she gives him the illusion he seeks to preserve because he is not really a man. Nevertheless, the relationship smells to high heaven of temptation—for the illusion of being a man, he becomes even less of a man in her hands. And instead of becoming the woman she had hoped to be by relating to him, she becomes a temptress, absorbing his male identity, and actually becoming like her male mother inside.

More often than not, a man not only has a naughty, willful wife on his hands, but her real mother as well. As for the wife, she is caught between her own need for her husband and her mother's need for her. She is torn between mama's appeal to her loyalty and her own ego's need to have her femininity restored to her with the power and the glory inherent in it. From this, it is easy to see that when we attack our wives, husbands, or children, we are usually fighting the wrong person.

In the case of children, especially, we must take care not to attack the habits they bring home with them, but look for the source and then promptly perform a "friend-*fiend*-ectomy" to cut them off from the corrupting influence and give them time to come back to their own senses. Occasionally, a man is able to perform this operation on a wife who is receiving too much support for her weaknesses and resentments from her family and friends, but of course it would be difficult for a woman to strong-arm a man in the same way. In any event, whether the person being cut off from his friends is a wife or a child, he will experience strong withdrawal symptoms that will prompt some ugly outbursts and tantrums. If you are the one doing the "cutting off," you may expect to be attacked as though you were the real enemy.

The enemy, of course, is the so-called friend who encourages the adventurous nature and excuses the weaknesses of your wife or child. For this he is admired—even loved—by the blind ego of his victim, but the wise parent or husband should see this situation for what it is and not allow his own egotism to trap him into "sympathizing" with his children's or wife's need for "friends." If he is so afraid of losing the love and respect of his loved ones that he is unable to do what is necessary, it may be that he is unconsciously allowing these exciting associations to finish the job that he himself began.

Every temptation adds another faulty layer of growth to a weak personality which tends to obscure the most traumatic and deadly influence in any life—namely, a mother without a true husband. She offers her children all kinds of freedoms and advantages in an attempt to buy their love, and in the case of the son, to outclass his wife-of-the-future and assure his return as a prodigal son.

A loving spouse or parent often finds himself doing battle with many allegiances and "loves" that cling to his loved ones like so many barnacles; "friends," mothers, fathers, grandparents, the whole blasted family. If you are not a strong and loving parent, your child can be so weakened by his associates that he will fall easily into all kinds of temptation, such as dope addiction, and you will be totally unable to help him until you find the strength to separate him from his "friends" for his own sake and hold him firmly until he runs out of curses for you. A child is not strong enough to separate himself voluntarily from temptation, and once he has been hooked, he is not open to reason. Only force will prevail with him, but it must be a loving force, backed up by wisdom and insight into the exact nature of the problem. And remember, whether you are a mother, father, wife, or husband, your own failings are partly to blame for the hangups of your loved ones. "For we wrestle not against flesh and blood, but against principalities, against powers, against the rulers of the darkness of this world, against spiritual wickedness in high places." (Ephesians 6:12)

In the light of what has been said, we can perhaps appreciate more fully another aspect of the biblical account of man's fall. ". . . and for this cause shall a man leave his mother and his father and cleave unto his wife and become one flesh . . ." In other words, he must come back to the scene of the crime, either to recommit the crime or to observe what it is all about and admit it. If he confesses before God, then he is given grace whereby he may love his wife in true and proper manner. At first, however, the male is compulsively attracted to the female through his need, so he leaves his mother and father and takes a wife—just as Adam "took" Eve, the daughter of his flesh, "bone of his bones," and made her his wife when they became male and female after the fall.

So male and female came together in the beginning as the result of a common need, but if the relationship is to become meaningful and holy togetherness, the participants must learn to transcend that psycho-sexual aspect of need. And in light of the suffering they inflict upon each other as man and wife they will have ample opportunity to observe and question their "natural" relationship.

Husband and wife are not physically of one flesh and one blood, as father and daughter are, so it must come to pass that one day man must overcome his masculine need with the godly love that is more appropriate to man as he was originally created. When he learns to look at his wife through truly loving eyes, he will see her as a woman and not as a female animal whose only function is to serve his lust and pride. He will trade the love that corrupts for the love that corrects, and in his own freedom from need he will find the strength to say "Eve, put that apple down." In a spiritual sense, then wife becomes daughter and matriarchy is supplanted by patriarchy.

As for matrimony, it should be fairly obvious that man should have only one wife and be faithful to her. Otherwise, he could never fulfill his spiritual obligation. To go from one woman to another in the hope of finding fulfillment is sheer madness, for the kind of woman a man seeks under those conditions is the kind that will most perfectly testify to his greatness, and because such a man is far from great, the "right" woman will always be the wrong woman. A man who commits adultery is committing suicide by degrees. To this many a fool would raise his glass and say "What a way to die!" But such a man is gradually becoming a crazed beast, increasingly sensitive to the demands of the evil lurking in the kind of women who are willing to play with him. And the more he turns a deaf ear to his conscience, the more he must assert his maleness and maintain his illusions and sense of well-being by means of excitements, temptation, and "love" games. And every one of those silly female pleasure units will dig her claws deeper into him and goad him all the way to Hell.

11

Mutual Corruption—
or Correction?

If you want to take a wife, you must be prepared to be taken by her, and accept the consequences. For a woman to be a wife, she must first be a female, and to be a female is to be less than a woman, and for a woman to be less than a woman is to be full of guile. Nevertheless, a man makes a temptress out of a woman, because only a temptress will support and serve his ego in the way he wants it served.

Eve became the first female, because if she had remained an honest woman, she would not have been able to support the pride of a man who wanted to be wrong. Adam received his first orders concerning temptation before Eve came from his side, and when he placed her in the position of temptress to support his scheme, she was yet innocent. Her position, second to man with God, did not grant her power to deal with temptation. It was Adam's responsibility to protect and correct her in that moment of truth, and he failed her.

The situation is similar to that of the child who is tempted by candies that are bad for his teeth and general health. It is mama's job to deny him those sweets. The child is not technically wrong for desiring them. How could he know any better? The child cannot fully realize what he is getting involved with. But if mother happens to need that child's "love" and support, she may trade him the candy for it. The secret needs of a parent often compel him to stand by in "loving consent" to the irresponsible behavior of a child at the very moment the child stands in greatest need of his parent's loving strength to "deliver him from evil." And, of course, mama and papa play this game with each other, too. He allows her some outlandish indulgence with the understanding, usually only implied, of course, and not openly expressed, that now he has the right to whatever it is he wants from her.

As humans, we are all tempted to get things that are not good for us to have. Animals have no desire for the forbidden, so they are not subject to temptation, but human beings all secretly desire the forbidden glory. Until we find correction for this desire we are subject to subtle beguiling forces which masquerade as our own wishes. On all sides, someone has something to sell us that will make us wise. We even come into this world crying (as animals rarely do), moaning, groaning with anguish, fear, and guilt, with all kinds of false needs and a latent dissatisfaction with life before it has even begun. And we can never be truly satisfied until we hunger and thirst after righteousness and are filled.

Since the Fall, our heritage is a separation from Truth. This ego separation causes us to feel an insatiable craving for support or real love. That is what a baby cries for, but the answer he receives is his first violation.

The female is still crying for true love, but what does she get? Sex! A male without understanding cannot understand a woman's need to be loved for herself alone. He interprets her demand for love in the only way he knows, as a brute would. The same kind of gap exists between mother and child. Mother, not having been loved by her husband, but having been given sex instead, bears a child. Now she is guilty of being a mother who does not know how to love. After all, her own demand for love was met with sex, so now she is a frustrated female accepting sex in lieu of love. And if she should cry out because she is worse off for sex, she just gets more sex. What can she now give in answer to her child's need? Ah! She will give that child the love it needs. But what kind is that? Well, it must be the only kind she knows—lenience.

The ego demand persists, and mother is on the spot to extend real love, but she has never received real love. The child is tempted and crying, but he doesn't know what he is crying for. It must be for the love that says "no, it's wrong to let you have things that will harm you"—in other words, correction by one who knows that love and correction are synonymous. He wants that thing his ego was made to crave, and if mother's guilt bothers her sufficiently, she will give in to the child and bestow the luxury in exchange for his appreciation and "love."

Mothers will often throw everything but the kitchen sink into the crib in the frenzied hope of finding the one thing that will make Junior happy—and make Junior love her. The more she gives, the more the child cries. Remember the sex-love game? You see, she is giving in order to get support for a sense of righteousness. As Adam does to his wife, so his wife does to the children. Children are subject to the same kind of beguilement a woman is subject to when she is without the protection of a true man.

The "crying need" of Adam's soul was to have power and glory—his very own purpose—just like God. But because Adam did not love and obey God, God's love and God's power were not in him to provide the authority he would have needed to correct Eve. So *his* need caused him to nod his head in approval of the temptation. When Eve was tempted, she appealed to Adam, who should have admonished her to abstain, but because he needed her support, he comforted her in her guilt. This made him feel right and free in his own guilt, so he also ate of the fruit. Most of us at some time have sympathized so much with a person guilty of wrongdoing that we have wound up committing the wrong with that person—especially if that wrong was what we really wanted to do all along. Coming down to another person's level assures us of his love at that level, and more importantly, justifies us in what we do at that level.

Now do you see how every dishonest, frustrated, wrong woman, still serving the pride in her husband, can affect her children? And how she "gets even" and obtains a sense of right for herself to replace the real right displaced in her by evil by serving her husband's ego need? For this she is wrong, and the presence of error in her affects the child in many ways. She leads temptation into the child, beguiling him by lenience, giving him what "he" wants and approving of his needs and of him, just as he is, in exchange for the child's respect, which approval restores a sense of dignity to her falling, guilt-ridden nature. God help us all!

Becoming better people does not imply an improvement or refinement of our personalities through our sexual performance, but a return to the state in which man and woman existed before they became male and female. As Adam and Eve once related somewhat as father and daughter, became male and female as a result of temptation, then husband and wife, then parents of new little males and females, they set in motion a downward spiral of nature in which the male comes back to degrade the female increasingly.

Therefore, if a man wishes to see his beguiled female wife restored to her proper dignity as a woman, he must find his way back to his own lost inheritance, and with his dignity restored by God, stand as something more than a male to her—a father, or at least a big loving brother. As a matter of fact, until he gets his foot on the first rung up, he isn't going to be much interested in relating to his wife as a woman, a fellow human being. It was probably the last thing he had in mind when he married her. And the same goes double for her if she is a typical female, full of guile. She knows that she will have the upper hand as long as she keeps him happy in his weakness and doesn't let him get anywhere near that ladder! If he persists in wanting to humanize their relationship, great will be her withdrawal symptoms. Like a dope addict, she has learned to need a male to supply her with a "female" sense of identity, and a sense of superiority, power, and righteousness appropriated from him, even though she might be aware that something is wrong. And she may well be somewhat aware, for deep within a potential woman-child of Light there stirs a craving for the true *father* image in an honest man. The weak father and husband has been the male for her femaleness, for the identity her ambitious ego craves and needs but should not have. Happiness is slow to appear, but it does arrive in the perfecting of the relationship, when husband and wife eventually become man and woman, then father and daughter (man and helpmate), doing God's Will on earth.

In every wife there is a mother, not only for her child, but to serve her husband's unrecognized need for a mother as well. A wife may have two sons: a natural son and one through original sin, her husband. Total maleness is not a pure or normal human state of being. Maleness owes its existence to femaleness and cannot exist unless a female is encouraged to support it with her guile. For it was the presence of temptation in the female that originally caused man to fall from "spiritual" man to "natural" male, to the environmental stress that can eventually strip a man even of his maleness.

Father compulsively fails in his loving responsibility toward his wife, and then, because he inherits a need for her support, he places her in the ancient role of temptress-female to assure and cater to both his physical need and his ego need. As a male, he needs the body presence of a female; as a sinner, he needs the reassuring temptation that lurks ominously inside that female body. There is a dual need here. His maleness demands femaleness, and his ego demands the ancient ego companion. The male animal who needs and demands a female to be a female cannot tolerate an honest woman, for such a woman has no guile and does not play games or spin dreams for proud egos. No longer totally female, she is a human person, and that is something quite different. For one thing, she cannot be used; and just as a pet takes on character from having been tamed by its owner's presence, she also has taken on character from a Presence, or ground of being, that is unfamiliar and even threatening to a proud man.

A male being standing obediently in the Presence of God is so stabilized and tamed by His Spirit that he is more than male—he is man. Because he is stable in his God-given identity, he cannot be tempted, but his very presence can tame and stabilize the temptress and enable her to become woman.

However, and unfortunately, today's male stands not in the Presence of God, but in the presence of the possessed female, and is tamed by her and the spirit that overshadows her. She is the tiger and he is the pussycat. It serves him right, of course, for he invariably seeks out the kind of woman that will serve his twofold need: the need of his flesh for pleasure and the need of his ego for reassurance. He seeks a female for his body and a "devil" (*her* devil) to serve the aspiration of his soul toward the same ancient forbidden quest for power and glory. The "devil" part in his wife is the "familiar spirit" of his mother who started him out on the road to male-hood, and his choice of a wife is the measure of mother's success in getting him off on the wrong foot. The less of a man he is, the more rotten a female will he need to reassure him that he is a normal man. And needless to say, the bigger the lie, the more guile is needed to make it "ring true," and it is this dishonesty that distinguishes a female from a woman.

The quality that a man looks for most assiduously in a wife is the spirit of vain love that so beguiled him in his mother, but it is the very quality that he may despise the most once he has succeeded in converting his wife into a mother. As the hunger of his body grows less imperious, the need of ambition to serve his pride takes over, and he becomes *dependent* upon his wife to keep stoking the fire of ambition that his mother started in him.

But the egocentricity of every male requires him to rebel against and resent any "god" who requires his obedience, love, and devotion. There are times when he would almost rather be a good-for-nothing than owe so much of his "success" to his wife. But instead of inquiring more deeply into the nature of that ambition and that success, he usually escapes his dependency and seeks a new boost for his pride in the arms of another woman. In her he looks again to "capture" and use the reassuring spirit of his mother, which he needs either for love or for revenge, and his second lot is worse than his first. He is enslaved again.

"And so for this cause a man shall leave his mother and father and cleave to his wife, and then they shall become one flesh." What does this mean? Look now a little deeper into yourself. Reflect a moment. Let these words become understanding and then let them fade from memory. When we return to the subject, that understanding will penetrate to the Reality that words cannot reach.

Until he matures spiritually, the male is always drawn to the mother principle, the basic temptation (now a necessity) as it first represented itself in the form of the female. He falls for it in his mother, seeks it out again in his wife—and perhaps in still another wife, another woman, and later still, in a bottle or a needle in the arm.

The first man recruited the female to support his vanity. Because of this support he fell to the order of an animal, and as he became more and more of an animal, he needed more of her body and more of her guile. The more he got, the worse he became, until today many males have degenerated to a point where they need stronger reassurance than one or many women can give. The stimulation a woman provides a man is an opiate to his mind, in that it feeds his illusions so skillfully that he becomes absentminded about checking the situation out in the light of Reason, if indeed he can even remember that there *is* such a light. It is good to remember that the error of man's soul is represented by nature in him; a nature subject to the wiles of women.

The ancient Greeks offered condolences rather than congratulations to friends who had *fallen* in love—and with good reason. A man in "love" is a man stripped of reason, a sleepwalker in a world of fantasy. For the female who snared him only the night before, he is capable of killing a lifelong friend. He is powerless to resist the lure of the temptress and the hope of retrieving that missing rib. Once he takes a wife, he feels that his rib has been restored to him and he is suddenly a whole being, like a god, infallible, king of the mountain. Every man's ego, if not his body, craves this experience, even though he might suspect that it will be the death of him in the end.

If you are a woman-hating bachelor, repulsed by the very thought of touching a female, why do you suppose you react so negatively to women? Is it not because you are aware of their potential power over you, thanks to what you remember of your mother—and are you not also stuck with a terrible need for what you fear to need? Adam's need for ego assurance has come down to us as the need we now have for *re*assurance, and if we do not reach out to woman for it, we still reach out for a substitute that our psyche equates with the female principle. We are all born in sin, overshadowed by woman at birth, and in the process our selfhood is violated, so we proceed to "take it out on" the woman we take to wife. The male body, brought into being as a result of the temptation in the female, turns around to use the body of the female and so adds fuel to the fire of her temptation.

Scientific studies show that animals draw strength from their environment, or territory. They are far more courageous and daring when they are fighting to defend their eminent domain than when they are trying to muscle in on another animal's territory. Also, the more territory they dominate, the more powerful they are in defending it. Perhaps we can relate this principle to the case of the falling male. The female represents his territory, the ground or environment to which he has fallen as well as his gateway to the world of glory. Could it be that without this psycho-physical environment backing him up he has no vital force to motivate him to prevail over obstacles and get ahead in life? We have seen how environment shapes and maintains the animal by means of an invisible vital force. It seems logical to assume that insofar as man comes down to the way of the animal he must be governed by the same laws.

They say that behind every successful man there is a woman—pushing—but no one has thought to ask what is behind her. Such a woman draws her psychic support from her instinctual environment, the spirit of temptation that lurks in the depths of her person and conditions her to rise to her man's need of her as a temptress. While the male needs the female form for reassurance, his unstable pride insists that this female be subject to the same corrupting lying intelligence that beguiled Eve in the garden.

217

She must be less than a woman in order to be acceptable to his ego. He uses her not only for the relief of his sexual burning, but to satisfy his pride of possession. He delights in strutting around with "his" woman, all dressed up like a dog's dinner.

Suddenly he is somebody. "Look what I caught," he crows. Surely the tempting dish on his arm is the big prize, and through her all the other prizes are obtainable. The sky is the limit, she is the key to everything. And for a little while, until the bubble of illusion bursts, he feels that everything is possible. He is free from inhibition, free to dominate his world. He is a big man with big ideas and big responsibilities. All his troubles, including motivation, are solved! He is, without realizing it, a big fat nothing, a slave of what he "owns."

A man may be quite aware of the illusions involved in what he needs to experience. He may even know what a fool he is going to make of himself just before he does so for the second time. But by then the little fool in him has grown into a bigger fool, and the fool in him that could not resist the first time certainly cannot resist the second time. Besides, if there is a second time or second woman, he will be foolish enough to want to get high again on a second one, if only to forget what a fool he became as a result of getting high on the first one. Women have the power to make a man forget his guilts and limitations and, in his own mind at least, change him into a superman.

When women begin to hurt a man's pride to the point that his "love" affairs are self-defeating, then he must seek other remedies based on the same theme. That is, he must find something to help put his conscious mind to sleep, to make him oblivious to what has become an incriminating conscience, a terrible "inhibiting" conscience, that insists on showing him what a fool he has been, possessed by the woman he thought he possessed. When this realization dawns on him, he no longer has anything to be proud of, so he must find something stronger than anything he has known before to heal and maintain his pride. Something that will assure him that he is not wrong and that he is therefore right, at least in his own eyes.

Man's first principle is woman. She is his first opiate. Mother church may be yet another diabolical form of the same temptation, intoxicating both men and women with self-righteousness. The minister may even be a mother figure in disguise. Men, more often than women, turn to narcotics, alcohol, smoking, and gambling, and entice their women to go along with them. In time, these escapes become attractive to the female because, if she is to maintain her advantage over the man without suffering conscience, by lying with and to him for her security, then she is quite likely to need a little snort or two herself.

Most dope peddlers and bartenders are men, but they are men who incarnate the spirit of the woman, and they know, having become like women, how to tempt a man and maintain their hold on him by increasing his susceptibility to temptation. As the male falls to need new and

219

stronger crutches, he must reach out to other forms of temptation to keep pace with his need. And the varieties of temptation are endless.

Smoking, drinking, and narcotics are actually female substitutes, since a man uses them to dull his mind to reality and preserve a sense of rightness about his faulty male identity. The principle that compels the dope fiend to become an addict is identical with, though one step removed from, the idea he first entertained about his dream girl at puberty. His relationship with his mother predestines his male need at puberty, but as he falls lower and becomes more guilty as a result of his relationships with females, he gets to a point where they no longer provide him with the amount of reassurance he needs. It is then that new temptations begin to appeal to him in exactly the same manner as the one that started him on his descent, and for exactly the same ego-building reason.

The new and exotic forms of temptation are simply "more of the same"—extensions of the first violation. In times of failure and frustration, the ego-conscious mind will conjure up images associated with the support it received from the tempter at the time of the temptation. And of course a male is high and hopeful as he is getting what he needs. He does not see that he is falling. He thinks he has it made—that he is being loved and considered by his tempter. And the tempter caters to his victim's need for ego support, his need to escape guilt, and his need to obtain what no man can obtain in good conscience. The moment of glory releases him from the anguish of conscience; it is also the exact moment of failing, falling to a new low, and because it is so "good" to him, he fails to see it for what it really is.

Thus the ego's need for a variety of crutches grows. It begins with mother, then goes on to wife or female substitutes for mother, and finally deteriorates to orgies, drugs, liquor, and other excitements. But all are mother female substitutes. Each succeeding pleasure or security is false and weakens him to need it in addition to the others. His need for all of them is just like the "love" he has for his wife, and the relief they afford him can well be sexually gratifying, equivalent to sexual relief.

When the ego cries out for escape from the pain of observing what it has done, it automatically draws the image that has assisted it in the past. The familiar appearance and assistance then throws a temporary mantle of pleasure over the pain and muffles the condemnation of conscience. But our hero never sees that the temptation represented by drink, drugs, women, and so on, is related to his present low. His ego associates it with "good" because it felt good, relieved his pain, and gave him a right and secure feeling.

The ego need calls up the image of its "god," and the image restimulates a physical hunger. And the hunger reaches for filling from the thing itself. The tension and terrible needs created by the reaching distracts the ego still further from the conflict raging deeper within the psyche. So man experiences a terrible obsession with sex, and as long as his ego needs support, assurance, and escape, he automatically fantasies "love" and escapes into daydreams. If the ego does not receive its "real" support in fantasy, its demands grow stronger, largely because of the additional burden of guilt it carries for using fantasy as an escape rather than facing the truth.

The growing need of the burning ego calls up various images, and the images stimulate the body to desire and to call up more images to whet the desire. When the tension becomes unbearable—comes the moment of truth: the sex act, the needle, the puff, or the snort, usually shared with a tempting accomplice. Now the cycle is complete. The body has found relief for its physical pain and the ego has found relief for its guilt in the rites of "love" with the beloved object or person, and the ritual itself is enshrined in memory—in a handy place, of course, so that it will be available for recall as "the way to solve the problem" the next time the problem arises.

Do you see now where you must draw your first battle line? If you love Truth, you must learn how to reject the image that presents itself to your mind as the "answer" to your problem. But bear in mind that to reject the image is not to repress it, or certainly not to distract yourself from the knowledge of it. Repression and distraction merely compound the problem because they are wrong answers, and as wrong answers they will present you with more image problems. For instance, if you decide to fly airplanes as a means of getting your mind off sex (distraction), you just might wind up having a problem with sex in sexually exciting airplanes.

Most hungers are just phantoms of the mind. You conjure them up to satisfy your ego's craving for an old friend-fiend in need. And when you fail to find that "need-mate," or when you do find one and proceed to abuse him (or her) to the point that he has to run away from you, then you are forced to rely on the phantoms of your mind—and the more you entertain them in your imagination, the more real they become.

It all boils down to one basic fact: that we find our greatest pleasure in relieving the pains that we should never have had in the first place. That kind of pleasure is the only joy we know, and the hunger for it is the only "love" we know. Sexual tension is usually the first manifestation of our failure to find our true identity; sexual tension is a pain that arises in a male as a result of his being less than a man. The real answer to that male's problem is to become a man, not to use a woman. When his soul is in need, it is represented by an erection. At this time a male would do well to meditate for the relief of that failure rather than find comfort and security for it at the hands of a female.

We will never be able to find correction or modification of our sex need as long as we use the sex experience to support our ego. We must disabuse ourselves of the notion that we are "loving" or being "loved" in the sex act—or that we are "making" love. What we are almost always doing is using sex to feed our own ego, or being used sexually by another to feed his ego. In the moment that we make this discovery, sex becomes wrong for us.

Sex, of itself, is not sinful; but when a person *uses* sex to obtain for himself a sense of security, an escape from reality, or an elevation for his ego, he is using sex in a wrong way, and he is therefore sinning. In the same way, when a person uses alcohol to feel good he substitutes the spirit of alcohol for the Spirit of Truth. Drinking to feel right is a wrong that his conscience will not allow to pass unnoticed. When he sobers up, he is bound to feel the pangs of guilt and anxiety. (A hangover is something more than a headache.)

The attempt to escape our conscience in sex is even more ill-fated than the attempts we make by means of drinking and drug addiction, though all three are merely variations on the same theme. Sex, which always starts out by looking like a natural handy *solution* to a problem, soon grows to be such a problem itself that it distracts us more than ever from the root problem; but as long as a man or a woman uses sex as a means of achieving ego security, he grows more dependent upon his sexual experiences, even as a drunk develops a growing need for alcohol, and a dope addict develops a growing need for drugs. And just as the pusher and the bartender are guilty of being accessories to the weaknesses they promote, man and woman grow guilty in respect to each other, not only for what they are doing, but for what they are encouraging the other one to do and to become.

As long as you need sex to support your ego, you need someone to provide it for you, and you must encourage (tempt) that someone to play his part. But sooner or later, you will become aware that something is wrong with your marriage. It no longer looks like the rosy solution you imagined it to be. You see that your spouse is a weak, demanding, unreasonable, evil person. And if you are capable of objectivity, you see how much you have contributed to his deterioration. After all, you cannot expect anyone to improve all the while some meddling "considerate" friend keeps him intoxicated. Nor can you waken your spouse while you are busy "putting him on."

Some needs are quite normal and some are not and, especially if you are a man, you must have the good sense to know when you are being used. At times, you must even have the *love* to deny sex to your wife in order to free her to come to her senses. This is especially good medicine for a man to "give" to his wife because women have very little honest desire for sex anyway. Properly executed, it will reveal that your attitude toward her has undergone a change. She will suddenly see that you are becoming a man capable of compassion and consideration for others, and that you are no longer simply promoting her for your own selfish gratification. She may be shocked, of course, to discover that you are capable of being loyal to her without her having to do anything to guarantee your loyalty—that you can do a right thing without her having to stand over you. Her ego can be greatly disturbed by this sudden loss of power, but the experience will be valuable to her. In time, she will see the love behind the denial.

At first, she will complain bitterly. "You are driving me into the arms of another man," she may scream in frustration. And now you must stand your ground, for you are being put to a severe test. As you may be aware by now, one of the most difficult things for a man to do is to resist the invitation of a woman pretending sexual need (when what she really wants is the miasmic vitality of the animal given off by the decaying man). Her invitation can be so tempting and reassuring to his pride that unless he is very *right* within himself, it can produce in him an overwhelming sexual drive, a burning for the female, and he will have to give her the "love" she has *tricked* him into giving in order to satisfy his own needs. At that moment, he will be so caught up with the illusion of doing some "divine" good that he will forget all about real love (correction).

What happens when a man observes a pleading, tempting, apparently innocent sex-needful woman standing before him? In effect, she is saying "It's your *duty* to be a male. After all, I am a female, with human wants and needs." This *is* a strong argument, isn't it? It is also exactly what your ego would like to believe, because it comfirms the "only human" aspect of your own fallen nature. Fallen males have one thing in common on their minds, and they are always wishing a woman would invite (tempt) them to "have at it." Either that, or they themselves are tempting women into sex. Men, not women, are the real tempters.

When we are wrong, we all need reassurance.

We have to know that it's "all right" for us to be as wrong as we have become. But of course we know that we *are* wrong—if we didn't, we'd have no need for reassurance. The drunk, even after he has sobered up, can be enticed to take another drink not only because of the conditioning factor of the bottle, but because he is guilty for drinking and for the things he has done under the influence of drinking. So, though he may be relatively sober at the time you offer him a drink, his soul agrees because of need and his flesh is conditioned to obey. So he will reach for the drink to escape his weakness through the "naturally" aroused impulse. In the same way, a conditioned man is self-conscious about being a male.

To get back to the drunk—even though he may have no troubles to forget, no overwhelming desire to drink, he is still vulnerable to the entreaties of a fellow drunk, demanding that he be a sport and join in the fun. He finds these pleas hard to resist because his conscience is secretly bothering him, and such a man, not being a real man, does not know how to resist temptation. His very inability to resist temptation from a platform of virtue actually increases the power of his tempter. He will seize on the flimsiest of excuses to justify his compulsion to indulge.

Similarly, a woman in distress is reassuring to a man's malehood. Almost every time a man has sex he becomes guilty through it, even though sex itself is not all that wrong. Through tempting and being tempted, and promoting females, he has become a weak person, less of a man, more of a male, and therefore more susceptible and guilty—because as a male, he is guilty of not being a man.

Now do you see that even though this poor chap might have no particular interest in sex at a given moment, he can be easily aroused in the old way by the tempting morsel before him? Regardless of what it is, because the average man does not know how to respond to the pressure of temptation properly, he has little resistance to it, especially if his soul is hungry for adventure.

Usually the temptation before us, whether male or female, drink or drug, has a twofold power over us in the way that all things do when we are hung up with them. Whatever promotes us to fall to its level has power to restimulate our attention to it, and if we have not found a godly power to resist it, we must at least physically respond to the pressure of its call. If the soul still has need, it will agree to the indulgence and will then go all the way through the cycle, and voila! Another layer of alcohol-sensitive flesh.

Things have power over us only because we lack grace, and when we lack grace, the need of our ego is such that it seizes on anything that promises to satisfy it. The more we reach for it, whether it be drink, sex, or whatever, the more obligated to it we become, and what started as a relief from the agony of burning desire ends as an agony of guilt, for we add guilt when we give in to our desire. But before the time of understanding, we nearly always misinterpret our needs as "love."

The resistance that pride prompts us to put up against temptation only makes matters worse. The tempter sees it, not as a true strength, but just as it is: false, vain, and vulnerable. From this observation the tempter gains strength to tempt us still more, all the way to the breaking point. As we respond, and we most certainly will, *we feel the guilt of responding*, so that if we don't give in to the temptation out of desire for what it offers us, we give in to it simply to relieve the pressure and the agony of our guilt.

For example: An alcoholic's response to drink awakens guilt in him for having responded to the drink, and the tension that results from the guilt feeling increases his need for the drink. For a time, the conflicting desires (to drink and to resist the drink) grow up in him side by side, but when the conflict becomes unbearable, he experiences a twist in viewpoint that enables him to excuse what he is forced to do. He looks at the physical desire that he is now unable to contain another moment, and then he looks at the guilt feelings that have been growing in him alongside his desire to drink, and he comes to a crafty conclusion as to the relationship between them. "Aha," he says to himself, "I feel guilty because I have not been honest with myself. I've been denying my 'natural' inclination!" So now he is free to take the drink.

The truth of the matter is that his conscience has been trying to tell him that he was wrong for responding to the temptation in the first place, and for needing to give in to it in the second place, but the alcoholic fails to get the message. Temptation in all its forms has a way of first bringing us down to its level (through desire), and then showing us how to misinterpret our guilt feelings in such a clever way that our need increases, along with a feeling of loyalty and gratitude toward our corrupter. On a spiritual level, we are guilty for needing as well as for responding to temptation, and our conscience continues to point to the ego failing that we are trying to avoid or cover up by means of the temptation, both directly and as the result of using it again and again as a refuge from our guilt feelings. So it is that evil claims our loyalty and devotion in subtle ways, by using and manipulating our ego needs and the compulsions that remain with us as the results of former needs and our excuses for them.

We misinterpret our guilt feelings in the presence of temptation and pressure. Temptation appeals to us with such intensity that we fail to be objective enough to evaluate what it is that is producing guilt in us.

For instance, you are invited to a party and even though you have made up your mind not to take another drink, you go to the party. Your rejection of the drinks is noticed immediately, of course, and it offends everyone there. How can the others relax and give themselves up to the "fun" of drinking if you are going to stand there watching them with your bright sober eyes? To relieve their anxiety, they start needling you to join them in the drinking. So what happens if you stand your ground in spite of all their blandishments? They begin to isolate you (as though you had bad breath), to cut you off emotionally from the group in many subtle ways, and to withdraw all the supports and approval that you have grown to need as a result of your associations with them and others like them.

When they take the pressure off you to conform and withdraw their ego support (having decided that you're a confirmed "party pooper"), they begin to tempt you with a new pressure, the pressure of rejection. You may even begin to see that your sense of security as a person has depended on the kind of support they were giving you. More of their attention will make you guilty, but less will make you aware of the guilt of your past association with them. You are certainly not a right or good person at all, because if you were, you would not require emotional support, from them or anyone else.

All your life, your sense of well-being and security has depended upon people like these. Here at the party you face two forces: drink and friends. And even as you resist the idea of drink, you begin to doubt yourself and feel less sure. You begin to feel the twinges of conscience, and your friends become alarmed when you show signs of "defecting" to the "enemy," your own conscience. To do so would be to withdraw from your friends the kind of ego support they have been depending on you to give them; so when you do not do as they do, you make them feel insecure. Alarmed, they try to coax you back to conformity, and if they fail in this, they grow hostile toward you. Now it's your turn to feel insecure. You resent them, and because you do, you add guilt to guilt. The more you have depended on them to support your ego, the more you will feel the sting of their judgment upon you.

Your resentment, of course, is a tit-for-tat judgment of them; but it adds a large measure of guilt to the conflict going on inside you, and it isn't much good as a tactic because there are too many against you. At this point you may interpret your guilt to mean that you feel like a heel for making your friends feel so unhappy, and even though you are lying to yourself and making yourself guiltier, like a little boy holding his nose and jumping into the deep end of the pool, you relent and have "mercy" on your friends—you become a good guy and you lift the glass.

At that very moment, your friends come rushing up with all the old support for your ego illusions, and buoyed up by their approval (with a little assist from the booze), you glow with power. Once again, you start the process of blotting out your anxiety in a way that you will soon regret. The morning after the night before, you will start to see everything in its true light insofar as you have the understanding to do so. The one thing you *won't* feel is happy. If you're extremely dependent on illusion for your life support, you may even need a "hair of the dog" to get to feeling like a "good guy" again. With very little imagination you could substitute any other hangup in place of drink.

If you lack grace, you will see the same ego-, friend-, temptation-needfulness at work in your sex life. Does the sex act leave you feeling vaguely uneasy, bothered? Does it bother you enough that you feel the need to play at it again as soon as possible?

As we discussed earlier, women are more aware than men of what is going on in the sex game. Basically, a woman's ego security rests upon man's being an unprincipled animal, one without real authority over her. She can rarely justify a real and natural sexual craving. Like the bartender, she gets a ''dry drunk'' by encouraging the drinker. Her uncorrected ego needs the man, not so much the sex, but she can't stay in the business of being Eve without serving Adam his sex. After a season, she begins to consider sex less of a violation and more of a necessity. Soon the pressure of her husband or boyfriend can produce the same effect on her as the drinking friends produce on the person with a drinking problem. If she tries to be honest with her man by admitting to feeling guilty as a result of having cooperated with him in the sex act, he gets mad and may threaten to go out and find another woman (like the drunk threatening the bartender that he might take his business elsewhere). Because she has never known the true fulfillment that would blot out her transgressions, and is dependent upon sex for ''love'' or money, she is in agony. She not only suffers guilt over what she has done, but feels powerless to cope with the temptations and problems that have arisen as the result of what she has done. How does she react? She hates the man? But that makes her guilty. She lets him go? Well, then she will feel guilty for being lonely and missing the bum. So she winds up ''loving'' him, giving him what he needs, thereby achieving a feeling of safety for a little while longer.

The first drink is a violation, but all the others are "necessities." Sex acts on a woman in much the same way through a little-understood ego need. She has no real need for sex. What she does have is an old-fashioned ego craving for "love." This ego need, uncorrected by true love, does not draw the love of God into her heart. Instead, it attracts to her the same kind of uncorrected "love," or ego need, in others, and she looks on the offerings of her needful counterparts as her divine dues, manifestations of her power and her glory. That need for a wrong kind of "love" and unmerited "devotion" excites men to "answer in kind," to try to rise to the challenge and meet it with their sex drive. Under the circumstances, when a marriage is based on a mutual need for "love," it is bound to end in mutual corruption and disaster.

And so it comes to pass that modern Adam, with his burning need, places his woman right back in the old Eve role through his animal-ego need. He instructs her in sensuality as he originally coaxed her to be his temptress in the garden. And to her this kind of love (ego security) covers a multitude of sins. It can even make her dependent upon the sex relationship. Once she is violated and deeply involved, she feels damned when she does and damned when she doesn't. What a dilemma!

It is wrong, of course, to use sex or anything else to provide oneself with a feeling of righteousness or security. When a woman is tempted to "help out," she becomes weaker and more wrong, but she has to depend on what made her wrong for a renewed feeling of being "right"—a vicious cycle. In her frustration and confusion, she may learn to demand from a man what it is not good for him to give, and if he truly loves her as a person, he will see that this is so. He will gradually become less and less excited by her "needs" and will begin to love (correct) her in a new and proper way. And not until a man has succeeded in experiencing and imparting this kind of love to his wife can he have sex with her, for fear that he will be perpetuating the old process of making her drunk with power and self-righteousness and serving her the last drop of his life along with the sex.

We can observe this principle at work in all our human relationships—the need (weakness) in us spoils others to need us in turn. Take the case of the father who wants to be a buddy to his son because his own father was always too busy for him. He becomes a friend to the child's weakness in order to satisfy his own old need for assurance through the boy, and spoils the child in the process. Had he not been needful he could have seen the propriety of remaining a father, aloof, with the authority to correct and love his son in a proper way. But because he himself has emotional needs, he loses authority and comes down to the level of the child for the sake of his approval, "love."

12

Struggling with the Ties that Bind

If you are truly considerate of another's well-being, you understand the hazards of trying to be a "good" wife, or a "good" mama, or a "good" doctor, teacher, politician, or a "good" anything in an archetypal way, along some preconceived lines of what is socially acceptable. Yet few there are with enough consideration for others to stop trying. We all know how easy it is to eat more than we should when the food is tantalizingly prepared and served; yet to many women, being a good cook is synonymous with being a good and wonderful person. They spend hours in the kitchen fussing with the tasty dishes that will show daddy and the kids what wonderful cooks they are—and turn them into pigs at the same time. Any truly objective and disinterested observer—a visitor from Mars, perhaps—could see at a glance that these "good-mama" cooks are actually tempting and degrading their families and friends to satisfy the needs of their own vanity and to justify the position of power they hold in the home.

The worst of it is that, once addicted to the bountiful repasts dished up by these good cooks, family and friends find themselves "hooked" not only on the food, but on certain ego satisfactions they themselves derive from the proceedings, and they actually encourage the cook to bigger and better gastronomical achievements. They see "mother" as a servant ministering to "their" epicurean desires; and as fellow egotists, they see this service as loving consideration for their "love" of life and appreciation of all that is good. Food, like sex, can be used to comfort and fill the void of the ego and raise the spirits; and when it is used in that way, the eating of it becomes a "religious" ritual. Anything that makes a person feel good and comforts his soul by its presence is basically a religious experience.

The ego with an acquired need does not like to believe that need to be in error. Once tempted by food, it will need and demand it as a "right" kind of thing. The natural desire to eat simple food for sustenance becomes adulterated, so that wholesome food no longer suffices. Remember our discussion of food and ego need? Food, to tormented abnormal people, must do more than satisfy the body's requirements—it must also gratify the ego and replace the soul's lost substance in an "ersatz" kind of way. Tempting food is like tempting sex. The spice communicates itself through the food or sex as the tempter, the ego offering that secretly assures us of the rightness of our unnatural voracious appetites, that will come to depend increasingly on the spice or excitant that started our juices flowing in the first place. Thus we are brought down lower, a step at a time, to require more of the spice, more of the exotic and unexpected.

Doing its thing, the temptation communicating through the food or sex says something in the inscrutable language of the Devil to us, his "sons." It approves our exotic needs and rewards them with pleasure; it assures the ego that it need not question its growing need for food or sex as an abnormal manifestation of the false identity that is secretly taking shape inside us. Since they are feeding more than the simple needs of the body, food and sex become objects of craving to our hungry egos. We need them to feel gloriously right, even though overindulgence brings on guilt feelings, which are soon followed by feelings of deprivation, and finally by a greater and more unnatural hunger than the last one. A person caught in the devil's web of food or sex addiction is never satisfied with a simple wholesome diet, or the natural sex act. His lusts are his gods, and he must make a "religious ceremony" of his indulgence in them.

Let's try to wipe the illusions out of our eyes long enough to take a really good look at a familiar character. There she is: Mrs. America. She may be sitting at the overloaded table, but she seems to be smiling down on it from a height, lapping up the complimentary sounds of approval issuing from her pigs as they eat until they are bloated, grunting their approval, clamoring for more. There she sits, the hostess, the center of whatever attention is left over from the food for a human being, pleased as punch with her great accomplishment. She may not eat a mouthful herself, for her ego gets all the satisfaction it needs from her family's piggy devotion and praise. On the other hand, she might have to overeat with the rest of them and get fat as a pig, not because she enjoys eating her own offering, but to keep pace with the family so they will think "fat is the only way to be." When they're all fat, they can't accuse her of treating them any worse than she did herself. And because they are in the same boat, it may not occur to them to accuse her at all.

Unconsciously, mama allows herself to get fat along with the family so that they will remain blind to what is happening to them. They will keep clamoring for her concoctions while her ego gorges on their praise and burps of approval. She might not even have to fill her belly because her ego is so amply stuffed.

You see, don't you, that a woman is capable of applying the same tactics to the sex act—making a hog out of a man by giving him sex with all the trimmings, enjoying it or pretending to enjoy it herself as the final touch, so that he can't possibly feel uncomfortable (like the hog she has made of him, or tempted him to be) afterwards. As he becomes more of a hungry animal, he will clamor in the usual immodest fashion of hungry animals and *demand* to be served with "hyped-up sex" lest he take his patronage elsewhere. So if she depends on his attention and admiration for her ego satisfaction, she has no alternative but to serve him spicier and spicier sex to keep him interested. And this can only end in his becoming a vicious, unprincipled, lustful animal (to say nothing of exhausted).

When we try to deal with this problem of appetite, *we must be careful not to overreact against sex and eating* by forcing ourselves to give them up entirely, nor must we give in to desire or pressure. We must understand the ego-need aspects of our body functions, so that we can reject the idea of using food or sex as an escape, distraction, entertainment, or support for our ego. A woman who has not found values within herself will allow herself to be put in a position that is degrading to her. To fill the hollow in her soul, she finds herself serving up spicy food and spicy sex and using the new experience to blot out the guilt of the one before, or she will try to "make things right" with herself by rebelling, pulling the bait out of reach.

A female always feels guilty about a show of love or hate, but many escape the awareness of their own guilt by deriving a secret satisfaction from observing how their husbands degrade themselves in their part of the unwholesome sexual ritual. A woman may pretend to enjoy sex for the pleasure of judging and hating her husband while he partakes of it. Then she may conceal her guilt for comparing him unfavorably with herself by the pleasure of eating, offsetting her guilt over the eating by cooking a tasty meal, and drowning her guilt over this in the praise of her family. The guilt of receiving praise she relieves by watching her hungry little pigs degrade themselves, and the guilt of this she relieves by worrying about the sicknesses overeating can produce in them. The guilt of making them worse by worrying about them she offsets by taking too much care of them, overdressing and overprotecting them. And she hides her guilt for this behind their love for her as a doting mother and their need for her protection as they grow weaker at her hands—or behind their rebellion, should they reject all mama's loving efforts to use them in the service of her vanity. So mama judges the ungrateful offender and thereby forgets the judgment upon herself.

Of course, this little drama is all hidden from view. What we see on the surface is a "good" wife, a "good" mama, a "good" anything, but beneath the surface she is corrupting the victim with "goodness" and care in order to escape the guilt of corruption.

A vain proud woman is constantly thinking up new tricks with which to please and hold her temptation-needful husband and family. She is forever dreaming up new ways to keep them "happy" (insensible to the facts of their weaknesses and needs), so that they will keep their attention lovingly and admiringly focused upon her. If that doesn't work, then she focuses her own attention hatefully upon them, hiding her own ugliness behind her observation of what she deems to be their greater ugliness. When she "loves" now, it will be to enjoy her secret contempt for the animals she has made of them. While this is going on at the various levels of her own consciousness, they are becoming more self-indulgent than ever, more dependent on the escapes that food and sex provide. They may even lean on "good mama" hard enough to wake her to the fact that while she has been puffing herself up at their expense, they have also been using her. At this point, she might pull the meanest trick of all: give up the ship, withdraw her largesse, and leave them all in a perpetual state of anxiety. A woman will sometimes give one great memorable performance (in the kitchen or in bed, no matter), then quit while she's ahead. Her man will long in vain for the exquisite pleasure she will never give again, and that no one else can duplicate.

In a moment of defeat, frustration, or guilt, a male's ego draws to mind the image associated with salvation and he dwells upon food or sex in an unnatural way, so that naturalness can never hope to satisfy his hunger. Only unnaturalness can, and when it does, he grows worse than he was before. He values only sex that has been adulterated, "souped up" in some way, and food that has been spiced. He is offended, even threatened, by the offer of pure food or sex, unadulterated by temptation or guile.

Make no mistake about it, meditating Lady, your male will not take kindly to your newfound innocence, and all your hungry friends will seek out another fool's home to stuff themselves in. So you may be left alone with your own hungers (for them, alas) and needs still uncorrected. Or, they may hang around to curse and criticize you for what appears to them to be your unloving coldness. Prepare yourself for a bombardment of criticism designed to make you feel guilty enough to come to your "senses."

All of us are grounded on this worldly spaceship because of an ego need to belong, "a sense of belonging," we call it. But if you are the least bit perceptive, you will see that you are really a stranger in a strange land, and the more you cater to the world for the sake of the only kind of belonging you have known, the more abandoned you will feel. The egocentric need for identity in you will tempt you to please the crowd, and for a while you may live by that approval and base your false being upon it; but this false being is always untrue to your true Self, and you will become as a stranger in an unfamiliar world. We look to the crowd as a mirror to reflect our identity back to us, to comfort and support us, and "lovingly" fill us with the indigestible goodies of the world, so that at first we don't see that we are asking them to support a wrong in them and in ourselves. We see the interchange as love *for* them and *from* them. So we fail to see that we are degrading ourselves for their "love," and that *we* are "loved" only because we degrade ourselves *for them.*

We "love" others in the way they need to be served, and get our fullness as reward. But that fullness depends upon our approval of their weakness and serving up something of ourselves to maintain their strength. By giving more and more of ourselves, we develop an illusion of our own worth, but the time comes when we have no more to give, or we can't stand the drain on our resources. It is then that we might be able to bring some light to bear on what has developed under cover of darkness, to see through the illusion and experience a wave of disgust.

As people pleasers, we are tempted to add a pinch

of dishonesty to all our relationships with others. From the cradle to the grave, we are trained to be "nice" (insincere) in the way of the mob, because it disturbs people to discover that you are without guile, without ulterior motives. They reject you for the honesty they don't know how to handle gracefully, and in doing so, they try to make you feel that you are the awkward one—and if you are not well grounded within yourself, you will accept their judgment upon you.

The more you serve these hungry "people eaters," the more you give up to them of your own identity, so that in the end, their very acceptance of you can feel like rejection, as though Heaven cast you out when they took you in. To be accepted, we have to degrade ourselves and cater to a sickness, and in doing so, we alienate ourselves from our true Selves. The moment we see that this is the way we are going, we should stop still in our tracks, suffer the pain of our observation, turn within, and await the True Comforter.

What we usually do, however, is work harder and harder at our people-pleasing labor, never stopping to wonder, never ceasing in our efforts to buy acceptance, adding "spice" upon "spice" to our offerings (burnt or otherwise)—all in an effort to escape to the self-alienation that will only grow worse as long as we look for salvation in the acceptance of the world we are serving, or falsely identify our loneliness with the world's rejection of us.

When we wake to discover the trap, we feel betrayed and threatened, even at the moment of acceptance, because in the final analysis, worldly acceptance IS the trap. It hurts, betrays, degrades, and threatens. It lures us deeper into a meaningless existence as IT gives ITS approval and ITS rewards for our craven "loving."

Do you see how our ego mind misinterprets everything? We try to experience self-acceptance, but always in an egotistical way. We kid ourselves that we are all right (because we know we ought to be, in order to earn our self-acceptance), and we put people "on" to help us fortify the self image we're trying to create with their help. In doing so, without realizing it, we sin against them and ourselves. As long as we cater to the world, we give it power to blame and abuse us, and no matter what we do to appease it, we will feel the sting of its (or, even worse, our own) rejection in the end. This is often the story hidden behind the headlines that scream the suicide of the young unselfish mother who was "loved" by everyone.

Nothing we can do for anyone can duplicate the process of being right that results from our being rightly related to God. The spirit in us will always condemn us for the "documentation" and "evidence" we conjure up to attest to our worthiness. In the final analysis, the shaft of pure light will pierce the bubble of our illusion, despite all our efforts to find self-fulfillment in our own way on our own terms. At the time of enlightenment, we will reject, even hate, the world we once "loved." We may want to take revenge on it, to hurt and destroy it before it destroys us, but of course this is no answer. People who take this course do so to their bitter regret.

For instance, a person who has hated his mother for having tempted him to eat may eventually become so guilt-ridden that he will overreact and revolt against the whole idea of eating in the hope of attaining to righteousness. In his confused mind, he thinks that if he became guilty by eating, then by not eating he can become "not guilty"—at least, by comparison with that fat pig of a mother who tried her best to make him into a hog to feed her own vanity.

When we lack insight to our problem, or self-control to modify the basic fault, we always go to extremes. People have died because they could not bring themselves to eat, or because they could not stop eating. The idea of not eating is, to some tortured minds, the same as not sinning, and not sinning equivalent to being right. But to a proud soul, feeling right is more important than anything else, even life itself; so that the victim of the righteousness-by-not-eating aberration becomes dependent upon fasting for the thrill of false virtue, the triumphant feeling of overcoming evil that his fasting gives him. So he wastes away while the people around him implore him to eat. He just looks upon them as tempters and delights in frustrating their intentions toward him, thereby "defeating" the designs of evil on earth. He even learns to derive his own nourishment from their frustration.

The ego and the body are so related that one can often "stand in" for the other; that is, the ego can receive so much nourishment that the hunger of the body diminishes in proportion to the ego's filling, just as a perfect person, perfectly fulfilled by God's love, would eventually transcend his physical needs entirely. Young people in love traditionally lose their appetites, for instance, and cooks often "fill up" on the smell of the food so completely that they have no appetite for it when it's ready to eat. We can also convert certain types of excitement to the satisfaction of our ego needs, and as we do so, we do not hunger as we did before. Confused people can become so high on love and hate that these emotions perfectly fulfill their spiritual and physical dietary requirements, and they lose their appetite for food and sex.

Women who finally revolt against sex become more frigid and self-righteous as their husbands grow more demanding. When the guilt underlying their rebellion has been caused by sex (with guile or ego need), they falsely associate their resultant frigidity with righteousness. The frigid woman, then, strong in her sense of righteousness, freezes at her husband's approach, and the needs that she has helped to promote in him now threaten her and fill her with revulsion. She may learn to take exquisite delight in overruling his beastly demands, and when her rejection makes him work harder to win her over, she feels more "superior" than ever in her insistence on complete abstinence. Of course, she became afraid of sex in the first place because it produced guilt in her, but if her man should leave her because of her coldness, she may begin to experience even more guilt in the absence of "love," or someone to hold in contempt. So at this point, she may thaw out and seek the sex experience again, thereby doing penance for her mistake—and assisting in the creation of another sex fiend in the bargain.

If two searching married people were suddenly to cease and desist from sex for a while in order to take a good look at themselves and their motives, the woman would soon feel guilt for what she has been required to be for the sake of the man's animal ego security. The man, however, would not feel too much guilt at first; he would just burn. A man is engrossed in the flesh too deeply to understand the implications of his burning. He would burn physically for his wife to return to her role of temptress, but he would not be aware that there was anything abnormal about his demands on her, because he does not consider himself to be abnormal at all. He just burns to "love" all the time, and to be accepted for that "love." Because he has not accepted his true responsibility, he wants to play all the time. He finds a woman irresistible if she will play with him, no questions asked.

During puberty, young males masturbate frequently, and many feel guilty about it. But if "Miss Right" should come along, they would not feel guilty, but manly, in their enjoyment of sex with her. From this point on, their manliness begins to depend upon this "right" one, who is unfailingly the wrong one. When this "right" one becomes too demanding (as she will, because she is guilty of using his need to forget her own failing) and he sees himself being used, and his whole existence converted to giving her attention, he may learn to delight in frustrating her demands on him by returning to masturbation. Now he doesn't feel guilty about it, as he did in his boyhood, because the fun of frustrating his wife's unloving demands is providing him with so much excitement and ego value.

Usually, in the absence of a substitute ego gratification (as above), masturbation makes men feel guilty and unmanly. They resolve this problem for the most part by imagining or fixing their attention upon some lurid form designed to take the place of temptation's actual presence. Or the "other" women a man needs, and often gets, provide the vital factor of "spice" for his ego and relief for his body, and his problems begin all over again on the sly. His paramour seems to adore his frolicking, irresponsible, and burning nature, and helps him to put aside the important doubts he might have entertained about what he is. She is full of guile and is constantly "at him" for a commitment to her. Such women fail to see that a loyalty that can be wrenched away from a prior and rightful commitment is useless to anyone who captures it.

Masturbation is the flowering of maleness without the guileful presence a man needs to reassure him of that maleness. Hence he feels guilt at the very moment he releases the sexual tension without the benefit of the spicy female presence to give him that invisible assurance.

Wild animals do not abuse themselves; their needs are seasonal and compatible with nature's intent. But man's need for sex is inordinate because of his ego hunger that "thrives" on sensation but can never really be satisfied by pleasure. His guilt causes him to become more needful of sensation all the time until he arrives at the big hangup or block. What we "love" hurts us so much that we become afraid of whatever it is that we need.

Maleness has a genetic memory like the homing salmon for its place of birth; and this genetic place of birth, along with the memory of it, is inimical to the psychic, or spiritual, "place of birth," for the "male" identity came into being through the presence of temptation. As a male, a man is not taking his proper place in the scheme of God's plan for him, and identifying himself solely with his maleness makes him a faulty person. Until he discovers his pride, it remains uncorrected, and uncorrected pride goes merrily on its proud way, inclining toward play and irresponsible antics to prove that it's a free spirit. The soul committed to God would prefer a helpmate to a playmate, but pride cannot exist as pride without a playmate. It's no wonder then that naughty girls are so attractive to men. (Males, that is.)

The ego reaches out and the mind's eye sees the playmate "doing her thing" to serve his pleasure. The image, in turn, awakens the dormant beast of sensuality, and the sexual burning forces the male to find a woman in the flesh. But when he does so, he behaves just as his father did with his mother. He makes a pig of her for the sake of his own ego need, and she plays along for her own ego's need.

If a man is a seeker at heart, he has to work very

hard to overcome his "inhibitions" with girls. A sensitive male is disturbed by the whole idea of sex (and rightly so). Still, he has needs in this area. That is, he has an uncorrected-female-based ego need, which he feels as a burning physical desire. Until it is corrected in a proper way, he is fascinated and distracted by his own desire. He can't work or think, but is totally preoccupied with the pictures that parade before the grandstand of his soul. His body is drawn hypnotically toward naughty girls, one of whom he usually weds, and their troubles begin.

The sperm of man is an unborn threat to the health and sanity of a woman who does not need or welcome as many children as he is capable of providing with his lust. She should protect herself against his weakness (or wickedness) with every conceivable contraceptive device. Ideally, however, contraception would not be necessary if the man and the woman were searching partners. The lesson of sex could be learned in the youthful years of their marriage, so that after they had had two or three children, their natural needs would have been resolved through the true love each has matured to know and extend toward the other. Failing this ideal relationship, in later years a woman might have to relieve the sexual needs that her presence might still produce in her husband, but she should not pretend to be a "friend" to it, because that attitude makes a man secure in his unprincipled beastliness and increases his appetite for the "serving," the love potion of security. Just as the father who is a buddy to his son does not realize how he is hurting him, so the lover is blind to the damage he inflicts on his beloved. We like others "just as they are" because we need to be liked "just as we are," and in so doing we impart to one another the "courage" of our weakness.

The principle of correction (love) is one, the same in all our relationships with one another. An overly-dependent, overly-affectionate child is one who has not been corrected (loved), but has known only the cruel extremes of rejection or encouragement. A child is naturally weaker and more needful than an adult. He must be embraced and reassured, but in such a way that the embrace will cool his need and leave his inner connections to his own indwelling strength intact. You must not excite him to need you, to look only to you for his fulfillment. If you do, his needs will grow to dominate your life. He will drain you dry. And when he has used you up he will find someone else to give him "love" and affection. If you do finally resist such a child, it is with hostility and rejection, and the child responds first with anger, then guilt. The guilt whets his appetite for affection (to hide behind) and makes him more persistent than ever. Or he can learn to thrive on the hatred your rejection inspires in him. Normally, it is "love," encouragement, that makes us feel right, but we can use hate to serve the same end when the love is not available. Again, you are wrong when you "love" and even more wrong when you reject.

A woman must divest herself of her ego needs, because it is her ego need that accepts and promotes bestiality in her partner. He always interprets that need for love as a need for his sexual services, and the guileful woman will keep him thinking in that direction. When he believes that women need his sex, he imagines himself to be God's gift to womankind, OK as is. Each moment of reassurance makes him worse as a man, and more of an ugly beast to serve the "beauty," but that beauty will one day reveal herself as the ugly old witch she really is for having lived on him in this guileful, tempting way. Eventually that "old witch" will be forced to reject him to feel like a queen again.

If a female will take the temptation, guile, and pretense out of her relationship with her husband, the chances are that she will seriously impair or paralyze her husband's sexual desire. He may demand that she return to the original unspoken marriage agreement (to play the game of boy and girl, remember), but if she stands firm in her newfound honesty, he will at least see what a pig he has been requiring her to be. The contrast she now provides for him shows him something about himself that he has never seen before.

A male's concept of manliness, or manhood, rests totally upon the sex act. The mother principality violates him in the beginning, and the changed male comes to need the female principle that he has become acquainted with, and fixed to, through his mother. The young faceless woman of his dreams, to whom he projects his ardor, remains the young mother that tempted him when he was a child.

During the age of puberty, a boy feels embarrassed, awkward, and clumsy, because of the urges created by his animal female need. He is an animal, of course, but a human male suffers from his animal nature in a way that is unknown and unknowable to the lower animals. A young boy's sexual desire is invariably attended by a subtle form of embarrassment and eventual slavery. When an adult male is ready to face and overcome his sexual hangups, he will reexperience this shame. The knowledge of it may return to him if he is left alone for a long enough time, or if he finds himself loved by one who is correct enough to reawaken him to his own conscience.

A seeking young male would prefer to date respectable young girls, but he is prevented from doing so by the invisible monster of sensuality stalking secretly in his mind. A respectable young woman increases his self-consciousness; in fact, she causes him to "stew in his own juice." To remedy his ego-animal need he must look further down the scale, to where adventure is not embarrassing, but highly possible. So he seeks "self-expression" with a physical equivalent, who, as far as women go, is less than the woman who would be truly good for him. She is good for him in the wrong way. In fact, she is usually very much like the "good one" his father before him found for himself. That is to say, she accommodates him and relieves the anxiety he feels about being an awkward, clumsy male, and she does this in exchange for those aforementioned considerations. As a result, instead of setting out on his way to becoming a man, a son of God, he now goes on to become a son of a witch, a slave to another miserable brood.

If you have been a temptress, and you would like to try an experiment on your husband to prove that he demands "old mother temptation" in you to justify what he likes to think of as normal, then just serve him sex without the trimmings. First, of course, you must recognize that evil presence in your own self and watch it flee from you (as it surely will, when you are willing to see it). Once you have removed the pretense and game playing from sex, you can allow him all he wants, but you will not pretend to enjoy it. You will do it lovingly, as a proper duty, but you will not pretend to "love" that duty. If you will pardon the expression, you won't go "hog wild," but will simply do your duty quietly because you understand the male physical need, not because you approve of it.

If you can do this experiment with honest-to-goodness *goodness*, you must be prepared for the shock of your life. Your husband, if he runs true to form, will back away as though he has seen a ghost—and perhaps he has—the Holy Ghost, in contrast to the spirit of deception that has been shining through you heretofore. He may be unable to function as a male, or even as a man. In you he will suddenly see the respectable woman that he had sought to avoid in the first place by marrying you, the temptress! His entire sense of identity and malehood will be threatened, because it has depended entirely upon that old arrangement with the spirit of error and temptation lurking in you.

Poor ladies—you thought you were loved for your-selves alone!

The temptation of the female presence excites a man's ego to feel proud (as it did in the garden), but that very reassurance to his pride gives rise to and supports his male identity. And that kind of male identity, in order to feel "right" and remain secure, demands its counterpart, or foil—a female identity complete with temptation at its core. The soul that requires the kindred spirit inhabits a body that needs a body. The male animal, housing a faulty pride-needful soul, must find constant reassurance for his body and soul in order to remain proud; and as long as he can find an Eve, he may never awaken to Reality.

When a woman begins to fulfill her husband's sexual requirements lovingly, but without passion, he either backs away in fear, horror, and shame, or he tries to tempt her, even *demand* her to return to her rotten old tormented, lying self again. In his eyes, she is not only taking away her support for his ego, but she is threatening him on a still deeper level. Not only is she removing his ego support and old comforts, but her understanding, acting as a lens for the true light, displaces the tantalizing thing that once lived in her and drew his "love." It throws a wet cold cloth on his lust and challenges the very existence of the "right, great, manly, lov-ing" person that he thought himself to be.

Next you may find your "hero" looking for other women to supply his need for the "right" kind of fe-male presence that once lived in you. In this case, all you have lost is a problem you should not have had in the first place. But if your virtue should awaken him to virtue, then you will have found a true soul mate. In the meantime, the virtue you will need most is patience. While he is still looking for the missing ingredient his ego demands, he may take up pornography and girl watching. Looking at revealing legs which have been adorned to be admired will provide the excitement his ego needs to turn him on sexually. The sexual arousal then justifies him spiritually, inasmuch as he looks on that kind of maleness as evidence that he exists correctly as a man. Most female entertainment is designed specifically to degradation of mind, body, and soul, and to the ultimate hangup with bizarre, tantalizing women who cater to men's needs in return for a secret devil-inspired ascendancy over them.

If, knowing the risks and pitfalls, you can nevertheless persevere in your guileless way with sex, your husband can go one of two ways—on to true manhood, or into convulsions as a result of his resentment. You see, he will be unable to find any real fault with you, for after all, you will be providing sex, which is what he claims to need as a man. What more is there that a woman can give? He will see the answer to that question only when you no longer have it to give him.

What he wants, more than your body, is for you to embrace the lie, the fiendish indwelling spirit that has made him into the bigger beast he has become through you. He needs that old devil to serve him up the lie that he is right and glorious just as he is. As long as you remain a beguiled and beguiling female, he will sacrifice his manliness on your altar, drop by drop, until it is no more. The natural will yield to the unnatural as he falls lower by the "love" that pretends to have his best interest at heart. The unnatural will express itself in many perversions and will demand that you sink still lower to accommodate, support, and assure it in its fall. You will have to continue your guileful assurance that he is all right just as he is, and as you welcome him, you actually encourage perversion and the need for perversion, and together you both take imperceptible steps down the ladder to death.

That which tempts a man to pride is the very thing he needs to caress the degenerating body created through pride. What emerges from pride (in the fall) is the earthy animal man, followed by the unearthly need for reassurance in that fallen condition. Both demand the guile-ridden body of the female for satisfaction.

If the shoe is on the other foot; that is, if you are the male of the house, and you happen also to be the first to discover the "awful" truth, you may have to go easy on sex for awhile. As long as your motive is right, you will manage to gain a measure of control over yourself, though it goes without saying that such discipline is more difficult for a man than for a woman. A man burns, while a woman has nothing to lose but her guile (unless, of course, she has learned to become masculine and burns like a male). A man may wish to give up his pride, and through searching he may even find compassion for his wife, and repent of the harm he has done to her for his ego's sake. Nevertheless, he may still burn for a long season. Once he has understood and overcome his need for temptation (imagery), he will be heading in the right direction, but his body will continue to experience desire and will remain sensitive to his wife's "signals." She, on the other hand, lacking the physical burning, merely gives up her pretense, her ego use of him, and her wrong motives. A woman suffers differently from a man. In her, the pain is largely guilt, while man's pain is an anxiety that is closely associated with, and related to, his burning.

Until a man is willing to be corrected, he cannot know the beautiful sexual harmony that can be achieved when, playing with his wife in a weak moment for the old response, he fails to get it. In his willingness to know love's correction, he sees the love behind his wife's denial. He is therefore corrected by it, and greatly relieved.

Should a man be the first to discover truth, his beguiled wife will soon notice the diminishing frequency of his visits and his increasing self-control (and she will be a rare woman if she does not regard the change with suspicion). Now, she will feel her own guilt emerging. You see, she could not solve her problem correctly while she was successfully tempting her man to be a beast and being rewarded, "loved," for the temptation. Now, as he becomes more considerate, he will begin to have much the same effect on his wife as an awakened woman has on her uncorrected husband. She will redouble her efforts to tempt him back into his beastly ways, for her ego security rests upon his beastliness, you remember, just as his security once rested upon her guile. If she is not "loved" in the old animal way, she will relive her shame, and eventually she will see what she has been doing to her husband in the name of love. In the meantime, however, feeling guilty, she will be suspicious of her mate's innocence, if only because that innocence makes her feel so uncomfortable. She may resort to mud slinging, sly innuendo, and other below-the-belt tactics to irritate him—such as suggesting that he must be going out with the boys, or getting a little sex during his lunch breaks. When the devious tactics fail, she comes right out and speaks her human feelings, accusing him of driving her into the arms of another man to satisfy her sexual need, which is actually not a need for sex as such, but a need for the beast to worship away her sense of guilt.

There are three distinct stages of living possible to man: (1) the normal, (2) the unnormal, and (3) the abnormal. The normal implies absolute perfection as a human being. The normal man would possess a bright nature and disposition, with little or no inclination toward sex, or for that matter food and drink. This is the level on which Adam lived until he bit into the apple. Until we find our way back to the normal, however, we exist largely in the unnormal state. An unnormal person has "natural" desires that must be eventually resolved, but if he persists in excusing and justifying his desires as "only natural," seeking to feel secure and right in his possession of them (and theirs of him!), then he cannot help but drop another notch. He becomes abnormal, tormented, and perverted, with a horrible need for horrible people to help him feel secure in his newfound and abominable vices. After that comes death, in torment.

Rather than wait for the inevitable fear, degenerative disease, impotency, frigidity, or frustration to put an end to your sex desires (or you), it is better that you give them up slowly, through understanding, and that you help your partner to do so, gently, correcting instead of corrupting. It is far better that you open the door to your better self, through meditation, and seek the spiritual assurance you need to raise you from the fallen ego state and *sense* of salvation to *real* salvation. It is better that you give up the illusion of life that rests on flesh and temptation to allow a place for a newer and better answer to your need than flesh and blood can ever supply. Even the male erection is a tension that should never have existed in the first place, and like any other addiction, when it is relieved in the wrong way, it grows in the wrong way to become more demanding and addictive than ever. When we begin to have true understanding, we seek relief of that tension through meditation, and as our natures (slowly) become modified by meditation, our desires decrease.

What happens when you eschew the better way of meditation, and persist in giving in to desire? Your overworked glands degenerate and cease to provide your ego with passion, so that you are finally left with the torment of unsatisfied desire. You will experience a growing need for sex alongside a diminishing capacity for it. Even though your sex organs may continue functional, you may become deathly afraid of the sex experience because of the terror and guilt it produces in you. Finally, you will become hung up on sex and go to the grave, usually with some vile degenerative disease directly or indirectly associated with those organs.

The author would like to make it quite clear that it is literally impossible for us to change our (in)human nature by any act of suppression or by any act of will. Changes in the anatomy of our fallen being will come about only as a result of our awareness of the Truth and our willingness to face Reality and accept the Father's will. "If any man be in Christ, he be a new creature . . . Be ye therefore transformed by the renewing of your minds from within."

This text is written only to awaken you to the better way to go, and to warn you that you have missed it and are headed for disaster. It is in no way to be regarded as a manual of instruction for salvation—especially inasmuch as salvation could never be achieved on an intellectual level by intellectual means. Only the process of meditation, entered into with the right intent, can lead the student to the rediscovery of these truths for himself and gently clear the way for the action of grace that can transform him.

Therefore, do not be impatient. Meditate (with the author's tapes) diligently, and remember that the conquest of sex desires is probably one of the final achievements on the way to righteousness. Sex desires are resolved very slowly, moment by moment only, through quiet illuminations that go beyond the power of words to reveal. Sexuality is the house built upon sensuality, and much of what we have become has been motivated and sustained by sex-oriented activities. What we have made of our mates now depends upon our existing for them as they exist for us—for love's sake, we must not give up our sex life too quickly lest the shock be too great for our partners to bear. What we must give up first is guile, and we can accomplish this only by first seeing how we have needed and used our mate's corruption, and then deeply regretting the fact that we have done so. As we become more conscious of the wrong we are doing, we become increasingly disabled from continuing to do it.

Before we deal directly with the problem of sex, we have many mama/sex-based problems to face. The last problem to appear lies closest to the surface and is the first to be resolved through meditation and right motive. This problem may be smoking—or rather, the pride, guile, dishonesty, or resentment that caused us to take up smoking. As we sharpen our awareness of what is turning us on through our willingness to face it, and as we repent of it, the surface symptoms begin to fall away. Soon we are able even to see the wrong motive behind all the "loving" things we do. When we eliminate the false love from sex, we begin to know sex with true love. Guile or innocence has a way of communicating through the action or contact it inspires. When guile is absent, then true love stands in its place. It is just that simple, and so is everything else that we can say, feel, think, or do to one another. We do well to go easy on words, especially preaching. We correct others best by being correct ourselves— patient, calm, considerate of their well-being. They will see the difference between the new "you" and the old one that used to lord it over them, and when they see that the change is "for real," they will usually be more than happy to meet you half way and listen to what you have to say.

13

Sexual Problems and Aberrations

It has been said that man is nature's only mistake. The truth is that because of a mistake, nature has gotten into man, and until he is corrected, his soul is subject to the temptation that "opened" him to nature, and his body is in chains to nature herself.

The soul brought into this world through temptation needs temptation. And to a male, temptation is woman. When the image of woman appears in his mind, in answer to his soul's mystical need for security, he burns with an unquenchable thirst. Nevertheless, he reaches out for something—anything—to quench it. And of course, it's a wrong answer, and a wrong answer to any problem produces a bigger problem that needs a (wrong) answer. And the wrong answer, of course, is always at hand to lull the mind into a false security. But only for a moment. The thirst returns.

Each "come-uppance" produces an anguish greater than the one before, which cries out anew for reassurance. The psychic need calls more fiercely upon the genetic memory for the helper. The more that man thinks, the more he burns.

Now, the very act of thinking is a reaching for a wrong answer, and it produces guilt. Seeking to escape guilt, he reaches for the wrong answer again, and the image grows more vivid. Finally, to clear his mind, he masturbates.

Somewhere along the line, our man makes a discovery: he feels guilty about masturbating because it's unmanly! So he rushes out and gets a woman to prove that he is as manly as any man. He has, of course, misinterpreted his guilt. He feels guilty only because he IS guilty: 1) guilty for what he is, apart from God, and 2) guilty for being a male, a fallen man, whose spirit is still reaching out and being consoled by his old "friend in need," the genius of Evil.

Error can never be corrected by denying it exists, but that is precisely what we do when we indulge ourselves in anything, from sex to drugs. We can see that we are using the indulgences as a false salvation because when we try to give them up, it is so much like giving up "salvation" that guilt emerges when we try to do it. Under the circumstances, we ought to face our tensions in a new way, with understanding.

A male feels guilty because, being wrong to begin with (though he doesn't know how he got that way), he becomes more guilty as the result of trying to feel right the way he finds himself to be. As he does, he falls lower, and as he falls lower, he feels anxiety, and as he feels anxiety, he tries (but never with any real success) to feel right the way he finds himself.*

*NOTE: This is the basis of racial prejudice.

The idea of woman is the original factor in man's fall from his rightful condition; and it is this idea that recurs to him in his moments of desperation. And as he reaches toward her in lieu of the Divine presence (conscience), he adds his own part to an original sin.

When a man masturbates, he relaxes his pent-up tensions without the tempting female body presence to comfort and assure him; so naturally he feels that something is wrong. Minus the woman, he does not gain the assurance his faulty nature requires. And while he discovers his guilt in self-abuse, he compounds that guilt in female abuse—an honest look at the situation shows it to be just that, but most females will allow themselves to be abused in exchange for certain advantages.

A woman who loves her husband truly, disarms him as well as herself. She forbears to tempt him, and when she withholds that temptation, her husband may experience an effect similar to masturbation. He will begin to feel a similar awkwardness and unmanliness during the sexual encounter.

Here she is, giving him sex with true love, and how does he feel? Terrible! And unless he is willing to consider some honest answers to the question of why he feels so terrible, he will go out of his mind with rage and fear. You see, that's how true love works—it corrects. It does not corrupt. It is innocence that communicates, and innocence (guilelessness, honesty) makes all the difference. So the loving woman does feed the brute, even goes to bed with him, but in a proper way, a way that dashes a cup of ice water on his pride. Slowly, over a period of time, the seeker in him is cooled off and brought to his senses, and when that happens, he feels truly relieved and grateful to his loving wife for only lying *with*—and not *to*—him.

Females rarely feel the need to masturbate, and when they do, it is usually because they have somehow become sexually exchanged. They have developed the process of imaging to a fine point in order to satisfy their egocentric need. For example, it is quite possible for a woman to imagine, during copulation with her husband, that her man is actually making love to another woman, while she identifies herself so closely with her husband that she becomes one with him—in effect, she becomes a male making love to a female. She may even take over his male identity so completely in her imaging that she sees him as that other woman, the female. Actually, this tendency on the part of a woman to take on a male identity can often be traced to some early experience that has impaired her ability to function as a woman. Later on, just the thought of her husband making love to another woman while he is actually making love to her causes her to slip into the preferred role: his. She becomes the husband, while the other form in the picture, her husband, becomes the female that arouses "her" sex interest as a man. Through such images as this, a woman can learn to burn like a male, so much so that quite often she will become so aggressive as to force her husband into the passive role.

Then there is the woman who was violated by her

brothers when she was a young girl. She resented her brothers, of course, and she began to wish secretly that she were a boy, reasoning that if she had actually been a boy, her brothers could never have done such a thing to her. Besides, her mother favored the boys, the apples of her eye. She longed to be a boy, if only to get even. (Most women's egos wish to dominate. They envy the place of men; and by challenge and temptation, they often manage to usurp that place for themselves.) So gradually the girl begins to behave more and more like a boy. She may even burn like a boy at the sight of other girls. She gets married as a way out of the dilemma, but the man she marries is weak because only a weak man could possibly welcome and appreciate her aggressiveness, and even need her to light a fire under him.

That kind of marriage, of course, guarantees the perpetuation of the changeover process. Instead of becoming more feminine as a result of getting married, she becomes more masculine. And the more her husband tries to assert, or excuse, his malehood, the more he loses out. Women always gain the power in such an arrangement as this and become dominant, whether or not it is obvious on the surface. While the woman might have hoped to become more feminine by taking on the help of a male, she actually becomes more masculine, and as a result, more guilty and frustrated than ever.

The day finally arrives when her husband loses his masculinity altogether, thanks to her over-aggressiveness, her determination to use him as the means of finding a female identity for herself. When his powers (such as they were), desert him, she is left with a greater burning than ever, and she relieves it through masturbation. Masturbation becomes her way of relieving the need that has intensified rather than diminished as she had hoped it would.

Now our female not only feels unwomanly—she feels unmanly, too. Because "being a man" holds so much promise for a man, many women feel that by helping a man to BE a man, they themselves will become more feminine. But the reverse is actually true. In the sexual relationship "males" have fallen from being men, and because they are descending rather than ascending, they eventually lose their manhood and become sexually exchanged. The man and the woman, responding to each other and living from each other, finally yield up their identities, each to the other. On the surface, it's "down" for him and "nowhere" for her, but in reality, both are falling. Falling in love, they both fall further from what love really is.

Assuming the lead over a man, a woman becomes masculine, if only by virtue of holding a place that is not rightfully her own. The male in her, excited by the man's sexual passivity, wakes and takes shape in her physically as she subconsciously appropriates his body along with his identity. How often we see the prototypes of these two in a restaurant—she, the sergeant-major wife, sitting there straight and tall and hawkeyed, while her shriveled little dried-up prune of a husband cringes over his bowl, slopping up his soup.

A woman who succeeds in ruling the roost and becoming masculine may make a last desperate attempt to conquer the guilt of the male role and become feminine again through her son. (Now she is like her mother, favoring sons because she hopes through their love to become queen and woman again.) May God help the daughter born to her—she will surely be rejected unless she is secretly masculine enough herself to earn her mother's respect in unspoken competition.

As for the sons, the favored ones, some of them (if not all of them) are in danger of becoming homosexuals, because the kind of men that worship mothers are not really men at all. Early in life, the sons of very overbearing women are programmed to be mother worshippers—long before they reach "malehood," they already have the characteristics of females. (And the mother, of course, becomes more masculine than ever in the exchange of identities.)

A young man can become so sexually exchanged as the result of responding to a dominating mother for fifteen or twenty years that he has more female than male characteristics and feels most at ease in the feminine role. When he is sexually aroused, it is not by a woman, but by a man. He has no erection, just a twinge of excitement. The era of Eros has passed by quickly for "him," just as it might have for his father (who probably flew the coop at some point to try to get his manhood back with other women, who would have aroused and got what's left of him anyway). For a moment the effeminate sees "her" ego advantage over mother, who in the eyes of the effeminate is playing the male role of serving "his" effeminate ego. In this topsy-turvy situation, it is what is most truly feminine that wins the dominant role, and the effeminate boy, being more female than his masculine mother, quite often snatches the scepter from her hand.

Now the effeminate homosexual, not wanting to see his own faults, may justify "his" existence as a female by relating to "super men," who are actually no more masculine than he—they also are in rebellion to a mother, but have chosen to arm themselves with a false, perhaps exaggerated, masculinity. The masculinity is an armor, or shell, that conceals a trembling fear of women, an overcompensation for their utter inability to relate normally to the opposite sex. These fearful males are excited by the weird concoction of effeminacy that offers them "something" of a woman, minus the fearsome form of woman. So the "female" homosexual justifies his/her existence by playing his/her part well and making "superman" feel like the man he likes to think he is.

Now they are like husband and wife. His masculinity becomes increasingly dependent upon the effeminate's playing the part of seductress. For a while this one will become more and more effeminate, and the physical relationship will become established and hardened. Then comes the switch. "She," guiltier than ever before, is now dependent on his being a loving beast to conceal that guilt, and "she" begins to demand so much of him that he gets to the point where he has no more to give. One way out of the stalemate is to switch roles. "She" (like her mother before her) may become the aggressive male-woman. Or, insisting on her feminine prerogatives, she may nag him and drive him off to another "love," another homosexual union. It may even happen that "superman" will try a real woman for a change of luck, and to stifle the guilt of the homosexual experience. But there again, he experiences the loss he feared in the first place. Guilt, fear, and anguish arise in him as the result of the way he uses the real female. So he may swing from men to women and back to men again. Remember the principle of extremes? If we are guilty at one end of the teeter-totter, we expect to reclaim our innocence by switching to the other end.

In the case of women, when a female perfects her changeover to the opposite sex, she can almost completely assume the functions of a male, complete with sexual excitement in the presence of another female. And when she is unable to find a satisfactory sex partner, she will dream of "love" and sometimes implement her dreams by caressing the sensitive parts of her body, sometimes but not always or necessarily achieving orgasm in this way. To a woman, the feeling, the sentiment, the ego need is paramount, and the physical need does not become an imperative until her erogenous zones have been stimulated or irritated beyond the point of no return. When a woman masturbates, she is usually impelled to do so by a psychic need for "love," rather than a physical pressure. Her fantasies will include a penis, an instrument of torture, the hand or mouth of another woman—almost anything—depending on her past experience and the kind of images she has conjured up to fill the void of her longing for perfect, all-consuming "love." (A nun would have no trouble keeping her vows if some of her sisters were not so seductive and sophisticated in carnal ways.)

Married men frequently take up the practice of masturbation when they begin to sense that they are responding slavishly to their wives. It becomes their own personal "Declaration of Independence." Although they allow themselves to be aroused by the temptation of woman, because they need the vitality, the evidence that they exist, they switch to masturbation at the crucial point to slip away from female domination and feel that they are free souls once more. The wife reacts to this with extreme frustration, and she will try all kinds of ways to "save" him for herself, thus giving him an increased sense of his own importance. In fact, she can become so aggressive and he can become so passive, and his ego can become so stimulated by her demands, that the ego satisfaction can take the place of his need to have erection at all. Frustrating her then, completes the satisfaction he needs.

Through such devious ways, men can become women through and through. You know those petrified trees that have lost their wood substance and turned to stone? A man can become so identified with woman that every atom of his being can be replaced by her presence, so that by degrees he becomes almost like her. Furthermore, he can be similarly transformed (and better he should!) by relating himself in the same way to God, so that by degrees he becomes translated into a representation of the Divine Nature of God.

Both man and beast must have support—something greater than themselves to impart to them an identity and character. An animal needs only his environment, but fallen man needs the devil in woman. In the beginning, man was supported and maintained by his identity with God, but he fell to a lower order when he fell in "love" to his wife, who, without Divine Love, is coached by Satan himself.

As I have pointed out, boys masturbate during puberty because their unrecognized ego need conjures up the ancient image of female to soothe the daily hurt to their weak and failing male pride. When no female is present to relieve the burning and to assure his ego, the boy has no recourse but to relieve himself. But when he does so, he does not receive the female assurance for his ego, and he therefore feels unmanly.

The solution, until he learns from bitter experience, is to get a woman, so that he can feel manly about his maleness. What happens then is that, while he is reassured of his maleness, he is actually becoming more of a beast, even effeminate, a slave, totally dependent upon the demands of that "friend" in need. So when he discovers that women make him less, not more, of a man, he may become impotent and revolt against the idea of allowing himself to be used in intercourse at all. So now the original "solution," marriage, becomes the big problem, even to the point of being a threat to him.

Yet our fallen man cannot exist without the woman or some substitute for her. He still needs her, even for his rebellion, the impotence or masturbation he is using to produce a renewed sense of independence in himself. The sense of right for his ego is always relative, dependent on something wrong elsewhere. Were it not for the evolving sequence of experience, his pride could not be maintained. To satisfy his need, the male ego enjoys "looking," and he allows himself to be entertained and aroused through his eyes. He enjoys the tempting gyrations of the girls as they walk by, and for a while he naturally enjoys their bodies as well. But as he senses the enslavement and the increasing anxiety associated with sex, he learns to achieve a new ego escape: conquest by masturbation. In other words, he is still using the temptation of woman, but not giving the devil her dues. To him that is "real" independence, and for a season he can find it very satisfying, but all the while he is drawing closer to and embracing more directly the spirit of Evil itself, and his guilt is growing. He gradually takes on a female identity, and he may lose all sexual desire as a man, becoming involved in bizarre mystical rituals and fiendish practices of a religious nature.

A boy feels his malehood to be a stigma—it is awkward and embarrassing to him. Masturbation relieves his burning desire, but leaves him with an inarticulate anxiety over what he is. The masturbation itself is not the real guilt producer he believes it to be—what really makes him guilty is reaching in his mind toward the images of the female as an answer to his problem. It is like a man looking to a drink as the answer. He burns for that drink, but the drink makes him worse in the guise of making him better—again he sees the drink as the answer to his problem of getting worse. He cannot give up the idea of drink though, because through it he escapes reality, and that is his real need and wish, which is answered by the form of the image that helped him before. It is a vicious cycle: the ego need produces the ego image answer every time he is wrong, and that image answer is always productive of guilt, and the answer to that guilt is the image—until he is going out of his mind with the physical desire that the persistent imaging awakens.

So it is with the young man. The female is the classic answer to his problem, so when he feels anxiety he gets ideas about women, and those ideas make him burn. Masturbating is like drinking alone. Both are more enjoyable with company, because sharing a wrong answer with another person somehow makes it seem more nearly right. Drinking can also become associated with manliness, but no matter how man relieves his passion, he is still left with the anxiety over his maleness, which he misassociates with the guilt of masturbation. The next step is to get with the right company, so the young man gets hooked. He discovers too late that the "girl of his dreams" is a nightmare of schemes. He finds he has fallen in love with a witch. For a while, she is his answer, his compulsion—he is nothing without her. He is like the man who falls apart without his drink for "moral support," even though he is constantly being made worse by it.

Then come rebellion, change of sex, and senility. The problems that can arise from a sex-based marriage are legion. When sensation is their god, men often become dissatisfied with normal positions in sex, and they demand that their wives or mistresses do tricks that degrade them. The degradation acts as a spice to restimulate their jaded appetites. They demand that the woman become more and more and more exciting. As a man sinks lower, he looks still lower to a still more exciting lower ground to stimulate him, as he becomes accustomed to the degradation that he finds at each succeeding level of his descent.

As a man sinks lower, he can derive vitality only from what is immediately beneath his own new "low," and if his wife is not obligingly lower, the fact that she isn't turns him off. So he forces her to degrade herself for the sake of his ego stimulation and elevation. He will leave a woman who is too "good" for him for a woman who looks good to him for the simple reason that next to her, he looks great and good and alive—and this is the woman who becomes mama to his children.

Children suck their thumbs to reenact past security. Sucking brings into play the comforts associated with the presence that violated the child in the beginning. It now makes him feel secure, as though he were back in the presence of truth. So a child will suck his thumb in an unconscious effort to blot out his problems. Later, his thumb or his security blanket will give way to "woman" as the great comforter.

Woman's magnetic field is so strong to a man that he often feels aroused by the extension of mama— feminine underclothes. In extreme cases, men will sometimes don their mother's clothes in order to fortify their identity and function as a man with their wives. The lingerie is reminiscent of a presence they identify with security, and with this talisman they can act like "men" with their wives. They are nothing without the mama presence, just as some men are nothing without money; but with it, they are alive again, virile he-men.

You see, don't you, that the problems posed by homosexuality, like those posed by sexuality, are rooted in an unrecognized quest for identity? There is an attempt to recover the lost role, or to obtain the needed essence (in the way a female emasculates a male), to support a faulty existence by establishing a relationship with another weak and corrupted person. Thus two homosexual men live as "man and wife," with the "man" justified by the other's femaleness.

In much the same way that a heterosexual is guilty for loving (using) his wife, the male homosexual becomes more guilty as a person. And, like the heterosexual female, "she" is more guilty with each round of intrigue, and will do anything to keep the poor fool around. That "anything" means being obliged to play the role of female to give the partner his security, while becoming more effeminate each time he provides the security.

The effeminate male, because of his relationship with his mother, has become basically a female. If his female nature is to be justified, it needs the "love" of a pervert "husband." With this need "she" will corrupt, encourage, and tempt a "man" to play the role which will provide security in the form of a sense of identity. In other words, "she" will cater to his existing weakness and weaken him more to bring about the traditional female slave relationship. The setup is identical (but in a more perverse way) to the real male and female war of the sexes, except that this perverted relationship devolves no further because of its sterile nature.

We see then, that the homosexual is a sexually exchanged male who may seek to maintain and justify "his" existence the way "he" is, or, if his ego cannot face the truth, engage in a perversion of the male-female game to support a false sense of security.

The variations in the development of such a relationship are legion. "She" can make so many demands on "him" as she becomes more guilty, that "he" will become disloyal and run around with other "women." Their personal guilts mount up to the sky, and are "remedied" by the making of ever greater demands, until there is nothing left for the partner to "give up." Then, as in "normal" unhappy homes, we have all the same arguments, jealousies, petty bickerings, and "divorce."

A woman is wrong in a way different from that of a man. She needs love to feel secure, whereas men need sex. A female needs love "lust" to help her forget that she created an animal for the sake of her ego need for lust, and her need puts the stamp of approval on his sexual lust.

Although it is not always apparent to the misty eyes of natural men, woman's nature happens to be the dominant influence in this present world system. As long as this is the case, the ultimate stage of devolution for the male victim is devilution. A male's proud unstable nature falls pejoratively from one level to another; some are almost completely transformed to the opposite sex. If the male devolves without becoming a female, he will often become a living demon, a "Tasmanian Devil" or a dictator, certainly much worse than the "wild man of Borneo."

Until he finds his true identity, he cannot resist the influence of women. He will conform or rebel. Conforming means becoming a woman. Rebelling means he must find the strength to resist from the error in the woman, and this process makes him a raving maniac.

All men fear the loss of their malehood, and, in a last desperate bid to maintain it, they lose out altogether and become demons or women. All efforts to find or maintain their malehood bog them down and involve them more.

The last stage of devolution for a man is that devil incarnate. The evil he once loved in the woman makes its home in him. It becomes his guiding spirit; whereas, in Truth, the guiding spirit of God might have communed with Eve through Adam.

So now we can see the wrong roads traveled by

both the heterosexual and the homosexual. All of our mistakes follow the classic mistake of searching our environment for our stolen identity. What we have really lost is the contact with our True Selves—nothing more. To restore that communication would be the real solution to all our problems.

Instead of establishing this contact with our True Selves, we mimic the person who steals a dollar from someone because an unknown person stole a dollar from him. He feels he is getting even, but loses a value as he seems to gain a value. Without realizing it, he assumes the identity of the thief who stole the money originally.

How much better it would be to face the loss of that dollar with dignity and to find the reason for the loss in order to prevent a recurrence. Instead of this, most of us turn around and do to others as was done to us. In this way, instead of improving our lot, we make matters worse.

We degrade ourselves in the process of pickpocketing people's brains and substance, associating with "nice" people from whom we hope to obtain that "nice," but elusive, self-image. So it is with females and some effeminates. They hope to become normal or to feel justified the way they are through associating with and receiving love from a man. In our attempts to gain or regain an identity by association, we try to become rich in virtue, but we become poor in stature. By stooping to such measures we are going the wrong way, becoming worse in our attempts to become better.

Remember that, once a male is perverted and has

become a woman, a cannibal, a Communist, a beast, or what have you, his ego will always seek to excuse that failing by clinging to what corrupted him.

The heterosexual union, which we all consider to be natural and normal, brings out all kinds of abominable traits, down to homosexuality. Women reach out to men; men lose out to women. Women become masculine and emasculate their sons who, in turn, grow up like women. Each person makes himself look good at the expense of others because he does not want to appear wrong as he is.

Again, remember the rule: as egotists, we cannot admit that the state we find ourselves in is wrong, so we forage for supports to prove that it is right. Because we feel humiliated by the dawning of Truth, our ego demands a sense of correctness. That need of the ego is a temptation that corrupts another to go along with us. That need, which can never be satisfied, is absolute proof that we are afraid to face ourselves. The war begins with what appears to be a normal and natural love a man and a woman have for each other. Everyone who reaches outside himself for love is escaping the knowledge of what he has become.

God cannot be wrong, neither can He fail. A real God does not need reassurance. Only what is not God but tries to be God needs the support of temptation to prove that he is God.

We are all beasts, devils, perverts. Someone has made monkeys of us, and we are descendants of original sin with displaced identities. We are all still seeking security for that displaced nature and are desperately embracing the same evil in others for the illusion of security. But a security gained by cheating is not a security at all. Neither is there honor among our thieving friends.

The cure for the failing status of heterosexual and homosexual relationships is to recognize the ego need for true identity. But vain egos will not and cannot reach up for illumination because of pride's need to be "right" the way it finds itself. Until that proud ego is awakened the painful way by reaching down to corrupt and be corrupted, there is no hope, until, through sheer agony (at any point along the way) it becomes willing to face the truth.

True identity is within us and, if we keep a firm grip on that Higher Self, it cannot be stolen. Only a God (conscience)-centered identity can produce the ingredients of contentment and the fullness of a restored being.

Restored to our inner identity, we will have no need to violate others for our existence, happiness, and "life" support. What we lose to our environment can never be retrieved from that environment. I repeat: we have merely lost contact with God within, and only atonement (at-one-ment) will restore the true identity to and in us. A God-centered presence will replace the woman presence in the male and make a man of him. Then this kind of man inherits the authority that alone can love hell out of a woman, and never again embrace the hell in her.

By this time, the reader must be familiar with some of the principles of evolution, such as the way animals take shape from their environmental influence. If this is true of animals, then surely man also has some type of influence acting upon him. Now, if it is proper for man to relate to females in the same way that animals do, then natural malehood should be maintained and perhaps even improved.

But look carefully at this present natural relationship between man and woman and see if this is the case. Look and see if the only love he knows (animal affection) improves his lot, or even maintains that status quo of his manhood. If you can be that objective, you will draw aside the veil of illusion to see the natural inheritance of woman for what it is—"reverse evolution." Men are born in sin, in bondage to the error in the female.

In the upward process of evolution the natural takes shape from the environment and is properly supported by that environment. In the devolution of man, instead of a man's remaining a man in the female presence, he becomes emasculated. When woman becomes dominant, the unstable male slowly takes on female characteristics. Then the unstable female, having been affected by this female environment (god) becomes masculine.

Until the time of actual change, the error in us causes us to develop an unhealthy craving for each other which we should call need. But we call it love, and this "love" nourishes the error in us and extends it to others.

The children who come from this kind of union have no enlightened father to obey, so they respond to their mothers. Children naturally respond to the most dominant force or spirit to which they are exposed. They then take upon themselves the mother's spirit of authority.

Except where scientists meddle, animals do not exchange roles as a result of loving. It is natural for a male animal to come out of a female and to re-experience maleness with a female. A bull surrounded by a herd of cows does not lose his identity as a bull. When he responds to the female demands, the evolutionary order does nothing but make him a jolly popular bull—and that's "no bull."

Now look about you and observe the sexually exchanged couples everywhere. Do you see that the love of a woman pulls a man down even as it props him up?

The female animal precedes the male animal and the maleness of that creature is appropriately maintained by the female without reversing nature's order. Courage in an animal is maintained by the fear of other creatures. When people fall to the animal level, the positive effect called courage is supported by frightening a victim, and it is like the maleness that arises from femaleness or anything of the like. The principle is the same. When the human male identity falls from God to being supported by the fear and hate of female principles, the entire process of existence has been set in reverse gear.

If man had come out of nature, there could not be any possibility of a problem between the sexes. If a man were of nature originally, he could properly feel like a man in doing his duty answering to woman's call. But when we see men becoming "women" and beasts, we know that something is wrong. We see that the call of the wild drives men wild. Obviously, the inherent power of the female is a faulty one, a detriment rather than an asset to man.

The stimulation a woman provides is supposed to bring out manhood, but it draws out a host of unmentionable traits instead. Only when we have blinked the illusion out of our eyes do we see this startling diorama. There, upon the chessboard of life, we see man and woman. The spirit of good and man is on one side; woman, with the spirit of evil, is on the other. Man moves only as his pride is tempted by the spirit lurking in woman. Alas, it is the spirit of the four horsemen of the apocalypse—of war, of pestilence, of famine, of disease.

For the sake of clarity, let us replay the drama of the classic human failing, so as to see more perfectly the subtle details of error.

A female finally emasculates her husband and assumes the dominant role. The masculine wife begets a daughter who, because she is of the same sex as mother, is rejected. This kind of mother demands boys as fodder for her ego; unconsciously the daughter responds to this demand. She then grows up feeling unfeminine and, to offset this deficiency, affectionately turns to her father to recover a sense of femininity. To achieve this end, she puts daddy on a pedestal and idolizes him to make him feel like a man. For this service, he gives her his approval. Unfortunately, the girl does not become more feminine through the father's approval. Unknown to her, the male syndrome in her is enlarged. Under cover of the smoke screen of emotional security, which gives her a sense of improvement, she unconsciously appropriates what is left of her father's malehood.

Appreciating daughter's weakness because it is feeding his own, the father becomes "nicer," but less of a man. Because of his "love" (approval), she secretly suffers frustration and even has secret resentment toward him. Still uncertain of her identity, she grows up with a craving for the kind of man (like her dad) who will provide assurance of her femaleness. Through her growing need, she is attracted to men like her father, who obtain the illusion that they are more manly because she supports them as they are. Of course, they are less manly and, in time, she becomes more inadequate and more masculine because they support her as she is. The male in her burns and makes her appear to be a hot mama to uncertain, feminine men who are slowly losing their aggressiveness by the same means by which she is losing her femininity. These men are excited by her coaching, which maintains in them an elusive sense of maleness.

The woman, being a male inside, is actually attracted to the type of male who is a female displaced. As the relationship continues without correction, they exchange roles. The principle again is that *we exchange places with what supports us.* Reader, do not lose sight of this startling statement, as the author intends to elaborate on it later.

During the season that the man-woman and the woman-man have sex with each other, a male child is born. For a moment, the masculine mama breathes a sigh of relief. Having been promoted to the rank of mother, she feels her female identity is assured. She has a male child whom she can also use to refurbish and refresh her sense of identity and authority.

No wonder mother swells up with pride! Now bearing a child is no great accomplishment, but it is a source of pride (support). Mama "el supremo" is strengthened and encouraged with renewed hope and confidence, which give the appearance of love. She now proceeds to emasculate her son for the continued sense of being a right person. Her demands weaken him; he becomes subjective, therefore feminine. She feels so good feeling proud that she does not see what is wrong with feeling good.

Proud mother's hungry presence tempts and usurps the boy's authority from infancy, because she must eliminate the threat of possibly having a real man around—a real man who could never serve her with helpings of ego "security." Such a man would shake her to her very egocentric foundation with the Light of His Reality. With sufficient desperation and hard work she corrupts him; then she dotes on him, while pretending to love. In this way, she succeeds in stripping him of his masculinity, and the woman in him begins to take shape.

Growing up uncertain of his malehood, the boy is attracted to "friends" who are compensating in the extreme. They are beastly rebels against the same type of female tyrant. So begins a tempting boy-to-boy relationship that may appear to be as "innocent as apples." But the apples have worms in them, as it was in the beginning. There was man and woman, then boy and girl, and the girl became boy and the boy became girl. Heterosexuals really are daughters to their patriarch wives. This is the reverse of what it was in the beginning when God created man in his image.

The young boy, seeking security for his corrupted identity, is attracted to another who appears to be considerate and fatherly. Unknown to him, this friend too, has a weakness that he is seeking to remedy by using someone. The admiring young "boy" appears to be the son who reassures him of his male identity.

Unfortunately, that son is no son . . . they have come around full circle to duplicate, in a perverted way, the typical set-up between a male ego and a female ego.

So, the respect he receives from the younger "boy" excites the father type into sexual desire for his "son," while the sex drive becomes a temptation that excites the larceny of the female which lurks in the young boy, and promptly brings it out as femaleness.

The older male does not know how to relate properly to the opposite sex, he always loses out and becomes more insecure as the result of each encounter with girls. On the other hand, the young boy is so exchanged that girls can no longer be used to make his ego feel secure. The girlish nature in him forces him to look to boys for that emotional security. He may not realize what is happening during the early stages of the "innocent" boy-to-boy friendship.

A boy who looks up to another boy as if he were a man makes the other feel first fatherly, then masculine. Then he becomes sexually excited in favor of what brought this feeling about. The young man becomes, in his eyes, a girl substitute, which he was all along. The female in the young man is playing the game with the male in the fatherly type. The love-lust this "masculine" sexual being feels toward that boy is the same demand that excites all women to become female temptresses.

The corruption seeded by the mother, aided by the weak father, is completed at this point. Mother is the original "god" of these two extremist pathetic "male and female" creatures of hell on earth. What began as friendship for this pair turns into a homosexual union.

Once the seed of a man's new identity has been transplanted, the male nature is assembled through "emotional security," but that male nature has a female source and a devil inside that core. As each identity reaches the threshold of completion, it is shocked to "life" by a new love. Lo and behold, there is that sudden fascination for the same sex, as if it were the opposite sex.

So we see more evidence that temptation has the power to change. As man became male in the garden, so he becomes woman on this earth. The sexual experience then goes on to become a transexual one to harden us to, and justify, what we have become. We cling to it for more relief and security until the time of our next change. The nonsexual experience provided to satisfy our need for approval changes us physically to burn sexually for what tempted us . . . and our course is plotted for us—be it from Heaven to earth or earth to hell.

I repeat, people are not tempted into a sexual or a homosexual union by sex alone, but more through an ego need for emotional security. Homosexuality is a third fall for man. It follows his fall from man to male and from male to female. The transsexual transformation appears at the completion of "construction," where he needs the shock of a tempting new mate to give life to what he has secretly become. God created Adam and, if his soul had been obedient, he would have been stimulated, stabilized, and electrified to the changless image of God with life eternal. Instead, in secret he came to "life" by the shock of temptation. The shock of temptation first "kills" us, then temptation revives us to a new and zombie-like existence.

Do you realize that just being a friend can destroy and corrupt? We are always being violated by all of our "considerate" friends, even as *we* are also corrupting *them*. Each "loving" experience edges us closer to the blossoming of a more decadent state of being, specifically, for the sake of this discussion, from sexuality to the perverted state of homosexuality.

The love we need in order to forget how rotten we have become makes us more rotten. When we are loved by others for what we are (so we will love them), that association brings the corruption that was developing in the dark of the soul. The dead

Frankenstein creation receives the electric shock that brings it to life, and we see what we could never otherwise have believed about ourselves. Now we can see the assembly line evolutionary pressures and the process of creation by watching it all take place in reverse inside ourselves. It is quite an education, to say the least.

Most people are too weak to relate to others without using "friends" as a source of ego self-acceptance. Not infrequently, when this happens, out pops a sexual desire for, first one of the opposite sex, and then later for a "friend" of the same sex. Men burn for women, not only because they are females, but for the familiar guile that made them what they are. People can be sexually aroused by anything that excites them, especially a warm furry animal. The homosexual theme is reiterated as an education to heterosexuals to make their own sexual dilemma more clear to them.

Temptation is a non-sexual "friendly" experience that our ego needs, and it alters our nature to need sex and to love lust for what altered it. *Man's sexual desire for the woman form is there because the woman was first used to tempt him into the animal realm.* From the beginning to this very day, through the security of woman's "love," all men sink lower. A man's sexual desire is not natural, as we are led to believe. The evidence is destroyed because sexual burning for the opposite sex appears as natural as the "birds and bees," but it is natural only for animals and what has evolved out of nature. It is unnatural for what has fallen *to* nature by default of

God's command.

An anxiety-ridden young lady tells me that, whenever she remembers her "kindly" father, she has a flashback in which she reexperiences the sense of her father's presence. At the same time she experiences a certain sexual thrill or twinge, although she cannot remember that her father was ever anything but kindly. He was a far cry from what we think of as a tempter and a "dirty old man"—what we would have expected to produce this effect in her. She is quite sure her father never made any passes at her; nevertheless, the whispering presence of what identifies with her father always produces erotic feelings.

In probing more deeply, she unearthed the classic mother rejection of a daughter because of her need for a son. A vain woman is usually possessive and guards her male "meal" against the wily needs of other women. Daughter was a threat.

One answer to this female dilemma is to add more men to her sty, in which case she becomes a tramp or a nymphomaniac. Another answer lies in using male children as husband substitutes, to glorify her ego mind.

So the mother rejected the girl for being a girl and, by subtle innuendo, demanded that she be a male. This type of mother violates the child with resentment and withholds approval until the female child gets the message to work hard for the "love" she now needs from the violator. The girl can rebel, but, if she conforms to get approval, she begins to feel masculine.

In her case, the girl's masculinity disturbed her, and she turned to her father in the hope of retrieving her femininity. The unconscious wish was that his maleness might give her back her female identity and erase the guilt which followed her violation by mother's resentful rejection of her. Her weak father in this case, and all cases, was delighted to accommodate her (for the wrong reason).

Remember that Dad had lost his malehood to his wife, so his daughter's need pleased him. It put the stamp of approval on his failing nature. He was a man again (in his eyes). Now his daughter, in idolizing him and supporting the fault in him, was actually being used to tempt him. He, by accepting the support of his daughter, was also corrupting her.

This temptation had the effect of making her feel like the female that she (in reality) was not. Her father's assurance made her more wrong inside, more needful of him—and more of a temptress. As a temptress, she was on her way to becoming more of a man inside, burning as a male burns for a female. The female was her father and then all her husbands.

The mother in this case would not, or could not, play the female for daddy because she had assumed the male role. So, emasculated daddy, thriving on his daughter's need, encouraged her weakness by his "love." And, there again, we have the age-old setup. A man's love of temptation (error in woman) unconsciously encourages the error for its support factor—a prerequisite to being "loved."

Even though there was not (in this case) a sexual

advance made by the father at that time or since, she will be forced to seek a sexual experience with a "man" like her father as ego support for belief in the idea that she is a woman. Her burning male aggressiveness will clash with egos of aggressive males who find satisfaction in seducing those girls playing "hard-to-get."

This young lady's experiences will mostly be with the same type male as her weak father. So she ends up either just like her mother, or she keeps on becoming more masculine until she becomes a lesbian. With her last love affair with a "male" per se, she will stand at the threshold of a need for a stronger support. The opposite sex will cease to be a man. It will be a woman to reassure the full-grown male in her.

So, here again, we see how daddy's "love" (growing need) for temptation ruins yet another woman, this time his own little girl. True to the classic tradition of weak men, his need, posing as love, tempted his daughter. While he did so, he could not see, from the vantage point of his own security, what he was doing wrong. Neither could daughter.

In fact, no one enjoying the security of his various luxuries, vices, evils, and the like, can see what blinds him to Reality. The prelude to change, aberration, abnormality, and sexual need is violation of evil love. Sex tempts only to the degree that it reassures, and that confirmation always comes by way of what made us wrong to begin with. It leads us through another process of change to a transsexual experience by another evolved "love"—form of support.

Is it all clear enough now? Do you see how the goading, irritating, or approving "love" of the tempting presence of mother can change the level of a child's consciousness? This can be done in simple or complex ways and set the pattern of miserable sexuality and transsexuality. Do you also see that this could not happen were it not for the failing of a husband?

Tempted man becomes male animal, then changes places with the female, and then with the devil himself, as you will see.

The effect that "love" and motivation have on a man is always pejorative, which is to say that they make him worse, not better. A man cannot accept the support of a woman and expect to remain the same. In fact, he cannot depend on anyone or anything if he is to remain a man. Until he finds support within himself, all the support that the male receives from the outside only weakens him and leads inexorably to homosexuality or bestiality.

The corruption that took place near the time of birth could not have occurred were it not for the weakness in the individual soul (pride) that allowed it to enter. From that time on, this corrupted pride seeks to escape the knowledge of its failing and causes it to seek "love" and security to support it as it is—corrupt. This search leads it into the embrace of various forms of temptation that finish off the job which all parents began.

The loves of this world, then, are subtle forms of temptation that tease you through your need to need and to be teased, and embrace you when you use them, convincing you that you are doing the right, the natural thing. Scripture tells us that love of the world puts us at enmity with God. The cunning beguiler disagrees and asks, "Can loving be so bad? After all, don't we all need love?" To the unenlightened or the egocentric, this is the irresistible argument.

I hope that, by now, you can see what is wrong with the type of "love" the ego needs. Can you see what is in us all that needs emotional security so desperately that we are blinded to the dangers that lie inherently with that security?

If I tempt you to become a thief and then love you to make you feel secure as a thief, you will become more of a thief by that "loving." This example frames the underlying principle behind all of our wars, sickness, disease and all other human suffering. "To love those who love you," says Jesus, "what profit a man? Do not thieves and robbers love their own?"

As long as we have an egocentric nature, the original weakness of the soul, we shall also have a growing need, an insatiable appetite, for false devotion by what has been made false for this purpose. All the time that our ego gratifies itself on people's approval, it is growing more sickly and more desperate for that "love" that soothes but makes the soul sick for more love. It is, at the same time, shutting the door on God's love—the real assurance and fulfillment.

There comes a time when "thieves' love" is no longer sufficient to make us feel secure against our conscience. When we have gone as far as we can, developed by these wrong supports, the stage is set for another change—one similar in nature to original sin.

If a person is not growing from God's motivation, he is devolving without a real pattern of unfoldment; therefore, he needs to *feel* a sense of growth and achievement. "Emotional fulfillment" is provided at different levels by "thief lovers" who understand our needs and cater to them to make our enslavement to the devil, their father, complete.

Homosexuality is an outcrop of an experience with one of those friends of our ego needs. There comes a time in the life of a certain male when the love of his mother (who corrupted him) will no longer support his ego satisfactorily because he has become so much like his mother that he needs a man to provide his ego security. When he finds that manly-appearing boyfriend, the female in him hatches out of the egghead. In the twinkling of an eye, the female emerges out into the open.

It is not unusual to see a male change sexes right before his startled wife's eyes, the male in her being the catalyst and accomplice to this change.

A woman can be so much like a man that she is aggressive and burns for a man who is passive and dependent upon her aggression to light a fire under any virility he has left. In one moment, having given his all as a male to obtain ego support, he is tempted over the line by the male nature in the woman, some of which she has appropriated from him. He becomes effeminate.

The male personality acquires female roots and is a displacement of the real self. Now, when he comes back to a female as an animal, to assert his maleness, he loses that malehood also. This is the second stage trauma, which I mentioned earlier. It is similar to what happened in the Garden of Eden, where Eve, considerate of Adam's needs, appeared to love him, and gave him the forbidden fruit. Today's Eve gives her Adam sex, with similar "consideration" in mind. This time, though, the assurance changes him from a male to a female, as it changed Adam from a man to an animal.

The fallen male may not become an overt homosexual. He may be content to live as a soft man, served by his sergeant-major wife. However, we are all sexually exchanged and are latent homosexuals and devils.

We are far better off before temptation, which justifies our greed and comforts us in our fallen state. Temptation changes places with us; those who tempt each other assume each other's identity. We serve and support those who tempt us, and they do the same for us.

A woman who lets her husband be the boss is still the boss. She becomes the man, and he becomes the woman. Quite often a woman discovers she is a slave playing the masculine role. A woman who prides herself in making a man out of her husband is doing nothing more than making him into a female. She will do the same to her sons.

The closest thing to hell on earth is a guileful female. Too late a "man" may discover that his wife, not he, is the boss, the power and the glory. Then, when he tries to assume his proper role, all hell breaks loose. Unmasked, his wife is seen as the spiteful demon she was all along. She is the boss or there is no marriage! If this arrangement is not changed, then God help that man and his ill-fated sons.

Quite often, the woman in this position will divorce her husband for another sucker and take the kids with her—to keep her pride fed.

The courts of law do not realize how often they are being used to serve the power of evil in the land. Occasionally, we observe a male becoming a man for the first time in his life. He stands before the judge.

"Your Honor, I've been a mouse all my life. I've given in to her. I thought I knew what love was; I thought I was a man when, all the time, I was a frustrated weakling using my wife. Now I want to be a real father to my children and a real man, a real husband to my wife, I am accused of cruelty and incompatibility. If I can't discipline her, who will? She is permissive with my children and spoils them. When I put my foot down, she brings me to court to get the law to make me tow the line. If you do this to me and others, you will have a nation of women who are men and men who are women."

But the judge doesn't care about love, justice, and mercy, and the understanding and wisdom which supersede the law. The law is the law and, because it has no discretion in it, can be used and abused until it, too, is a tool of evil and oppression. The judge is interested only in money and possessions, and divides up the property "fairly." Mama gets the children, Father is kicked out, and matriarchy wins out—with or without him around the house.

All transition to lower states of being takes place as the result of the cunning of temptation. Temptation "love" has the power to change us by degrees. Eve, under the devil's expertise and guidance, understood Adam's ego need. She offered him the forbidden fruit, and that experience changed him into the animal he is today.

The undue "respect" today's female shows for this fallen sexual animal is responsible for the sexual exchange. At every level of descent, the strongest urge for that particular changed living form is procreation. So, when we find a mate, we find a subtle agreement . . . and there we go again. . . from Heaven to earth, and from earth to hell itself!

When anyone agrees with what we are at a low level by having sex with us, it communicates to us that all is well and, imperceptibly, we sink even lower. Then the sexual experience hardens the course of our mutual inheritance. The progeny of such a union become the next confused and perverted generation.

Some boys are so thoroughly violated that most of the preparatory stages leading to transformation take place between him and his mannish demanding mother. Some become effeminate before they experience girls, while most boys remain latent homosexuals. They have not reached the point of change, but are prepared for a certain kind of encounter which could bring it about. The experience that will change his identity from male to female will be similar to the nonsexual experience of original sin. The male experiences a sexual desire for what changed him by its "temptuous" love support—this time it is a boyfriend.

The reader should recall that I mentioned how young boys can be sexually aroused by nonsexual objects, the stimulation of the desire to steal cookies being cited as one example. Any exciting experience which pulls us away from our center of dignity produces desire associated with the object of temptation.

Some people must experience the sex act, in the position, or with the thing or person associated with the first arousal. A boy might have to steal before he can cohabit, or dress in his mother's clothes. At any rate he usually marries the girl most like his mother.

We might need a full moon for that romantic effect. It may be plain to see that if a woman is wooed by the light of that full moon, or seduced with the gift of a diamond bracelet, she is being tempted to become an animal. So that temptation, and not the man's body, becomes the cause of her sexual desire because it was the temptation which caused the male desire for her body. So you see that it is possible to make love to anything. We may find we have a sexual feeling for whatever we use for ego support.

A male can be aroused to sexual feeling by temptation associated with any form or object. It does not have to be a woman; pardon me, but if the doughnut were the original sin or source of enticement, then it could be the doughnut that makes him burn sexually. As a result of the fall to the tempting doughnut, he may suddenly be possessed by a passionate sexual desire. Then every time he would see a doughnut he would burn with sexual fire. He would bring the world to that doughnut, if only it would keep on being a doughnut for him alone.

Whatever it is that represents temptation excites us further away from the truth in our conscience and results in erotic desires. If you can add one plus one, you can see why young women are so irresistible to men and not the other way around. Young women are the embodiment of temptation.

The moon becomes a sexual symbol for a woman because it is not as bright as the sun, and by its dark "light" the male needs seem more attractive. They are not seen in a clear light.

A woman is often placed in a romantic mood by moonlight and soft music. Here a symphony of "love" is played to her pride. Tributes in the form of gifts and flowers are laid at her feet. Such "love"—all the things her ego cherishes—is the excitement that produces whatever lukewarm sexual desire she has. Temptation transmitted through male sexual desire has its day again by being responsible for her change, or, at least, by bringing it out again—this time with the help of a tempted, corrupted male. (Little wonder why older women "love" tending their flowers when their men are no more. They are left alone with a lust for the symbols of their sexual fall.)

Considering yourself to be natural, you'd feel it unnatural to make love to the moon, so you make love to the nearest logical thing. This is usually the person associated with the process of change.

When woman tempts man to steal or conquer the world, it is that temptation which creates the desire for her. It also produces a dependence on her goading and nagging, while she also provides a natural outlet for what he becomes in the process. Remember then, that a male is not sexually excited by the female herself, but by the assurance she affords through the temptation she also represents.

We are all latent or dormant homosexuals. There is a little of the opposite sex in all of us. If we continue, unmodified, in our affections and responses to each other, that opposite sex is bound to emerge, in varying degrees, in us and in our offspring.

Temptation now in the form of "love" and emotional security, then, is the catalyst in the transition of man from a higher state of being to a lower. The spirit of evil could not have power over a real man because a real man would be true to his conscience. To be of service to the devil, a male must be subject to a woman (and not realize it) or he must become a "woman" with that power over her "husband."

When we have become weary of all that human "love" can offer us, we can know that there is another kind of love. The love God has for us is not the same kind as that offered us by the tempter or temptress. God's love, through our repentance, changes us for the better, while the "love" of people corrupts as it changes. The fleshly affection, devotion, and admiration for what we are is sustaining to all ego-related faults. What feeds our ego keeps developing us in the wrong way, apart from God's restoring grace.

Human love is the great corrupter. Temptation makes emotional reassurance, or false love we need, irresistible to us. In his love affairs with women, a male becomes more of a beast with an even greater hunger or, losing his masculinity entirely, he becomes unable to relate as a male to his wife or mistress. The descent and suffering of a man will continue until his direction is reversed by his seeking the security of God's grace within.

14

The
Tangled Web

Finding yourself lost in your thoughts is positive proof that you have failed to cope with a pressure, a personality, or a condition. A trauma has occurred with dangerous future repercussions. Unless you can awaken from your trance-like state of fantasy, worry, and prepared speeches, more tragedy lies ahead. It is only a matter of time before you will experience mental, emotional, and physical suffering, accompanied by fits of depression, hopelessness, and despair.

Happily, there is hope. Read on and learn about your principal weaknesses, and awaken from the nightmare of false forgetfulness before any more harm is done.

Dwelling in a thought world can cause any dream to become a reality. Brood too long over anything at all and a hellish reality will hatch out.

Any time you cannot cope with the pressure of a dominant personality you are drawn into a dream state, and because your ego is afraid to fully awaken to the realization of the condition you are in, you are obliged to remain in your dream world, fascinated by worry and by the memory of the person who made you fail.

It all begins with your ego's employing dream mechanisms to reach certain goals. Unfortunately, the very process of dreaming denies the unfolding plan of God. To the degree that you lose sight of Reality through your ambitions, you become sensitive to pressure and you are led by deceit.

Now the trauma of the fall introduces to you the imprint of the dominating lord personality, and your ego deals with the rude awakening to the harsh reality of its actual inferiority by escaping into thinking. In your thinking world you can play with those indwelling images and make them do your bidding. Only in the dream state can you see yourself as lord and master, because in Reality you are not. And now, because you cannot have the real security of being the Lord in fact, your humiliated ego descends to the false-security world of dreaming.

Setting a person on a pedestal is the classic means of mind control, subjugation, and degradation. But the one being worshipped cannot know this beforehand, only after the fact, which is the principal reason why the victim's ego falls prey to the dream state. Down there amid his fantasies he can forget to be aware of his failing and shame.

You see, there are actually two realities, one of them seen in the light of the other. The ugly world reality emerges through denying the light of reason, playing God and letting others put you on.

To let someone set you up as a god makes them the god-maker, better than you, the elected god. This subtle trick causes your foolish pride to feel good about itself, and the guilt of this makes the dream world attractive. You escape into the dream world to solve the problem of failing by reducing the awareness of your failing. Your mind now becomes converted to something not intended by its Creator. Your mind becomes a private universe with you the fallen-ego god in its center, a world where you try to make your own thing happen.

Notice the difference between the two roles. You are either the one who does the setting on the pedestal (for the purpose of manipulating) or you are the victim who, for a fleeting moment, thinks he is lord. The resultant fantasy of being worshipped is the lord's or loser's syndrome; this sad state results from being put on the wobbly throne.

In real life we all live out one of two roles, or both. We manipulate and we are manipulated. When we fail to project, the shock of realizing our disadvantage frightens us and flips us into a fantasy world.

You become a victim through being foolish enough to allow yourself to be placed on a pedestal. The excitement of being accepted or recognized draws the "king" into a dreamlike trance, and as that dreamer you usually like it so much you may not wish to awaken to the aftermath of a painful conscience. You rarely see or wish to see what is happening to you regardless of the price you must continue to pay. A typical romance has these elements.

In order to obtain a high, the "king" must come down from true Reality to a mental world to accept his homage. This is where the "king" loses his protective, intuitive, awake awareness. Later, the wretched "king" is too ashamed to come back to Reality and preserves the ego state by losing himself in his thoughts.

By now you must realize that there is a disadvantage in any advantage the world holds out to you. The result of any put-on is a come-down, no matter what it is. Anything from a religious high to a drug high involves you and you fall.

Manipulators end up with every advantage they hold out. Evidence of their power is the rage and inferiority that wells up inside. This is one reason why the ego-sexual adventure often causes a male to feel resentful.

Not understanding the mystery of his come-down, and being equally unwilling to face Reality (still desiring to be God himself), the male ego is left with no alternative but to take a nosedive into his (emotionally aroused) sexual fantasies. Humiliated in a brawl, a male develops the type of fantasy in which he sees the other person as the victim. Only in his dreams can he be the conqueror. But bear in mind one thing about this: it is the energy of resentment that draws him into his dreams and the same energy keeps him there. The abuse of sex also results in trauma.

Lacking the special manly grace to which sensible women would gladly submit, the male always loses out through his use of the female body. Only in the dream state can he force the image (the one that got inside through his failing) to serve him, because in real life this is becoming impossible. Fantasy is the loser's way of being in control, while being had is the catalyst for this sad state of mind. The law governing human nature is immutable: whatever you use (to get high) uses you.

The seeds of violence and rape are planted through mother's undue influence, and later by a female who offers relief (by her pretentious submission) from the painful inferiority caused by mother domination. Alas, surrender turns out to be the same means of conquest that mother used against father.

And so it comes to pass that all humiliated men dream of being worshipped and doing the humiliating, going so far as to degrade the worshipper in the act of worship. The best they can do is dream.

Because sex drive and lust are (and always have been) the evidence of man's fall from grace, man's ego tends to overreact (to cover embarrassment) by degrading the woman with sex and teaching her to excite him and worship the sexual outcrop of his soul's failing. You realize what that does: it makes his mortal animal condition worse, and that in turn leads to blame. He sees the woman as the cause of his wretchedness, and in a sense it is true. But by viewing her as the cause and blaming her, he fails to see how she came to be that cause—through his wrong use. Blame, which is based on resentment, is an escape from his own responsibility.

The more he falls to any sort of temptation, the more the failing man dreams of sex, and more often than not is drawn dreaming into an actual experience resulting in more and more humiliation, resentment, frustration, and rage. Each new trauma reinforces the sensual, mortal way—and blame.

Trauma causes a downward change from one way of life to another and from one kind of person to another more lowly and beastly. And it is the observation of the changed identity which causes guilt in the observer. It is the presence of Reality that provides the contrast. Unwilling to bear the guilt, you nosedive right into your blaming dream.

Soon new fantasies begin to evolve. For a male, the first dream scene is usually one of sexual worship and then sexual degradation. Later on, because of resentment, scenes become violent. The male is compelled to satisfy his need for sexual worship as well as his judgment toward the deceitful female worshipper. He is first excited by the sexual put-on and later he is upset by the switch. Sex produces one type of mental fantasy, and upset another. But let us devolve this process one more step and see how resentment welling up inside a man can trigger evil sexual desires.

A punishment scene adds fantasy to a fantasy. Violent thoughts arise from sexual frustration and rage, which now evolves to dissolve the painful realization of being conquered by the sexual experience.

He who starts out being a king ends up a queen, with the identity of his tormentor inside him. Here the male victim often becomes sexually impotent. He becomes afraid of losing his manhood in a real experience with a real female. He fears and hates the very thing he needs to sustain him in his ailing, failing pride. He is terrified of a submissive woman, simply because her willingness to surrender always ends mysteriously in his defeat.

He discovers now that revenge and resentment are just as effective in producing erotic desires as the sex tease was. So he uses thoughts of violence to excite him to feel potent. He dreams continuously of *forcing* women into *unwilling* sex acts. Because fear excites potency, dreams of love change to nightmare thoughts of violence, of rape.

Fantasy, being sin added to sin and another reason for guilt, also needs reinforcement fantasies based on new forms of temptation. The power-mongers (also victims), too, need food for their sense of "security," and that food happens to be their victims.

"Food" for fantasy is packaged in the form of pornographic magazines and movies, violence on TV and violent sporting events where people get hurt or killed. Here the dreamer can dream more intensely and perhaps identify with the aggressor, the avenger, or the rapist in the play and in real life.

Through the process of identification we can once again take in the scene in what seems a positive way. Little do we realize that we are being defeated and used again by those who profit by strengthening our secret need for dream reinforcement. As men, we are now being tempted in a different way: by drugs, booze, and entertainment. At this point, the author must point out that violence on TV does not by itself originate violence. However, a weak mind uses the entertainment of television—the cruel street scenes, for example—to reinforce the fantasy of being in power and being potent, lest the

315

dream which is its refuge break down and give way to Reality.

Those who exploit human weakness are less visible and are, therefore, themselves invulnerable—untouchable. At this point allow me to introduce you to two excellent words to describe victor and victim. The victim is the psychotic and the motivator is the psychopath.

The dream-world security of the sinner, psychotic or victim, is secured by dwelling on rape and violent scenes. The obstinate sinner is a stubborn dreamer who seeks to stay asleep to avoid the truth of his failing in real life. Therefore, as sexually violent scenes are reinforced in his head by those psychopathic exploiters, the guilty victim dwells more intently and more securely in his dreams—that is, until the day the dreams hatch out to become horrible realities in the form of sex, violence, and murder.

Ambition leads to dreams and dreams lead to failing; failings lead to fantasy and fantasy leads to violence and lower forms of failing. From being dominated by a woman, a man ends up dominated by evil low-life people. At this point he can be used by those underworld characters as a pawn. For a victim, hell is what it takes to keep him sweetly asleep to what hell is making him do.

Sex energy and violent energy are two sides of the same coin and they are interchangeable as one leads to the other. Sex leads to violence and violence leads to sex.

In animals, anger regulates sex drive. Anger is the natural animal response to danger. As with animals, it is the amount of stress which regulates the reproductive cycle of man. Because they are so vulnerable and expendable, sardines, for example, reproduce more prolifically than do whales. Sardines compensate in bodies for their mortality rate. So, the more stress a man feels, the more sex drive he tends to have. In man, sex drive is directly proportional to the stress man himself creates by failing through his ambitions. Now it follows that the less he copes with life the more he must fantasize, and this in turn makes him fail even more, creating a growing threat factor.

Through lack of grace and faith, men fall to anger and then to fantasy where they conceive thoughts of "love." However, the weakness of sex, like the weakness of anger, becomes lust when practiced improperly; and it becomes just as shaming as the anger which gave rise to the sex, and that leads back to anger again. As men experience the pain and shame of one extreme they escape to the shame of the other.

Perhaps you are beginning to see the link between hostility and lust. Evidence of this is to be seen everywhere in nature: many plants will not produce unless they are stressed. Be careful not to water your tomato plants too well or they may give you no fruit. The vine may grow like crazy, luxuriating in its perfect surroundings, but you will have nothing but a nice, healthy vine without tomatoes. What is this saying to you? Surely reproduction has a stress relationship—less stress, less reproduction.

Some wild animals will not reproduce in captivity.

The reason is startlingly clear: the less stress reaction, the less reproduction. A certain amount of stress must be a procreating trigger to living things. And there are many kinds of stress triggers; what is stress to one living thing may not be to another. Surely you can see that if plants and animals had too perfect an environment there would be a lower mortality rate and therefore less producing. How much more does this principle apply to mankind.

Another thing: as you slowly but surely degenerate to the level of lower animals and plants, you will find yourself turned on by different triggers. You will feel aroused by the body warmth or the fur of a cat, or even by the rain. There are many different spurs to reaction.

Now let me bring forward what I said before: the more a male uses a female, the more inferior he is to her; and that produces the threat factor, which in turn produces the hostility, which arouses sexuality, which puts more unloved and hostile people on this over-crowded planet than it can support. So we end up killing each other.

As a man grows toward the perfect mental state, he becomes less sexually active. He also begins to see how much he has used stress to awaken his sexuality. All failing men see sex (evidence of their dying, really) as a virtue; they see more sex as more growth and virtue. But in actual fact it does not prove itself out. On the contrary—the more sex, the less virtue and less superiority.

Vain men wallow in intrigue. They revel in their resentments and hostilities because the excitement of it all makes them feel virile and sexually alive, while asleep to the Reality from which they have fallen. Man continues to use the presence of that which originally set the course of nature on fire in him, and made him the beast he is, to reassure him. Because of this wrong use of the woman, he sins; and as he sins he falls again and again into the pit of his own evolving sensuality.

Now let me point out that this critique is not aimed at proper sex relations. How can you find out what that is until you have understood what the abnormal—the lust aspect of it—is? As a man, you will discover what that natural sex is when you cease using the woman's body to assuage the shame of your mortal existence.

The woman you use (and fail to love) ends up using you and taking liberties, and here you are left with that vicious cycle threat factor, ending in resentment which leads to lust and violence. And anger sets aflame the morbid wheel of nature and the cycle of life and death.

Ambitious men are highly sexed through the process of dreaming. No man can dream without a queen in the scene, if you see what I mean. As the ego falls, it reaches for reassurance for what it is and so, through that need, thoughts of "love" enter.

"Security" leads around to insecurity and insecurity leads to need for love again. And so he descends into that love/hate cycle of dying until he realizes the trap.

Alcoholics "love" intrigue, simply because any stress creates the tension (pain) which is relieved by the drink (pleasure). The stress, the tension, and the relief are tantamount to sexual orgasm. The same principle holds true with drugs. Alcohol and drugs also conquer low-level men in real life through their falsely created need for them; and the guilt sends the victims into fondling fantasies through which they are led again to the doom of the real experience, just as it was with the women who drove them to distraction in the first place.

Dear reader, conquer ambition and you will soon conquer resentment and the effects of pressure. After that there will come a day when you can conquer the stress of sexual provocation itself. And then you will be numbered amongst the overcomers. You will begin living in Reality, not in fantasy, without fear and hate; you will become master of your own mind and body eternally.

With animals, season is the reason. But with men, reason must become the season. Reason must lead if men and women are to become friends and not foes.

Non-ego or normal sex is practiced on the way up and out of the sensual life. Lust is practiced on the way down to the sensual life where stress is the welcome factor.

What must be discerned is the difference between natural sex and lust. That difference boils down to allowing the natural act in season without letting the experience become the extension of the very trauma that caused that state to begin with. Don't tease; don't promote; don't use; and above all, don't fantasize.

Man is an unnaturally natural creature. That is to say, he is mortal through (original) sin. I have said that sin produces trauma and trauma alters the body through the sin-consciousness which is based in pride. This pride factor is still present today at the root of all our problems.

Through original sin a procreating, mortal, natural body appeared, revolving around the woman who was used for pride's sake. All descendants of the original-sin trauma inherit the sexual dilemma of how to express the natural state without going from "bad" to worse.

The principle is childishly simple. It is all a matter of emphasis—what is most important to a man. The perils of original sin are amplified through the stubbornness of the ambition of pride. The perils are diminished by the soul's seeking for the *original* ground of its being, by discovering how to care for the person more than the body. Such genuine concern for the well-being of the woman enables man to one day transcend his sensual nature.

Again, the secret of life has to do with the attitude of your ego. Are you willing to understand your nature and your spiritual origin? Do you desire to find your Creator, or do you wish to escape into fantasy, endlessly abandoning yourself to your senses and desperately struggling to force the female god to reassure your pride in its downward (upward to you) spiral?

If you lean toward the sensible, you will immediately see the need for a new reference point other than the woman's body, the one who already exists within, who now greets your seeking Him.

Never ever use women as a base, to preserve a

sense of security. "For whosoever shall preserve his (ego-animal) life (and breath) shall lose his spiritual life (God's life and breath)."

To use the female to support the ambition of pride and to use her to assuage masculine anxieties is to duplicate original sin; hence, to add trauma to trauma. And trauma leads to change, and change leads to guilt, and guilt leads to fantasy, and fantasy (escape) to more sin and trauma.

Are you getting the message?

Identifying with what is written here should be all the proof you need of what your origin was, and, in the stubbornness of pride, what your destiny will be.

There is no alternative to this vicious cycle except to awaken from the mortal's dream, to face the reality of your failing, to repent of the sin of pride and be saved from sex, sin, and death.

Becoming attached to someone makes you happy, but when you lose that person you are unhappy. Notice how the latter state is worse than the former, unattached state. Something negative occurs in the process of becoming attached that is not evident at the time; it shows up later on in the relationship or when we "fall" out of love.

We can never love the person we become attached to, although we may think that we do. Attachment is really a self-serving ego experience, destructive and self-defeating in the long run.

Females attach themselves to the weakness of a man and tend to feel what the man feels. They experience his strength and eventually gain ascendency over him. Males like that attach to women be-cause they think they are being served, accepted, and loved.

Acceptance is very important to the ego when it is guilty. Having someone attached to you is very exciting and comforting. Unfortunately, such a relationship reinforces everything that is wrong in you and this leads to more guilt, which in turn develops a greater need for those enchanting attachment personalities. This is the basis of addiction—to anything, from women to drugs. If you cannot see this point, you are probably asking why such a natural thing is so harmful.

The answer lies in knowing the truth about your origin.

The ultimate love goal should be to set your beloved free—not from marriage, but from your own selfish needs and use of him or her. Would you believe that the need for approval and acceptance is exactly equivalent to original sin? Hear me out, please!

The ego that became wrong cannot admit that it is; hence, the need for approval. Wrong people cannot stand alone; they must have support. It is that support which reinforces the error and makes them dependent on approval.

We come into the world with an inherent uneasiness over our state of being. That inexorably translates into the prideful need for acceptance and approval. All such relationships eventually prove out the fault lurking within.

You had better be careful about being too close to people. Romantic or emotional closeness inspires animal feelings for your daughter, son, dog, or cat. Closeness is not love; it is evil use.

The very first recorded close relationship was inspired by Adam's falling out of love with Reality and falling in with what made him fall out. Falling makes you "love" or cleave to what makes you fall, but cleaving or clinging makes you fall again. Man loves the lie, especially if it (she) loves him back.

It is only natural for a man to fall for a woman and for a woman to cling to that failing man. Unfortunately, it is quite easy for a male's ego to become sexually involved with other things besides women. Anything that accepts him or otherwise excites him can do the trick. A male can have sexual feeling toward anything or anyone that excites him to do something wrong. Thereafter, wrong, whatever it is, is exciting; and the wrong that has made a home in him craves excitement for its reinforcement.

If a dog had tempted Adam to fall, Adam would have had sexual feeling toward that dog. Thank goodness it was a woman.

Therefore, beware of all close relationships: man friends, girlfriends, and pets. Anyone or anything which makes you feel good agrees with you, accepts you the way you are and soothes the savage beast; but, unfortunately, this makes the beast more savage. Don't even let the shower soothe you or it could turn you on. Any form of temptation which excites and succeeds in its appeal to the male ego, as well as anything which is used to soothe the guilt of his fallen nature, can arouse a sexual affection toward it. Poor fellow, he can have sex feelings toward the strangest things—even war and violence. Gentlemen, read on and learn about your own nature.

There can be only one healthy close personal relationship, and that is with your spouse—and then only for a season. Hear me out please. There is a very profound metaphysical reason behind that statement.

Marriage is a physical as well as a metaphysical relationship. Only highly committed moral beings can hope to enter into a marriage relationship and allow it to run its natural course without being destroyed.

Marriage, even under the best social conditions, is a living hell. If you expect to find something more than that, you are very surely deluded. You are certainly not going to find heaven, not at first! Through the gates of enchantment you are going to find disenchantment, and it is just as much of a living hell for the man who is highly moral as it is for the one who is not.

The Scripture records that Jesus went down into hell to raise the dead from death to life, to lead the saints to their promised salvation. This is what He came to do and no ordinary, ungracious being could have done this marvelous thing. The ungracious remained forever where they belonged.

The next closest thing to this principle of salvation is marriage. As a man you can enter into marriage and save the guileful female from the hell she is in, or you can end up wallowing in it with her. If she is the type who welcomes a good man, she can follow him out; the other type remains forever wailing and gnashing her teeth.

It is the destiny of man born of woman to become emotionally involved with the opposite sex; and if his intent toward her be honorable, he can find the inner strength to deal with what he finds in becoming as one flesh with his wife.

Lacking wisdom concerning his origin, every man is drawn to his death through the woman he "loves." But from the depths of his private hell each one can cry for the grace to be saved from the woman, and the woman from the clutches of hell's grasp; or he can curse her and die. The vain, brutish type of man is deceived when he thinks he can use a woman endlessly, taking pleasure without paying with his life.

But if marriage is so bad, then why should there be such an institution? The answer is that spiritual marriage is the moral framework ordained for two people to work out an ancient curse they are born under. The social reason it has survived this long is that we are deluded into believing it to be a beautiful experience, disregarding ubiquitous evidence to the contrary.

You might never have married if you had really known what you would have to go through. Like a moth to a flame, the male ego is "karmicly" and irresistibly drawn to the hell-centered female, because there is a mystery to be worked out. This is not to say the state of marriage is necessarily holy. Marriage cannot benefit two self-seeking people. Most people are ill-prepared by the church, state, or by their parents to embark on the perilous voyage to Heaven through hell. Consequently, when we marry we are taken completely by surprise. We expect heaven—and get hell.

We are taught in school, in church, and in psychology and anthropology that sex is an animal imperative and that marriage is merely a man-made social rule for its orderly expression. But what they do not tell you is that people differ from animals in a special way: people are capable of governing their lower natures through an enlightened reason. And by that leading they are eventually able to raise the level of their minds and bodies above the animal realm. They must do this or perish miserably.

We must learn and understand our "natural" state because we, unlike animals, are mutants from Reality, here in an unnaturally natural way. The natural state that we inherit and awaken in is the one man originally fell to. That is not too difficult to understand, is it? There is no doubt that we are animal, flesh and blood, and that we also replace ourselves in the same way the beasts do. Now if all that were so normal, why the war between the sexes, the arguments, the need for "sex education"? What is all the controversy about? Why should we be so bothered by sex? Why do we need to be taught anything at all?

Could it be that there is something mysteriously unglorious about glorious sex? Perhaps the reason we glorify sex is to reduce a secret embarrassment concerning it.

It is the habit of vanity to see all the failings as virtues, all the way down from the first one—sex. Sex is not the noblest relationship a man can have with a woman. It may very well be the most meaningful in the animal world, but compared with man's true potential, it leaves a lot to be desired. A woman knows this far better than a man.

As the first man descended through the sin of pride, his mortal nature appeared and bothered him. With us, the sex drive must be understood to be what it is—evidence of our fallen natures. The expression of animal love should be limited to a framework of honor and responsibility, lest there be more disobedience, falling away, and sin. "Therefore a man must leave his mother and father and become joined to the woman as one flesh." Marriage, then, is the animal union that appeared out of falling. For Adam it was on the way down; for us it is on the way back to Reality.

The sex drive is amplified by a subtle under-current—the need to feel secure about being a sexual being. Female acceptance revives the vain hope of glory that all men inherit in the death-as-life Adam and Eve syndrome. In the process of using her in a blind and stubborn way, man enters into the sex relationship and is eventually destroyed. In this process he makes an ugly witch out of his woman. His displaced, sinful, fallen nature is going to encourage the serpent of old in her to support it, and without realizing it he delivers himself right into the arms of the ancient one, the living hell. At that point he could awaken, but most men do not. In fact, they do just the opposite. Stubborn fools!

What do they do? They cheat; they divorce; they

go from flower to flower, seeking to coerce a more perfect soul support. Little do such men realize that heaven lies just beyond the hell they find themselves joined to, if only they could realize the meaning of their condition in terms of pride and blame, staying with their wives in order to find the original love to save them.

Perhaps you can now see that a very special attitude is required for marriage. And if you have a close relationship with *any* woman other than your wife, it can be only for a selfish reason: to use that person to build your vanity. But there is always hell to pay in every embrace. The advantage turns out to be a disadvantage as the deceitful, heavenly aspect is seen to be the hell it really is. And it is the hell-created nature in man which seeks out the reinforcement of the hell-cause in woman.

So, there is only one hell-on-earth, close relationship that can possibly work out. It is the highest and noblest hell-relationship of all: marriage. All other relationships are more sinful and too far removed from Reality for salvation to be next in line.

This is why men are attracted to women in the beginning: the wickedness in the woman becomes excited by the weakness of the man. It is the female hell-self which is excited by the prospect of owning and enslaving the man, projecting its seed into him so as to be mother of hell's children on earth.

The naughtiness which excites the male is the same wrong he must one day correct or else die to it. If the fallen ego of man could correct a woman (it can't), it would not. The wrong in her is the basic security for the wrong in him. His false security requires that her sin-self be cultivated. He rewards her support with his falling love and for a time they are both lost in Hog Heaven.

Make no mistake: the woman is the cause of all the misery and suffering in the world, but the real fault lies with the man.

The tragedy of marriage and of life in general is the man's fault, because it is the responsibility of a man to love the hell *out* of—not *in*—the woman. To realize his heritage, he must first embrace the hell in her body. His prideful fallen nature is first attracted to, excited, and stung by the serpent coiled in the woman. Wrong is always attractive and exciting when we are wrong, and it is wrong that comes "alive" in the presence of what made it. It is the surrender of one's soul to evil which men confuse with loyalty and love.

I am speaking now of a metaphysical process, because animals, you see, are products of a lifestyle that does not arise out of choice. They are originally creatures of nature, not "falling into" nature through error as we have. And since no fault lies between them, it follows that no fault can enlarge in their relationships. But between man and woman there is an original sin or fault, a common error that is proved in coming together. Whether you are conscious of it or not (and most of us are not that aware), the very act of being drawn together without the leading of enlightened reason, but through strictly human need, reinforces the original sin and makes it apparent. That is precisely how you can discover your original-sin heritage. When you next read the account of original sin, perhaps something within you will then stir and awaken a new relevance.

In the course of your externally motivated growth you develop your natural body to a point where you can see what is right but you cannot do what is right, and in this state of anxiety you seek out the woman for your ego comfort. Then you reach the threshold of Reality where you feel threatened and enslaved by the woman you thought you loved. Here, also, you feel conflict in yourself for what you have become.

Originally, death entered through the woman, spreading abroad on the earth domestic horror, war, and tragedy. Man's every touch is a failing to extend divine love toward the woman and a failing to rescue her from her private hell. How she loathes him for this!

We could learn obedience through the things we suffer if we could only understand what our sufferings mean in terms of ego, sin, and falling.

Like the perfected man, the perfect woman has no need for marriage. The perfected woman cannot be turned on by man's weakness; it is disenchanting to the whole woman. Only wickedness is interested in weakness. Understanding this, the divinely-led man must eventually encourage his wife toward the state of perfection and wholeness. This can happen when he awakens from the agony and ecstasy of delighting in her "beautiful" wickedness.

So man is destined to become joined to the

woman, to become as one flesh: one the extension of the other. But the question is, who is the extension of whom? Should the man be the extension of the woman through his need for ego support? I think you know the answer to that. But in case you don't: in holy matrimony a woman marries or joins herself to the man. That must be the understanding at the outset. Warning to the ladies: be careful to marry the kind of man you can respect and follow. Marry the man who loves what is right in his heart more than he favors you. Never fall for a man who falls for you. There is no greater agony than to find yourself supporting the wickedness in a man.

As long as a woman remains the basis of a man's existence, she will continue to take power from his failing to rule her with love (correction). In every temptation relationship, power goes from one to the other, from the man to the woman, from the people to the dictator and from one friend to another. It frequently happens that when two men become too close one will play the female role, and thus develops a homosexual relationship. All intimate friendships eventually become sexual friendships, even in the case of animals.

Because of many wrong relationships, there has grown up in every man a little bit of woman, and a little bit of man in every woman and a little bit of hell in both of them. So what is one to do? What is the proper relationship and where is our original identity? I mean, is it possible in the light of what I have said for a man to have a proper sexual relationship? The answer is emphatically yes, but as a man you must learn how to give up promoting the female and you must stop using the tease. In general, you must stop using her as a means of entertainment.

The ruthless man appears to indulge in the same way as the decent man. Or does he? The difference between the good guy and the bad is that the bad man doesn't care about the person of the woman at all. Neither is he conscious of the harm he is doing to her and himself. The bad man cannot be "happy" unless he degrades the woman in the sex act, or unless she lowers herself to excite him. Every woman feels the effect of a man's attitude. She can feel his drawing something evil out of her. The proud ego cannot experience the sense of security it needs without lying, deceiving, putting someone down or on. That same feeling that troubles some women, delights others. The reason is that some women are enjoying being degraded because it feels like a high. Down is up in the kingdom of hell.

Men are not excited by good women, only bad ones. The naughty women will cling to the security of being used, which is really not security at all, but hell's grasp on the man. The strength and comfort that she feels comes from his falling and dying to her ego and this makes her feel like a goddess. Everything that is of hell lives at the expense of something dying to it. Some women like that; others don't.

In their youth, women are parasites by inheritance—they should not be, of course. But a man delights in a woman's clinging. Clinging does seem like love and acceptance, and he is often so excited by such a display of affection that he does not see her draining away his life and changing him into an unprincipled brute.

The sensitive woman feels a great deal of conflict. She may see herself as the mad scientist, a Frankenstein monster-maker with a terrible power over this nothing, netherworld creep. She finds herself joined to King Kong, compelled to love him for that loathsome security that only makes her feel uglier. What a dilemma it is to be joined to a man who is wrong! For when that is the case, everything she does to make him happy only makes him more beastly and her more vile.

The entire human family is involved in this ongoing dilemma. Man is constantly being traumatized and changed by the woman his "love" degrades. Mortal changes come from crossing a mental/spiritual border into an evolutionary realm with death as the last frontier.

15

Back to Reality

Let me illustrate the principles I have been expounding with some less threatening examples and then come back to the point. In the process of creation there are ecological links between living things. There is a border between the cloud and where it becomes rain. There is a positive and a negative, a cause and effect, cause becoming effect. The link between one natural thing and another is known as ecology. Each effect emits energy, much like the lines of force extending from a magnet. Each rock, plant, insect, and animal emits a special energy of its own that supports or makes possible refined, higher life forms.

Let us take two little fish in a pond, for example, and let us say that one is a slightly different species from the other, so slight that you can hardly tell. But each fish has its own way of life. Let us say that they could mate and produce a cross between the two similar fish, but they don't, simply because their differences program them to perform different duties in their pond environment. They both could not survive if they ate the same food and did the same things. To prevent one from crossing the border to become the other, our Creator has given them a special password ritual. Don't ask me how it works; I cannot tell you. But investigate for yourself and you will see that many creatures have special dances and noises—some of the most ridiculous antics you have ever seen. Only the bird of that kind or the fish of that kind could possibly find that sort of dance to be acceptable and be turned on by the mate of the same kind.

If you have any brain at all you must know an intelligent Creator has brought this about. Surely those creatures have not figured this out for themselves. If survival depends on those differences, there can never be any mistake. The rule of nature then is to protect the identity of the species, to keep one from becoming the other, so that there is no mistake and each species comes into the world programmed to do its own thing. Fish should not become birds, nor should birds become fish! Males are not supposed to be females; men were not designed to become women, nor women to become men. There are natural and metaphysical laws to keep every natural thing distinct in the flesh as well as to keep man separate from evil.

If there is an evil, there will be a law, a boundary or frontier to cross where good becomes evil. The knowledge of this law is wisdom and the power of it is grace. There are mind laws, protocol, such as whom to befriend, whom to marry and whom not to marry, and even in marriage when to indulge in sex and when not to. Everything is a matter of time and season, governed by wisdom which is grounded in God.

If you seek Truth, you will know your place and your time. You will not let others trespass against you. Neither will you push in where you do not belong.

But when you are not aware of that knowledge and timing, you step further and further away from the frontier of reason. You tend not to heed the warnings nor even care. The blind ego is excited by the call to adventure into the unknown where glory seems to lie. Crossing the border, the entire body becomes changed as it adapts to the female base and the death and hell beyond. This condition is called sin, and sin is a transgression of God's law for men.

Now isn't that a sweeter way to understand what sin is? You usually think of sin in terms of something not good for you, which is silly because that doesn't mean much. Besides, it makes sin more attractive. But when you see sin in this new light—involving delicate laws and rules for your well-being—then sin takes on a new relevance. Now you can say, "Why on earth didn't somebody tell it like that before?"

It is evil that says "don't" and "do," so that you "do" and "don't." Do-gooders lay down the law as if they were God, and so tempt you across the border into their realm through your rebellion and conformity. If I say, "Don't jump into the lake!" you may say, "Just who do you think you are?" You see, man was not made to be ordered from the

337

outside. So you rebel. But on the other hand, if I say: "Hey, look, there are crocodiles in that lake. See for yourself," then it is your own understanding that determines your options. This kind of awareness is your protection.

You will never develop any character if, through rebellion and conformity, you get pulled in and then try to hate yourself free. Had you grace and wisdom in the first place, you would not have been there in the second place. The rebellious pride that has fallen to the woman's charms blames, tries to use resentment to get free. It is folly to believe that "beautiful" people can save you from the ugly. (Out of the frying pan, into the fire.)

We are talking here about very subtle currents that can kill you, and there are so many of them. A million books could be written, and there would be no end to writing because evil is always dreaming up new ways to trap you outside the border of the Kingdom of Heaven.

I tell you that some of the "born again" Christians are no different from Nazis. Many are not "born again" Christians, as they are led to believe, but fooled again. Hitler justified the wickedness of the animal people. He was the savior of the beasts; he saved them from their conscience. There also are sweet Hitlers—for hypocrites.

Now when you are dealing with fooled-again Christians and their leaders, what are you dealing with? What do you think those sheep are excited by? It is the same principality in another guise, justifying rather than making just! It is just as wicked in the guise of religion as it is in endorsing wickedness as good. In the kingdom of pride, "good" is evil and evil is evil, a bad person is a bad person and a "good" person is a bad person. Bad women look good, and "good" women are bad. There is hardly a person to whom you can relate who isn't sick in some prideful way. Everybody is rotten to some degree and so you must be careful as to how you relate. You must become objective in the Light; therein lies your salvation, and perhaps theirs, too.

You need not avoid marriage or the world, because it is ordained that you learn obedience through the things you suffer. Pain can awaken you to what is wrong with your close relationships; hopefully, you will seek comfort in the laws of your Heavenly Father—presently felt as your conscience. Through your pride you lost understanding, and so it came to pass that you were attracted to evil as though it were good—and that, my friend, is love and marriage. Ladies, you married weak men because they made you feel strong. Can you see now how a weak man can feel like a great man at the same time?

What is most important is that you enter into every relationship, good or bad, with an honorable intent. When you enter into a relationship with that right intent, you cannot be completely destroyed; you may be devastated—laid waste perhaps—but not totaled. You will learn from your mistakes. In the event you are lucky enough to find someone like yourself, you can at once have a relationship that begins to work. If not, your spouse will run away, solving the problem by divorce, leaving you without the stigma of guilt. You will simply lose what you should not have had all along and you will be better, not bitter.

Your first line of defense is intuition warning you off, saying, "No. Don't have anything to do with that person at all." But the same guiding light may also allow you to enter (shielded) into a relationship with wrong people in order to teach you something more about life and your weakness. It may be good experience for your adversaries to find themselves involved in a relationship with you, because then you could rescue them from their wickedness if they chose. It is better for them to be involved with your goodness than you with their badness. You cannot rescue others unless there is some relationship. How can you rescue anyone if you are far away, if you ignore that person, never talk to him and put a wall between you? The difference between entering a relationship with a good intent rather than with a bad one is that the hell finds itself involved with you, not the other way around. The hell will sometimes flee from you, taking that person away from you. There is rarely any need to run from it. *It* flees from *you* and sometimes leaves the person that you love alone.

So shall it be with your wives, gentlemen.

Having entered into all kinds of business relationships, I want you to know I have lost some and gained some, but thank God I have never been hurt. In the long run those who sought to exploit me have become the means of my success and my personal character development. I have learned to be patient. I have learned to be calm and objective. I have learned not to seek revenge. I have learned about my weakness and seen where to close the gap in the border of my mind, for in the next situation I am that much more aware. I have gained awareness of good, having become more conscious of evil, while the other person has only destroyed himself emotionally, taking into himself the "hell" of my heaven.

Just as I might take on the identity of the corrupter if I responded to him, so do corrupters become imprinted with the nature of good through their emotional frustration. What they end up with is a case of psychological indigestion that can kill them or cure them. The more they hate that imprint in them and attempt to reject and dislodge it, the more power they give it to remind them of the good they wish to forget. They will live in fear of another encounter; it is very much like being afraid to get up in the morning to face the evil world that keeps getting to you, but this is far worse.

You must be bold and you must not be afraid of hurting these psychopaths. However, you can discover this kind of boldness or innocence only when you meditate with a pure heart to find the entrance border to Reality and step across.

My wife used to think she needed to protect me. That was her ego trip. In her zeal she was really protecting herself, her interests, you see. And her protectiveness was a mothering. When I couldn't see danger at the moment that she could see it, it was only because my innocence forbade me to see it. Intuition never tells more than is needed in the moment. It did not say "Don't go in there, and don't do business with that person," anymore than it said, "Don't marry your wife because she is not right." It was right that I married her; she needed me to save her. I always check with my conscience, and if there is no stop sign I enter with good faith and a non-suspicious mind. But the adversary may rub his hands with glee. The adversary often confuses innocence with weakness; this confusion is his downfall. Were I suspicious, suspicion would register in my behavior. Suspicion does broadcast. But if you have no suspicion and are completely innocent, with faith and without guile, this can attract a person who is full of larceny. And if there is a lesson in that relationship for the other person, then you are the deliverer—you kill them or cure them.

My wife thought I was an easy mark. It almost killed her. Fortunately, it cured her; she laughs about it now. But, believe me, I learned a lot. How else could I write like this?

Do you see, then, what your real protection is? It is innocence, through which comes the power to see and bear what is there and deal with evils with grace and long-suffering. There's a meaningful and loaded word for you: longsuffering. It means bearing patiently the horror in people in order to save them from the evil in themselves.

To return, then, to the man/woman relationship, the strongest pull is the death-as-life sexual attraction of the ego-reinforcement scene. The sex act involves two egos through their flesh. So man enters into the woman's realm of hell as heaven, sex as love. And there he finds himself with a devil instead of an angel, an enemy rather than a friend; he sees that he is a slave, not free. If you are destined to find salvation, then experience awakens you. You realize that you have been deceived. You see that you are somehow falling in your rising, dying in your living, that the womb is your tomb, and you discover the resolve to find the way out. You know that if you do not, your beloved will kill you.

As a sensible person you begin to seek. And from that moment on, through the perfect desire of the soul, you receive a little grace. Slowly but surely you back away from the ego values you once cherished in the woman. You rebuke the wrong in the woman, the very wrong you once cultivated and rewarded. As you back away, the woman loses her power and the hell in her tries to get back with all the meanness and cunning at its command, denouncing your stand as coldness, cruelty, and unmanliness. She may shriek with pain and with fits of crying as one being tortured. And I suppose in a sense there *is* torture: she can't get her way. But those antics are met again and again by the patient long-suffering good in you, the true man of God. You realize what is controlling her. She may or may not be aware of the deadly game she is playing. A female born in Timbuktu will play it the same as an Eskimo in Alaska. It will be as though they both went to the same school and had the same teacher. You know they have! She loves you for giving in to her and she corrects you for correcting her. Should your roots be too deep in her, you might think you are wrong for standing up to her. Even in those times when you are perfectly right and poised, she might denounce your new love and try to cultivate that old clinging allegiance to her. She could misconstrue your denying her power, your effective, commanding style, as being mean and selfish. Possibly, but you had better be well-grounded in yourself so you can know for certain, or else you will end up confused, a victim of her hell again.

You must go your new way with conviction. But there is also a wrong, stubborn, self-righteous sort of conviction, and very often you will be at loggerheads. You must be as sure of what you are about as your spouse is in her (or his) hell, so that your patient, non-violent force of love can get right in there and neatly separate the meat from the bone. True stubbornness born of love will patiently and persistently break down the stubbornness of hell.

So there are many tricks, and your woman won't take kindly to your manliness at first—perhaps never. The best of women will give you a hard time. Their favorite weapon is rejection. The male ego cannot stand rejection, because his entire false lifestyle is built on her (sexual) acceptance, don't you see? Sexual rejection reduces you to a suicidal whimpering dog or one prone to fits of violence; not so when you are grounded in yourself. Her schemes then backfire. She becomes upset for not being able to upset you. Again she tries and is met with grace. One of you must break, but it must not be you. Don't ever start this war to end all wars unless you are prepared to go all the way.

The sexual relationship between man and woman is a very difficult thing to resolve. Nevertheless, man must realize that he really is not doing the woman any favors, while a woman has to be sensible enough to stop pretending that he is.

Every male wills (teaches) the woman to want him sexually. But what she really wants from him is just the opposite of what he wants from her. She needs a fatherly love, not a sexual one. The flaw in his nature teaches her to mother the fallen man. That's the dilemma. He wants a mama to support him and she needs a father to correct her. He, however, is too busy making her into a mama while he is becoming a little boy.

There are no books written about the way, nor can I write them for you. By trial and error you will find it, by the leading of the Light from within.

So get married—have your sexual fling. But know also that there will come a time when you will be living with your wife as if she were your beloved daughter. Otherwise, there will be hell to pay.

And so it comes to pass that you find yourself involved with a woman, and once you have had a few children, enough sex is enough. It takes a few years—more for some than for others.

Because of the subtle intrigue involved, a woman feels guilty because she secretly resents what her husband demands from her. Then the guilt of resentment changes into a desire to make up to him—sexually, how else? That is her way of getting power and security. Making up to him excites him to fall. It turns him on. And so he becomes more of a beast, the wheel turning like the treadmill of hell it is.

When a woman joins herself to the beast in the man, everything she does for him makes him more of a beast, making the hell in her grow stronger. His "love" gives the hell in her power, and for a fleeting moment she feels secure. Then she discovers that she has been betrayed by his love; what was love changes to loathing, and loathing changes to a need to punish.

Here we arrive at divorce, and the making of even more complex problems. When you are unfaithful, you take your mixed-up identity and join it to another's mixed-up identity. (A woman can feel the presence of the other woman, even the mother of her husband, in her husband. She can feel contaminated by those identities.) You must see that divorce is a sin.

Marriage is no heaven, but through *staying* married you discover the awful but wonderful truth. You mature in the hell of marriage, and when its purpose has been fulfilled, you rise beyond that state. Not so with divorce. You must not run from your mate to find that other, more "perfect" soulmate; you must stay with your wife or husband and work out the ancient curse. The marriage relationship—or male/female identification—comes from man's falling away from God. A man must stay with the woman he betrayed until he can find the love of God he lost.

There are two ways a man can relieve sexual pain. The proper way occurs when he is motivated by concern, which wakes him up to the cruelty of sexual fulfillment, the harm being done for selfish pleasure and for that ancient ego reassurance—*the wrong as right*. Concern is love, which modifies desire and eventually replaces it completely. The more common method of relieving sexual pain is simply to keep indulging, but in this process of making himself "happy," a man makes his wife miserable. The relief produced by the sex act is only temporary, and desire itself continues to grow until it can never be satisfied.

Remember, insecurity drives the fallen male ego to seek refuge in the image that got inside him. He thinks about sex all the time only because he is not really a man and he is becoming less of one through the thought and reassurance process. He does not realize that the demon female identity is making a home in him. Through that weakness of needing a woman to serve him, up pops the devil and soon all hell breaks loose.

Anything can be seen two ways, depending upon who is doing the looking. A male can look at a female in a special way that fulfills a psychic need, but which becomes lust. The first effect of sin is to become sex-centered. When sex becomes a ritual of worship and reinforcement, it then produces guilt and violence. While corruption may appear in marriage, it *always* occurs in fornication; there cannot be any love here, only use. Just as sex fascinates and produces violence, so does violence fascinate and produce lust. And as we draw closer to death, death begins to fascinate and frighten.

In every wrong relationship, one tends to cross a border to become the other. As with the union of two fishes producing a composite of the two, so it is with man as he crosses over the line to join himself to sin and, eventually, death.

Man is either a son of the Light or a son of the darkness. He is related to one or the other spiritual dimension. The moment the bond with Reality is broken, the nature of the female seeps in and he adapts to her hell-centered environment. The man soon takes on the characteristics of his immediate environment, the female, and slowly but surely he approaches her guiding spirit, becoming part male, part female, part devil.

A single woman who wishes to find a real man cannot afford to be turned on by weakness, nor dare she play those girlish games. Remember, I said that a sensible woman cannot be turned on by weakness except she be violated by brutality. She cannot help but see men for what they are, while they cannot help but feel observed. That is her protection!

Such grace appearing in marriage can awaken the man to what he is doing wrong. Grace awakens, just as guilt puts to sleep. Once she awakens him to what he is doing wrong to her and he takes a new attitude toward her, she may revert back to the usual female behavior to provide the stress that will test his awakening manhood. The man once again finds himself involved with some kind of hell, but does not cry out to that woman or any other—he behaves in a manly way. Here is the crux of the matter: the weak male always seeks comfort from the very spirit to which he fell and from which he emerged as the fallen man. Hell is refuge from Reality, a false security for what is false in him.

Learn by experimentation, gentlemen. You have a great deal of latitude in your experiments with your wife—and, to be sure, *let it be only with your wife*. Live by trial and error and so prove the way. There are times when you must let the woman reject your amorous advances.

Respect her mood and her season.

Conquer your own burning with her concern in mind.

Consideration is what real love is about between man and woman.

Love eventually transcends sexual desire, beyond which lies the key to immortality.

Divine love is what gives true identity back to the man. And if you do not find this love, you will wander in the wilderness of life, searching for something you cannot find. You will, however, take on all the identities of those who comfort you.

Children do not aggravate for punishment. They tease you to love them. Loving them means overcoming your hostile, impatient, animal responses to their challenges, standing firm, not giving in. By the same token, your woman does not tease you to be sexed, but to be loved. Gentlemen, think of intercourse as a moment of weakness—a kind of giving in to the pressure of a tease. Be aware of the relationship between the sex act and your wife's depression, her unreasonable ways and demands. Observe how that uncorrected naughtiness (that which you have given in to) becomes a strong sexual tease to which you respond with animal lust.

Sex love is fascination with the cause of falling away. Animal love rises in man in his falling away from obedience to God. Sex love (worship, devotion, commitment to the female) is a displacement of agape (godly) love for God, who is everything to the real man.

No male can become a man overnight and no female could really stand the shock if he could. A woman is overjoyed if she can sexually join herself to a good man. But if she joins herself to an ego-maniac, all her evils are encouraged to grow unchecked. That is her dilemma and her conflict.

Correction should be a mutual thing. Both man and woman must respect each other's rights and sex should never be promoted. Let your own desire pass, for her sake—that is love. With animals, "love" is sex, but with man, love is the spirit to give it up. Marriage is the framework in which such loving sex can be practiced on the way to God's paradise.

Animal life is ongoing perpetuation by generation. Eternal life is UP-going—perpetuation by regeneration. Regeneration comes by giving up the ego-animal life, surrendering one's will and the things of youth graciously to God, gaining His reassurance and righteousness rather than surrendering the will to the female (god) for self-righteousness—

for her reassurance.

It is a delicate thing. Be together; lie close to one another if you wish. You don't have to have sex every time! Realize what your wife really wants from you—love, love that is always there in the absence of use. Otherwise, marriage becomes a jungle battleground and you will develop longings that create guilt, terrible longings that nothing can ever satisfy and that can cause madness.

Madam, *you are not being a good and selfless wife if you please your husband no matter what.* That you do for your own selfish security, in your fear of losing him. Give him a little resistance at times, or else how can he ever question the erroneous nature of his desire? You have rights over your body; exercise them—or lose them. Never engage in sex for feelings of security, to soothe the guilt of an argument.

The prostitute is super-obliging, and so is the other woman. Ladies, let them have your rotten husband if lying comfort is what he wants. Let them go to hell together, if that is what he wants. Don't you ever play that role if you want to keep your sanity. Never fear losing that kind of man.

Always be honest. All you can lose is a rotten husband, but you have a chance to gain a good one. Your commitment is the boundary that separates the good way from the bad way—it is the door. And this fact holds true for men and women in every situation throughout life.

The process of becoming whole is by the leading of the Holy Spirit. You cannot learn this mystery from your Bible, nor can you learn it from my book,

How Your Mind Can Keep You Well. You cannot learn this mystery personally from the author. The secret lies within you; you must discover it for yourself. You fail to find it only because your adventuring pride stands in the way.

A glib salesman is himself easily sold. In order to be successful he must set aside his own conscience, but conscience (knowing) happens to be the criterion he needs to keep from being conned himself. In your pride, in your supreme egotism, you have set aside your conscience once, for gain, and again, to forget what you have become. The female you need is the support for the wrong way pride must go. Every person who "sells" or supports your way is an evil in human form, and it is the evil in you, needing support, which attracts you to them. You must surrender your soul for that support, not knowing what you do. Indeed the wages of sin is death. Excitement is attractive to you when you are wrong. Excitement is life for dead men. Temptation can make such men feel alive.

The deceitful female opens wide the door to the male's glory. With her, man ventures away from God to be God in his own mind. He loses himself in the female completely. Sex (body acceptance) is how he gains more confidence, falling down further. An egotistical man makes a woman miserable while making himself happy! Sooner or later she will punish him for using her and not loving her.

Remember, when you are wrong, wrong is exciting and attractive to you. The ongoing relationship makes everything worse, but you are not going to see that fact if you continue involving yourself. Even though making love leads to war, there is nothing you will not do or give for that support. Man is in love with what lies to him and tells him what his itching ears want to hear. The woman lies with a physical body language that was the product of an original lie. Drugs, alcohol, marijuana, and tobacco speak the same body language; they lie without words.

Don't rush out and give up sex, thinking you are going to live forever. That is not the way it is done. Please be sensible about this. Simply be conscious that your animal heritage is represented by various lusts. Don't run away from realizing that! And whatever you do, observe your after-feelings and anxieties and let what is there in the ever-present modify your behavior next time. Especially watch those fantasies, for every man begins his journey into hell by dreaming about his failings being worshipped.

Become objective, and as you become objective, the Light in the objective state will come to bear and give you time to work this thing out. Marriage is a time for a man to work out his problem (of failing), and to provide the only kind of sex relationship that is acceptable to a decent woman. In the process, she bears children who also inherit the sin of pride. I assure you, you will have to dig a little deeper into your soul for something more than sex love in order to correct them.

Let me give you a rule of thumb. Check this out against your own experience: the more venial (sexual) you are, the less authority you have with your wife and children. The less venial, the more power and respect you will have and the less trouble, sickness, and tragedy there will be in your home. You will prosper in your business because you will be more aware, sure of yourself because you are more right.

Your salvation hinges on your commitment to the Truth; belief joins you to Truth. Belief in a lie also joins you to that which lies and changes you into a beast who believes in "love" and what lie-loves him.

No one works at making himself sick and miserable. Sickness and tragedy come from a way of life that comes through believing and joining ourselves to others through our need for and our false belief in them. That is why you must believe these words, for these words must have testimony in you. If you believe the inner witness to them, you can be saved from sin and death.

You must never believe those who tell you that sex is love, for that is the lie that all fallen egos need to hear and believe. Liars intensify failings as well as produce them. Sex is the death-as-life principle, the *physical* enslavement/commitment to that which lied and killed man from his beginning on earth.

Through the sin of pride man fell from immortality to mortality, represented by sexuality. The womb is the tomb, a dead end.

Read me well. If you love the Truth, a good spirit waits upon you and says, "Yes, that man is speaking truly." But if you are foolish, these words will not sit well with you; the spirit within you will be offended. Now I cannot tell you who are right and

354

who are wrong people in the short run. But in the long run, when all is said and done, when we have disciplined or indulged ourselves to our heart's content, there will be a chasm between those who have followed the good way and those who went astray.

You have a long life ahead. Many dangers will befall you. You will be surrounded by evil, as though you were walking through a pit of snakes. But if you are sincere, no real harm will befall you, not one single hair on your head will be harmed, because hell has no jurisdiction over those who are heaven-bound. The child of Light has authority over evil because he is simply not its subject; a person who loves what is right is subject only to what is right. But a person who loves what is wrong is *subject* to the wrong he loves and is lost in the exciting female or her substitutes, drugs or booze, even as the female is lost in hell forever.

I have found the answers myself, and you can benefit from the course I have run. I have not contradicted myself in anything I have told you. I do not wish to bring you a new teaching, re-indoctrinate you or implant new behavior patterns. I want you to be the extensions of what is true in you through being a witness against the evil way.

Every one of you can become a beautiful human being. But many of you are diseased, old, sick, and ugly. In time, you can change. You have changed from a beautiful child to being the ugly, decrepit creature you are now, so there is no reason why you can't change back again through a new commitment. It is all a matter of movement back across the moral border to Reality.

It is easier to find the way when you are married, because otherwise, your unfulfilled need and burning preoccupies you and limits your growth. You have to get past that stage and become disillusioned. That is what marriage is for. Men's minds are too much on women, and women, too, lust after men because the something missing in them feels it can find fulfillment from the other. May I suggest you read John 15 and John 18, verse 19 to the end of the chapter. Jesus is speaking about His being in God and God's being in Him, even as He is in those He has saved. Man suffers from an identity problem through sin; the woman is in him, even as he is in her and hell is in them both.

It is just a matter of knowing deeply within yourself the truth about your fallen identity. Realize this and let it settle in your mind, and by and by it will begin to bear fruit. No need to struggle! Merely observe your identification with the female. Observe lust as it is aroused. You are not going to die by denying yourself sex, even though you may at times feel as though you are. What will die is the hell self. As it dies in you, it will feel as though you are dying. It will feel as though you are missing out on something precious and vital. But let me remind you that to pick up your eternal life you must lay down your ego-animal life and breath. Your ego-supports of mortal life begin and end with the way you relate to woman. When a man dies, he often cries out for his momma; momma is God.

Now what you really need is the proper marriage

relationship. Purify your mind. Keep yourself chaste and wait until you can find the right kind of person. If you happen to be involved now with a beast or a witch, there may be beauty somewhere inside. It is up to you to bring the Light to the marriage. Don't look to the other person to do it first. Don't hold the attitude "If he (she) would be all right, then I would be OK." It may well be that if he (she) suddenly became right, you might jump out of your skin. You find the Kingdom of Heaven on earth by being right within yourself.

I began by saying that the very nature that seeks approval is wrong. In its uncertainty, the ego seeks to be assured that its wrong is right. Right here you can see the origin of all the problems that have been, are, and will be. Remember that the very essence of egosexism can be distilled down to a concept captured by the word "acceptance." The very thought of being accepted arouses unbearable sexual desires in the fallen male.

It has been shown that the brute evolves from the fall of the ego to pride. Reaching for power and glory, man's consciousness became changed, and through the altered consciousness came the animal nature with perverse sex passion at every level of descent. Eve certainly made a monkey out of Adam, and something that his ego weakness cultivates in her preserves his brutish nature by accepting him just the way he is.

The need for acceptance is the need for the lie, and when the liar loves or accepts you, you die a little more.

If egotism means being God in one's own eyes, then the form we assume in any phase of descent will not want to see its own failing. The now-animal being will always want to be accepted, and when it is, it descends again and again.

Let me reiterate that point: while it was ambition of pride that once separated man from God, acceptance of the earthy nature hardens the course of inherited sin and becomes tantamount to another fall. It is no wonder we speak of "falling in love," because love, or acceptance, produces the failing that emerges as sexual burning.

Female appeal to this craven need to be accepted (awarded sustaining worship) awakens man's earthy, brutish, death-oriented life as he dies spiritually because *that very acceptance of the sex nature is directly connected to the ego mechanism of failing.* Putting both those ideas together, we have: acceptance equals renewal of the inherent ego hope of glory, instantly translated into strong sexual desires, which, when accepted, cause a man to become physically as well as mentally addicted to what does the accepting, a woman, or anything you care to think of.

So any gesture, hint, or suggestion of acceptance triggers sexual desires and carries away our fallen man. Unless that desire is modified by an overriding, corrective consciousness, sex becomes a dangerously debilitating, enslaving experience.

Gentlemen, kindly bear this fact in mind on your way back to Reality through re-humanizing experiences. Do away with your need for acceptance and at once you take control of your sexual apparatus.

Observe from now on the faintest hint of acceptance as it arouses lust (which you think of as love). The so-favored female grows more unreasonable and thus more exciting sexually. Her naughty but naturally exciting nature, which really is crying for true love (correction), becomes interpreted as need for your sexual services. You surrender to the excitement source for physical relief, thus "favoring" the female, and her inborn error grows to excite you to the sexual surrender of your soul again and again, until you are mad—and then dead.

Kindly observe how, because of your failing to love her properly, your every thought revolves around maneuvering for sexual acceptance to relieve guilt and anxiety. You think of sex continually. You labor for female reassurance for your fallen existence and you fall or fail again. You think of it as life and hope, but you are really digging your own grave. You can never see the truth until you are ready to face Reality and abandon pride.

In the false kind of hope that man gains from female acceptance, there is always a great anxiety; this feeling comes from the God you are rejecting to be accepted as God yourself. You are not as great as you think. You are a beast, a slave of the beauty. Poor Eve, he has given you the mommy's curse. You can't get your man unless you play the ancient game. Gentlemen, the mommy's curse for you is really Daddy's curse, if you see what I mean.

She cries to you for godly love, and you interpret her cry as a signal to abuse her. You are like a worm crawling on its belly, a lowly serpent seeking the refuge of the womb to escape the reality of what you have become. You are the one for whom the womb is a tomb—a dead end.

Every woman, whether she likes it or not, needs the kind of love that has the power to deny itself. Such love will gradually reject and eventually correct the agonizing role in which Eve is cast, or, at the very least, take away her power.

Now it is true that men often end up rejecting women who cling too much, because they emasculate by that kind of loving. Fear and guilt can also produce rejection by men; however, that kind of rejection is not what I am alluding to, for it inflames a woman's passion more through her resentment.

Sex must be a living sacrifice, not a dead one, for when you have become impotent through old age and abuse, you cannot deny yourself for love's sake. Older, impotent married men often go through a sexual revival so that they may experience the sacrifice for love's sake, as younger men should. Wise, timely, and gentle rejection is the rule. Teach the woman the reverse of what you have taught her in the past. That is, you will love her for herself, so that she can rely on your love without any sexual performance. Sex is no longer necessary for your commitment to her, unless, of course, she wishes it for her needs. Even so, a man must be careful not to have sex with his amorous wife *if* she is making up for something she has done wrong, or is trying to keep him an animal so she can continue to dominate him.

The love that lies beyond restraint greatly satisfies the woman. A man's gallantry evokes genuine respect for him. But *here he is in danger of interpreting that love as respect for what is still left of his ego.*

Careful, or you're dead.

A female (as opposed to a woman) can feel threatened by the emerging superiority of a man's enlightened reason, and here she might give a man all the acceptance he could dream of—but only to feel the security of her dominance again.

Careful, and you will live forever.

Males and females will emerge as men and women when they learn to love God first, and each other—not as gods, but as people under God—second.

Most of us are the sum total of our experiences, but another way of saying this is that we are burdened down and bothered by our past. Unless we learn to respond properly in the present moment, the present becomes merely an extension of that burdensome past.

Roy Masters, author of this persuasive self-help book, describes a remarkably simple technique to help us face life properly, calmly. He shows us that it is the way we respond emotionally to pressures that makes us sick and depressed.

By leading us back to our center of dignity and understanding and showing us how to apply one simple principle, Roy Masters shows us how to remain sane, poised and tranquil under the most severe trials and tribulations.

Roy Masters has nothing less to offer you than the secret of life itself—how to get close to yourself and find your lost identity, the true self you have lost in the confusion.

The observation exercise materials consist of the book, *How Your Mind Can Keep You Well,* and three (3) cassettes of the same title. We suggest a donation of $30, or whatever you can afford.

Other Books Available

from The Foundation of Human Understanding
8780 Venice Blvd., P.O. Box 34036, Los Angeles, CA 90034

HOW TO CONQUER NEGATIVE EMOTIONS
Simple instructions by which anyone may learn how to eliminate guilt, anxiety, pain, and suffering from his life forever, completely and without effort. 325 pages

SECRET OF LIFE
A philosophical guide to the whole riddle of existence. 194 pages

NO ONE HAS TO DIE! Beyond the Known
There lives in this world an insidious evil force that understands and caters to our weakness, and we are delivered into the hands of the evil shepherd, and he is the author of our suffering or tragedy until we find the truth that makes us free. 243 pages

HOW TO CONQUER SUFFERING WITHOUT DOCTORS
The relationship that now exists between you and your healer is the relationship which should exist within yourself. This book shows the seeker how to look inside himself for common sense and answers that are meaningful and permanent. 222 pages

THE SATAN PRINCIPLE
The entire thrust of this book is to bring all the subtle causes of your problems into the spotlight of your consciousness. 261 pages

HEALERS, GURUS, AND SPIRITUAL GUIDES
ESP, psychic healing and mind-over-matter explained in this easy-to-read book by William Wolff. Several chapters are devoted to Roy Masters, informative biographical material plus case histories of meditation at work. 258 pages

HOW TO SURVIVE YOUR PARENTS
Since all parents were once children, the question arises: How can we survive our parents; how do our children survive us? In no uncertain terms, this book tells how. 190 pages

THE ADAM & EVE SINDROME
In our present state, we can hardly have a relationship that isn't wrong. It is imperative, Masters says, to see directly to the original cause with objective precision . . . and then, in that moment of realization, the curse is broken. 266 pages

EAT NO EVIL
The ultimate book on food—a delightfully shocking expose' of what is at the very root of all your food hang-ups. 127 pages

UNDERSTANDING SEXUALITY: The Mystery of Our Lost Identities
This work explains how man's failing ego expresses itself in terms of sex and violence and how husband and wife can eventually transcend their sexual problems. 361 pages

All books quality paperback, $9.95 each.